Reading Ideologies:
an investigation into the Marxist theory
of ideology and law

LAW, STATE AND SOCIETY SERIES

Editors
Z. BANKOWSKI, *Department of Public Law, University of Edinburgh, U.K.*
M. CAIN, *Department of Sociology, Brunel University, Middlesex, U.K.*
W. CHAMBLISS, *Department of Sociology and Anthropology, University of Delaware, Newark, U.S.A.*
M. MCINTOSH, *Department of Sociology, University of Essex, Colchester, U.K.*

Reading Ideologies:
an investigation into the Marxist theory of ideology and law

COLIN SUMNER
Institute of Criminology, University of Cambridge

1979

ACADEMIC PRESS
London · New York · San Francisco
A Subsidiary of Harcourt Brace Jovanovich, Publishers

ACADEMIC PRESS INC. (LONDON) LTD.
24/28 Oval Road,
London NW1

United States Edition published by
ACADEMIC PRESS INC.
111 Fifth Avenue
New York, New York 10003

Library of Congress Catalog Card Number: 78 18032
ISBN Hardback: 0 12 676650 9
ISBN Paperback: 0 12 676652 5

Text set in 11/13 pt VIP Bembo, printed by photolithography,
and bound in Great Britain at The Pitman Press, Bath

Contents

Part Three. Reading Ideologies in the Law: An Historical Materialist Method

For Maggie

Preface

Different countries have different Marxisms, each with its own distinct form and content. British Marxism has become particularly concerned with understanding the dependence of British capitalism on its supportive ideologies and reinforcive legal machine. A declining economy produces regular crises which need to be defused ideologically, and, in the last resort, resolved with legal force. This text is above all an attempt to conceptualize the way in which ideology is an integral part of any society and determines the course, content and colour of human history. I hope that the book makes it clear that ideology is integral to every social practice and thus acts as the cement which prevents an unstable social structure from falling apart. For I, like an increasing number of others, have concluded that ideology is a vital feature of social change and stability and not just a passive agency of infrastructural forces. I would not wish to deny the classic theses of the centrality of the mode of production in any society and of the practical importance of political power, but a Marxism without an understanding of the vitality and force of ideology is in danger of becoming antediluvian: if, indeed, it could be classed as Marxism at all.

The book represents an exploration into the possibility of establishing a general theoretical and methodological framework, along Marxian lines, within which we can study ideology and law more scientifically. In other words, it stands for an attempt to specify the concepts and methods of an historical materialist semiology, with particular reference to law.

It will no doubt be commented that there is too much general theory around and that it is often difficult to know what it means until we see it in practice, in empirical research. I would not defend the lack of empirical illustration of my proposed theory and method, however, there are reasons for it. Firstly, my investigation was provoked by problems that arose from an intensive (and extensive) piece of empirical research. Secondly, even to achieve some degree of satisfaction on the general approach took so long that its practical illustration must now be a separate exercise. As will be seen, the approach proposed is detailed and will take time to concretize. Also, if what I have put forward seems plain and obvious, let me say that the issues did not look that way in 1973 when I began the research. Several other people thought so too at the time and wisely advised me to avoid the problem of reading ideology altogether. Fourthly, what temporary overproduction of general theory there may be pales into insignificance compared to the persistent overproduction of untheorized data and to what social science stands to gain from its current theoretical revolutions. Finally, empirical illustrations of this approach will follow, in one form or another, and when they do they will be of much more value than the kind of readings produced in the early seventies, which tended to polemic.

Apart from the need for empirical readings of specific discourses (particularly legal discourses) and for studies of the role of ideology in socialist societies (particularly their legal systems), my analysis seems to give importance to three other areas of enquiry in future empirical research: (1) the effects on 'the balance of ideology' in a society brought about by the commercialization of the superstructural practices, (2) the historical classification and definition of the different modes of appropriating the appearances of social reality (or modes of observation), and (3) the relation between the growth of the 'surplus' classes in a declining capitalist society and the increased social significance of ideology and of cultural pluralism.

The chapters of the book form a cumulative development. I do not recommend reading them out of order since the same issues keep cropping up time and again and my comprehension of them developed gradually throughout the book. The last chapter is a kind of summary however for those who want one. The essays were written and rewritten between 1974 and 1977. They do not centre on authors or books but on the Marxian theory of ideology and law and the methods used to read them. All the readings contained within, therefore, are done on that basis. They are spontaneous and rigorous readings which are similar to those suggested for the first stage of my

proposed reading method (see Chapter 7). All this is to explain why
(1) some leading writers in "the field" (such as Hall, Goldmann,
Sacks and Habermas) have been ignored, and (2) some recent
materials do not get a mention. No major method of reading
ideology has been deliberately excluded: excluded authors employ
reading methods which fall under the headings discussed or which
count as hybrids. "The field", in any case, is too large for a
comprehensive review by one person. Moreover, many recent
British writings have often seemed unclear to me, or they have
produced little progress. They seem to be moving in the direction of
the Althusserian theory of the subject, Lacanian psychoanalysis etc.,
rather than in the direction I am advocating which is towards an
analysis of ideologies based on a more developed historical knowledge of social relations. Paradoxically, given the critique of
bourgeois individualism, recent Marxist work frequently points in a
traditional, bourgeois direction. Finally, recent translations of work
by Derrida, Barthes and Kristeva are simply too recent to be
discussed. Because of my view that ideology has been superficially or
confusingly understood, I have put a higher premium on clarity of
expression, precise use of language and punctuation, and sustained
interrogation of established ideas than on comprehensiveness. I hope
that I have clarified the key issues and concepts and generated some
valuable questions. If nothing else, I would like to think that I have
made a small contribution to the clearer understanding of method in
the social sciences.

The book began life as a Ph.D. thesis, entitled "Ideology and
Deviance", at the University of Sheffield (1976). That thesis has been
considerably developed and rewritten, and the sections on deviance
removed. Throughout the project, Maggie Sumner, my wife, has
been an incredible support and no statement of thanks could be
sufficient. She translated articles, typed and corrected some earlier
drafts, listened to me drivelling on about it, suggested ideas, and,
crucially, did the bulk of the housework during this period.
Apologies to her and Ben, I will organize it better next time. During
my Ph.D. research, my supervisor, Ian Taylor, was a great encour-
agement and helped me to develop my views considerably through
his perceptive and constant criticism of them. Also at this stage, Peter
Alcock, Peter Gibbon, Barry Smart, Christine Jennings and various
seminar groups in sociology, semiology and communications studies

were of great assistance in stimulating and criticizing my ideas—particularly Peter Alcock and Christine Jennings who had to live with this thing in one way or another. Since then, successive generations of students at University College of Wales at Aberystwyth and at Cambridge University have provided me with constant feedback, and Maureen Cain's editorial advice has helped to tighten up the presentation and some of the arguments. Finally, for the typing, my thanks go to Judith and John Blanchfield, Jane Cook and the unknown but hard-working typists of the University Typewriting Company (Cambridge). If the arguments in the book are right then apart from yet more people (such as the hard-working printers, sub-editors etc., and authors who stimulated the work such as Marx, Althusser and Stuart Hall) one should also thank the social structure for reflecting this particular combination of ideas. Instead, I suppose I have to face up to my legal responsibility for the text—whether you grant me any more responsibility than that depends on how you read it.

Thanks are given to the following publishers for permission to quote from their books:

Basil Blackwell, Oxford — Carver, T. (ed.), *Karl Marx: Texts on Methods* (1975)

New Left Books, London — Althusser, L., *For Marx* (1969)
Althusser, L., and Balibar, E., *Reading Capital* (1970)
Korsch, K., *Marxism and Philosophy* (1970)
Fiori, G., *Antonio Gramsci* (1970)

Free Press, New York — Cicourel, A. V., *Method and Measurement in Sociology* (1964)

Clarendon Press, Oxford — Robey, D. (ed.), *Structuralism* (1973)

Lawrence and Wishart, London — Marx, K., *Capital* I (1974)
Marx, K., *Capital* III (1972)
Gramsci, · A., *Prison Notebooks* (1971)

Routledge and Kegan Paul, London and Cornell University Press, New York — Culler, J., *Structuralist Poetics* (1975)

The Society for Education in   Screen 14: 1/2 (1973)
Film and Television
and to the Department of Sociology, University of Essex for
permission to quote from Slater, M. *Levi-Strauss in Fleet Street*
(1970)

Cambridge   Colin Sumner
October, 1978

Part One

The Concept of Ideology

1 Introduction

Since the middle 1960s, European culture and politics have undergone profound changes, inspired by radical students, innovative youth, militant workers and their suppression by, and frequent incorporation into, the dominant political and cultural institutions. These changes were not the effects of a class war in the classical sense. Rather, it became clear that one had to talk about class fractions, class alliances and intra-class divisions. Gramsci's conception of hegemony re-entered the currency of political language. The bourgeoisie did not rule alone, they had ideological consent and political support from fractions of the intermediate and working classes. Ideologies became very important in the analysis of social developments. It was not just a question of class but a question of consciousness. Political sensitivity to differences, perhaps quite small on paper, between various ideologies became heightened. As a result of this increased sensitivity, many people began to see clearly, for the first time, the ideological nature and underpinnings of the dominant institutions. This was especially true for the social superstructure—the legislature, the administrative bodies, the legal systems, the universities, the schools, the television industry and the press being the main superstructural institutions brought into question. Doubt prevailed: no longer was faith and trust put in the hands of the so-called benevolent authorities who ruled, they said, in "the national interest". And, as Weber said, doubt is the father of all knowledge.

Ripples of doubt, and sometimes tidal waves, passed through the academic world, notably the social sciences. Many classical orthodoxies were run aground, not the least in Marxist scholarship.

Perhaps the most important effect within the tradition of Marxist analysis was the re-examination of the nature and relevance of the concepts of ideology and consciousness. Previously restricted to an epiphenomenal reflection of the economic structure, the concept of ideology could not cope with modern developments. Its resurrection in one new form or another often left the bounds of Marxism itself. Scientific theory and humanist morality were often run together in a way which negated scientific enquiry at the expense of values and purposes. Only today are the two aspects of socialist practice being correctly distinguished again.

Radical humanism and orthodox Marxism often clashed, notably in the work of Althusser whose interpretation of Marx is given much attention in this work. Very often, however, they formed a twin attack on the classical orthodoxies of the social sciences. They frequently came together on the question of the social superstructure. This book follows in the wake of their twin attacks on this realm: attacks centred on the question of ideology. For me, the most relevant areas under doubt and scrutiny were the legal system, the institution of mass communication and the social definitions of morality and deviance. The concept of ideology is very central to all three areas. The legal system is founded upon a series of ritually articulated ideologies which work to benefit the dominant classes. Newspapers, television and schools constantly disseminate ideology, predominantly of the bourgeois variety. And definitions of social deviance are essentially expressions of dominant ideology in moral terms. What is more, the existing studies of these areas of social life themselves seemed to favour the status quo ideologically. Thus law had been seen as an expression of universal consensus, or the national interest, administered by impartial judges; the mass media were said to be presenting 'the truth' impartially; and social deviants really were sick people.

Ideology really is central to all the radical and Marxist enquiries made of the superstructure. Yet, its existing conception is inadequate. Moreover this inadequacy is compounded by the multiplicity in the range of conceptions offered. I deal with the range of conceptions here and there throughout the book, but for newcomers to the field it may be useful if I outline the main definitions of ideology currently on offer:

1. Ideology is a set of beliefs stemming from false consciousness. The falsity here is usually explained by class interests.
2. Ideology is a political thought system, usually motivated by self-interest or Utopian hopes.
3. Ideology is a superficial and largely mistaken view of things based on their appearances. This view entails the deceptiveness of all appearances.
4. Ideology is any systematic body of thought. This view usually holds that ideologies are distinguished entirely by their social origin (see Cornforth, 1974).
5. Ideologies are those beliefs which are necessarily generated by a particular mode of production or economic structure (Gramsci, 1971).
6. Ideologies are non-scientific beliefs related more closely to social practice rather than to theoretical enquiry (Althusser, 1969).
7. Ideology is the lived relation between people and their world represented in an imaginary way in their unconscious (Althusser, 1971).
8. Ideology is the site of the class struggle in consciousness (Callinicos, 1976).
9. Ideology refers to a complex of social practices and systems of representations which have political significance and effect (Hirst, 1976a).
10. Ideology is a specific social practice: "an articulation of the fixed relations of representation to a specific organisation of reality, relations which established the positions that it is possible for the individual to inhabit within the social totality" (Coward and Ellis, 1977, p. 78).

I have mentioned three basic conceptions and seven fairly recent ones in order to indicate that the problem of the concept of ideology is not a great deal nearer to solution. All these conceptions would cite Marx for authority: they are all interpretations of his texts. It is clear that someone, sometime, will have to examine and compare the different Marxist approaches and elucidate their real similarities and their definite differences. That is not my purpose here, however. I have decided to establish for myself the utility (for analysis) of a particular line of enquiry into the matter. If one looks at these ten definitions of ideology, several clear differences emerge. Firstly, some writers think ideologies must be systematic, others think that even a simple form of consciousness could be ideological. Secondly, some think ideologies must be mistaken and others think falsity is not a necessary feature. Thirdly, some people relate ideologies only to the economic structure and others relate ideology to all forms of social practice. These differences will arise time and again throughout this book. It must also be clear from my list of definitions that there are some common principles. Clearly, interpretations claiming Marxian parentage usually see ideologies as (1) elements of consciousness, (2) originating in social practice, which (3) are widespread throughout a society. There is a fourth common feature, and that is that in some way ideologies often reflect the main social relations in a society and the appearances which these relations give to phenomena. So there is a broad core of agreement: it is one which I develop in this text. Falsity, political significance, systematicity and economic origin are all contingent features of an ideology, in my view. Therefore, I will attempt to formulate the conception of ideology as elements of consciousness generated within and integral to social practice, reflecting the structure of such practice and the appearances of the practical context. This is in no way to find the lowest common denominator from the Marxist approaches, but to state the view of the essentials that makes most sense to me.

Ideology is a very difficult area of enquiry; at first it seemed colossal. However, I have tried to be as clear as possible. I hope that the reader will bear with me. This book is very much a theoretical investigation, an exploration, rather than a definitive review of the field. I have sprawled far and wide in my attempt to pursue the key questions I posed for myself. It is not an exploration within any one discipline, but has plundered any discipline relevant to the enquiry: linguistics, communication studies, sociology, politics, economics and law all enter the fray. Primarily, it is a philosophical enquiry within social theory which attempts to elucidate concepts, fix definitions, suggest future areas of enquiry and to establish a method of reading ideology. It was written for self-clarification and, like all such writings, it is cumulative and what fruits it bears are strewn throughout. It is an exploration which is geared to producing fruitful concepts and valid method for future historical/empirical analysis, rather than to establishing a 'correct' political line. Fundamentally, it is an enquiry based on problems arising from my own empirical research on ideology in press reports and judicial decisions; problems which stemmed from the apparently impressionistic and subjective nature of existing methods of reading ideology. I began, therefore, in search of an answer to the question: is a more scientific method of reading ideology possible or is the study of ideology caught up in its own ideological circle?

In terms of ideology itself, the main questions I was asking were: what is ideology? how does one identify it? what determines its forms of appearance? and, what is ideology's place and function within a social formation? In terms of law, I was very dissatisfied with the depth of understanding Marxism had to offer when law began to be re-examined by scholars in Britain in the 1970s. Everything seemed to be put down to dominant class interests based on the economic structure. The state was often mentioned but was quickly dismissed as an instrument of the bourgeoisie. Times have changed, of course, and the enquiry is now more sophisticated. I hope to contribute to that progress. In particular, I want to show that the basic theoretical premises of Marxist analysis demand that law be seen in its ideological aspect. Investigations hitherto have tended to focus on its economic and political features and functions. It seems to be that laws and their interpretation by lawyers are very much a part of contemporary culture. They are not just political interventions in economic conflicts. Their very character as discursive expressions containing meaning must also be examined. Laws are not just functional instruments, they are also displays of ideology. I am thus interested in legal discourse as a social form in the same way as other people are interested in the social nature of novels or works of art. I am also concerned with legality itself: the very form of law seems to have an important ideological function.

Law is a particularly interesting expression of ideology in many ways. It has a peculiar language all of its own. It has clear economic and political functions. It is clearly not just an automatic reflex of current economic social relations. And, very importantly, it seems to be closely involved in the hegemony of the ruling class. Law therefore represents a challenging phenomenon for the theory of ideology and the method of reading ideology. I hope to show that Marxist concepts and the method of historical materialism are in a position to make great advances in the investigation of the social nature of the legal form.

The investigation gets under way in the next chapter with a statement of my interpretation of the Marxian theory of ideology as it evolved out of my dissatisfaction with Althusser's work. This chapter serves to make explicit the theoretical assumptions which entered into the discourse of Part Two of the book. The latter section is a critique of some of the most popular methods of reading ideology. It is the dominant section of the book because that, essentially, is where the research began in practice. The critiques it contains are not focused on mere technique. They are concerned with method or theoretically informed technique. Because of this, they raise issues of epistemology and methodology of acute importance in social science. Methods of reading ideology seem to raise these issues more acutely than any other field of enquiry. More importantly, a focus on method is central in the book because it serves to demonstrate the substantial problems facing the general study of ideology in social science, and therefore the study of law. Thorny theoretical issues are raised, time and time again.

It seems to me that problems emerging from practice are usually more clearly understood than those posed on the basis of logical enquiry. Method is very revealing. It will be seen that when examined, the main methods of reading ideology are often appallingly inadequate. Some of them use fancy theoretical justifications which usually reduce to nothing, and some of them use no explicit theory at all. Their investigation demonstrates the importance of sound theory in the construction of method: inadequate theory usually seems to result in the erection of great methodological monstrosities which are nothing but common sense. The methods examined in Chapters 3 to 6 are those of content analysis, information theory, speculative criticism, structuralism in general, structuralist semiology and neo-structuralism. I conclude that they are inadequate and Part Three of the book contains, in Chapter 7, the theoretical advances needed to be able to formulate a more scientific method of reading ideology. That method is formulated at the end of Chapter 7.

Chapter 8 is an exploration of the ideological features of law. This is done by way of a look at previous Marxist theories of law and some formulations of my own. The concepts and method arrived at in the earlier chapters are put to work in an account of the ideological composition of law and the historical materialist method for reading the ideology in its discourses. Chapter 9 sums up and adds some final reflections.

Throughout I shall maintain that ideology is a vital feature of all social practice. It is vitally important, therefore, to know what it is and how to read its existence within its complex forms of appearance, such as discourses. Without it, the theory of law is much impoverished. The problems involved in understanding ideology are brought sharply to light when we try to identify it in practice. Consequently, although the book may seem at first glance to be outside the theory of law, it most certainly is not. The study of law will not be advanced by continually investigating specific pieces of legislation or specific legal systems. These investigations must be accompanied by enquiries into the theory of law and the methodology and philosophy of the social sciences. Since ideology is one of the two components of the legal form, the other being power, the conception and identification of ideology are of central importance to the development of the social analysis of law. Therefore, the continual reference to ideological forms other than legal discourse is not irrelevant or accidental. These references are instructive by analogy. More importantly, they anchor my insistence that legal discourse and the ideology of law must always be seen in relation to other contemporaneous forms of ideology, such as those in the newspapers and on television, because law is but one of several ideological forms which combine to form and reproduce the ideological kernel of class hegemony. Law is linked in reality with other ideological forms and apparatuses as a mechanism of domination by consent: it must therefore be linked with them in theory too.

2   *Ideology and Social Practice*

Introduction

My purpose in this chapter is to outline a conception of ideology and its location within a social formation (or society). This outline will act as a foundation for later critiques and expositions; the latter will, in turn, clarify and refine the foundation.

The conception presented here is itself founded—in Marxian analysis and the socialist movement. It represents the result of an attempt to draw Marx to his logical conclusion on the question of ideology, whilst at the same time still making sense out of the appearances of social reality. The latter requirement is uppermost, of course, and where Marx is silent I have drawn on others, such as Saussure and Vološinov, without producing any inconsistency. What becomes clear is that a sophisticated theory of ideology can be developed on the basis of Marx's existing formulations.

Given the difficulty of the issue, the varied uses of the term ideology, and the esoteric, internecine character of Marxist writings, I shall aim for clarity above all else. Many of the implications and issues I raise will, therefore, not receive much treatment: some of them will be dealt with in later chapters but others will need comment elsewhere. Given my prime aim, I shall only use one theorist, Louis Althusser, as a sparring partner. The absence of detailed critiques of writers such as Gramsci and Habermas may be unfortunate, but clarity and space dictate. This is not a comprehensive review of the field but is intended as a sustained investigation of one line of thought on ideology in order to see if that line is tenable.

My reading of Marx concerns itself with the letter and the spirit of his work from 1845 onwards. Before that time, he did not use a concept of ideology regularly, if at all; nor did he even have the basic premises of an account of ideologies. Even after 1845, what we have is mainly odd quotes and the implicit logic of his general position. In his major work, *Capital*, there is a detailed exposition of the laws of value, and ideology is merely an incidental theme. In short, there is not a great deal to work from: only a signpost and a few odd clues. However, what signs and clues we have will serve as a starting point.

Ideology and the Forms of Consciousness: Fundamental Propositions

To begin with, it is abundantly clear that Marx did not conceive of the elements of consciousness as the foundation of any social formation. Even where they appear to be, as in the Middle Ages, this is an illusion:

> This much, however, is clear, that the middle ages could not live on Catholicism, nor the ancient world on politics. On the contrary, it is the mode in which they gained a livelihood that explains why here politics, and there Catholicism, played the chief part. (Marx, 1974, p. 86n)

Marx believed that "the mode of production determines the character of the social, political and intellectual life generally" (ibid.), and that "definite social forms of thought" correspond to "the economic structure of society" (ibid.). However, whilst Marx held that the economic structure was the basis and dynamic of all social formations, he did not argue that everything non-economic was an immediate and direct product of the economic. His conception of the economic structure as "the real foundation" (Marx and Engels, 1973, p. 181) was that it assigned "rank and influence" to other forms of social practice: the economic structure "is a general illumination which bathes all other colours and modifies their particularity" (Marx, 1973, p. 107). So, whilst the economic structure does, indeed, produce certain elements of social consciousness, and does, indeed, act as the basic determination of the dominant ideologies of the day, some elements of social consciousness can arise out of other types of social practice (e.g. politics, law, mass communication). This is why

Marx and Engels can say in *The German Ideology* that "consciousness can never be anything else than conscious being, and the being of men is their actual life-process." (Marx and Engels, 1976a, p. 36).

For Marx, the form and substance of social consciousness are intimately bound up with people's everyday existence. Neither exist in a vacuum, like some brooding omniprescience in the sky, both are integral aspects of social practice. Consciousness originates within social practice and acts as a social determinant of its products. In *The Eighteenth Brumaire*, Marx develops this thesis:

> Upon the different forms of property, upon the social conditions of existence, rises an entire superstructure of distinct and peculiarly formed sentiments, illusions, modes of thought and views of life. The entire class creates and forms them out of its material foundations and out of the corresponding social relations. The single individual, who derives them through tradition and upbringing, may imagine that they form the real motives and starting point of his activity. (Marx and Engels, 1973, p. 117)

The forms and elements of social consciousness are not individual inventions: they reflect the total life situation of a social group and form the mental grid through which that situation is experienced by the group. This fact of life does not exempt theorists, lawyers, philosophers, priests and other members of the "ideological classes" (Marx's phrase) whose job it is to articulate and produce social ideologies:

> The same men who establish their social relations in conformity with their material productivity, produce also principles, ideas and categories, in conformity with their social relations." (Marx and Engels, 1976b, p. 166)

No person or group is exempt from the rule that social relations determine the modes of social consciousness. Such a thing is inconceivable as long as social relations exist.

What exactly did Marx mean, though, when he used the term ideology? Three things are definitely clear. Firstly, whatever ideology means exactly, its instances could include: sentiments, illusions, modes of thought, views of life, principles, ideas and categories. None of these things in themselves seem to be the sole referent of ideology in Marx's work; each is a form taken by ideology. Secondly, Marx saw the ruling ideologies of a society as those of the ruling class. Their economic and political supremacy also gave them supremacy in intellectual life. Thirdly, the "ideologists" and "ideological classes" of modern societies were consistently defined by Marx to refer to such groups as jurists, politicians, priests, lawyers, philosophers and professors. These classes were seen as the producers of thought-systems which justified or obscured the social relations of an epoch and thus contributed to the hegemony of the ruling class.

It is easy to conclude, as most commentators on Marx have done (e.g. Mepham, 1974; Evans, 1975), that ideology is composed of those representations which conceal real social relations. Marx and Engels certainly imply this in many places. For example, in *The German Ideology*, Marx and Engels say that ideology may turn social relations "upside down as in a camera obscura" and imply that the "ideological reflexes" in men's brains are mere "phantoms" (1976a, p. 36). In many places, ideology is described as "mist". However, I do not think that such statements warrant a conclusion that ideologies *always* mask and thereby sustain social structures. If Marx and Engels drew such a warrant, why were they constantly concerned to develop the radical spontaneous consciousness of the European working classes? Indeed, Marx argued that capitalism produced its own "gravediggers" because of its own internal logic as a mode of production. Moreover, he demonstrated in *Capital* that the capitalist economic system worked in such a way that, of itself, it concealed its own constitutive social relations. Whether one looked at it with a true or false consciousness did not matter, it still presented itself to the senses in a way that left its inner structure undisclosed. Therefore, it is not false consciousness (nor the ideological classes) that conceals the nature of capitalism, nor did capitalism fail to produce people who could, wholly or partly, see through its apparent form. We might also add that Marx and Engels are usually concerned with the ruling ideology when they are discussing ideology, so their statements would tend to overemphasize ideology's false or mystifying forms. Conservatism and mystification are merely tendencies of ruling ideology: they are not the defining features of ideology in general.

If we return to *The German Ideology* for a moment, I think that we can begin to unearth the complexity of Marx's conception of ideology. In this text, the glimmerings of a distinction emerge; a distinction which seems to run throughout Marx's subsequent work in one form or another. When Marx and Engels use the following apparently clumsy phrase, they leave us a clue:

> . . . morality, religion, metaphysics and all the rest of ideology as well as the forms of consciousness corresponding to these . . .
> (1976a, p. 36)

Ideology, here, seems to refer to specific elements of thought, whilst forms of consciousness seem to be general modes of thought. In a later passage, in the same text, particular forms of consciousness are discussed (e.g. sensuous consciousness, sheep-like consciousness and 'philosophical' consciousness or consciousness independent of manual or productive labour), and they again clearly refer to general modes of "conscious being" (1976a, pp. 44, 45). At this point, Marx and Engels argue that, once mental labour is separated from manual labour as a distinct mode of social practice, consciousness can "emancipate itself from the world" and "proceed to the formation of 'pure' theory, theology, philosophy, morality, etc.," (ibid.). I am left with the impression that, given a determinate level of the productive forces, a clear distinction can be made between general modes of thought ("forms of consciousness") and specific elements of thought ("ideologies"): neither of which are necessarily false. This historical-conceptual distinction seems worth retaining, even if we change the use of the terms used to define it in *The German Ideology*.

Probably more on the basis of philosophical elitism than history, Hegel made a similar distinction. In his *Logic*, a text Marx was closely familiar with, Hegel distinguished general thought from "the reflective thought of philosophy" (1975, pp. 4, 5). Hegel believed (like Marx) that consciousness in general distinguished man from other animals. It did not usually take the form of thoughts, but rather feelings, perceptions and images. In some instances, notably law, religion and morality, general consciousness took the form of feelings and images moulded and permeated by spontaneous thought. In contrast, Hegel argued, philosophical consciousness involved thoughtful reflection on these general "modes of con-sciousness" (his phrase, p. 5). It involved logical and reasoned thought about spontaneous thoughts, impressions, images and feel-ings which thereby brought the latter "into consciousness". Hegel did not agree with the view that philosophy was superior to general consciousness because it led to the truth. The truth could be contained in a mere image, although it could not be *known* in that form: the task of philosophy was to know the truth and not just experience it. As Hegel points out, if we had to have knowledge of chemistry, botany and zoology before we could eat, these sciences would not exist at all.

If we now look at Marx's "1859 Preface", we see that he talks about "the legal, political, religious, aesthetic or philosophic—in short ideological forms" within which "men become conscious" of explosive contradictions in the economic system during "an epoch of social revolution" (Marx and Engels, 1973, p. 182). It seems to me that Marx implied that, in all periods, people not only spontaneously experience the contradictions of the social structure but also fight them out under the banners of various thought-systems. These thought-systems bring the spontaneously experienced social contradictions to a fuller and clearer consciousness. In short, although he puts philosophy in the same category as law, religion and morality, Marx makes the same distinction as Hegel in separating out spontaneous consciousness and organized thought. It could be argued (correctly) that for Hegel, organized thought was only useful for self-knowledge, whereas for Marx it could also render the social relations of people's existence intelligible to them. It could also be correctly state that Hegel tended to see forms of thought as phenomena of the human mind rather than as thoroughly social entities. Nevertheless, I think that a similarity exists between Marx and Hegel on the point in question.

I am, therefore, satisfied that Marx, like several Marxists, drew a distinction between two general modes of consciousness. One was spontaneous and linked to the exigencies of productive labour: the other was more thought-based and linked to unproductive labour. One was not necessarily truer than the other; in fact, meditative or reflecting consciousness probably contained more organized untruth than spontaneous or practical consciousness. Neither mode bore any *necessary* relation of 'accuracy' to the real world. However, as Marx pointed out, "all science would be superfluous if the outward appearance and the essence of things directly coincided" (Marx, 1972, p. 817). Science is only therefore possible as a result of meditative or philosophical consciousness: "there is no royal road to science" (Marx, 1974, p. 30). If spontaneous consciousness could grasp everything on sight, scientific philosophy would be non-existent.

One should also realize that the distinction in consciousness was not class-based: it does not mean that the workers are thoughtless and too busy to think whilst the leisured classes are thoughtful and spending their hours in introspection. The distinction relates to general forms of social labour rather than labouring (or non-labouring) groups and thus cuts across classes. On the other hand, the above class caricature is not absolute nonsense, because the general forms of social labour are obviously class-related and exist in the context of a class structure. Basically, though, the distinction refers to the general forms of social labour; spontaneous or practical consciousness therefore being that general form of consciousness typical within the active production of/social wealth. Marx was strongly against the confinement of people to one kind of labour: either productive or unproductive labour on its own was a recipe for stunted "human growth" (see Marx and Engels, 1976a, pp. 46–49). Communist society would herald the collapse of the distinction in consciousness along with the abolition of the general division of social labour, provided the productive forces had been developed to the extent that privation was also abolished.

Let us stop and reflect for a moment in order to settle the terminology. In Marx, "ideologies" seem to be the specific stuff of consciousness and "the forms of social consciousness" seem to be general modes. I propose to label the two forms of social conscious-ness, given historical significance by Marx, as follows: (1) spontane-ous consciousness, and (2) philosophical consciousness. These terms have some suitable, historical connotations and seem preferable to the distinctions "practical/meditative" and "commonsense/reflec-tive". I shall return to ideologies in a moment but, first, let us examine the above distinction a little further.

The conceptual distinction between spontaneous and philosophical consciousness is an historical one, in at least two senses. Not only does it depend on the existence of basic developments in the social productive forces, but also its edges begin to blur and fade as automation moves towards its peak. General categories, said Marx "are . . . themselves likewise a product of historic relations, and possess their full validity only for and within these relations" (1973,

p. 105). At times, history has seen our two modes of consciousness separated socially by colossal gulfs. The onset of machine capitalism seems to be the height of the separation, where philosophy reaches its utmost in heavenly abstraction and spontaneity sinks to the hell of the struggle for survival. At other times and in specific places, the gap seems to be closing. The oldest capitalist society, Britain, seems to produce more and more people with practical and philosophic sense (of some depth) every day. For example, certain well-developed ideologies are profoundly and instinctively familiar to many: socialism, free enterprise, liberal democracy and egalitarianism. In the same way, philosophic ideologies have been thoroughly permeated by the pragmatism of spontaneous thought. The high development of mass communication technology has accelerated this interpenetration—without ever being a necessary condition for the existence of the intermingling.

The spontaneous mode of social consciousness could happily be termed practical or experiential since its elements are the flashing moments of consciousness in practice. Philosophical consciousness also goes on within the framework of some social practice: armchair philosophers need wealth and power to provide them with the time and the armchairs. But the practices of unproductive labour do allow more time for reflection, and often make reflection upon extant consciousness (of both kinds) the absolute centre of the work. In this sense, philosophical consciousness is more contemplative, interpretive and introspective: its world of reference is the world of social consciousness more than the world of practical social reality.

Hegel had seen philosophy as the practice of getting to know the phenomena of spontaneous experience. The two forms of consciousness had an order: spontaneous consciousness was the infrastructure and philosophic consciousness the superstructure. For Marx, the ordering holds but in a different and less abstract way. For him, the two forms of consciousness emerged because of an increased differentiation of the social division of labour. They were also embodied, confined and developed separately within the different corridors of that division of labour. Thus, I think Marx would say three things about Hegel's ordering:

1. The ideas and images of spontaneous consciousness may be taken

to a "higher power" in the cultural and political practices of the social superstructure, but the real question is: whose common-sense is being elaborated in systematic form? The workers' commonsense is not the commonsense of the masters.

2. Given that the practices of the superstructure have their own particularity, they enable the extended development of specific ideas and principles. This attenuation within the cloistered and carefully guarded confines of a cultural or political practice produces the possibility that the 'philosophic forms' produced represent the extension of no group's commonsense other than that of the immediate producers.

3. Spontaneous ideas, images and feelings are not converted into philosophic or attenuated forms without human intervention *in specific social circumstances*. Consequently, the nature and function of cultural or political practice, in a given society, needs to be understood before one can describe the nature of the extension and its social functions.

Finally, since spontaneous consciousness is generally more rooted in the hurly-burly of the productive life-cycle, it tends to be more flexible, more pragmatic, adaptive and less ordered or principled than philosophical consciousness. I do not think this view would offend Marxian method; although at first glance, it looks like a reification of extant forms of class consciousness. It must be remembered that our categories are historical and the extent of the difference between the two forms will vary; although, I would maintain that as long as the distinction exists then these differences will hold to some degree. Two further points must also be remembered in considering my conclusion. Firstly, historical materialism abandons the notion of forms of consciousness as an individual or group invention; we are discussing general forms of *social* consciousness which are linked to general forms of *social* labour. These forms of social consciousness must *not* be reduced to forms of class consciousness. Secondly, one must not assume that being ordered or principled makes a thought-system better, more moral and more true: everything here depends on the principles or categories used to do the ordering. The net outcome of this difference in the two forms of consciousness is that one must expect the formations or systems produced by philosophical consciousness to be intrinsically more slower moving, more rigid and less immediate as reflections of social relations. Their inner ordering principles are more effective in determining their products: the imperatives of social structure are thus mitigated to a certain extent. Research into forms of consciousness must be cognisant of these differences, and cognisant of them as reflections of the general division of social labour in itself: the differences cannot be explained away simply by more contingent determinations such as "the cloistered nature of academe", "the social isolation of judges" or "the bureaucratizing influence of capital".

I have said that it seems to be Marx's view that "the forms of social consciousness" (spontaneous and philosophical) are general modes of subjective being reflecting general forms of social labour and that "ideologies" are the specific elements or moments of social consciousness. I think that this view is correct and it is now necessary and possible to develop the notion of ideology. Clarity again forces us to examine terms. Is there a warrant to describe the more systematic products of philosophical consciousness as ideologies (as Marx did) and to find some other term (e.g. language) for the elements of spontaneous consciousness? I think not. Firstly, such a usage would encourage the conception of ideology as a false system of thoughts based on a political motivation, or as Raymond Williams puts it:

> Meanwhile, in popular argument, "ideology" is still mainly used in the sense given by Napoleon. Sensible people rely on *experience*, or have a *philosophy*; silly people rely on "ideology". In this sense, "ideology", now as in Napoleon, is mainly a term of abuse. (Williams, 1976, p. 130)

Secondly, elements of philosophical consciousness are, in Marx, not characterized *necessarily* by falsity, conservatism, radicalism, or political origin. Thirdly, elements of both kinds of consciousness are, for Marx, all reflections of social existence: terminological differentiation between them may lead to a view of spontaneous elements as non-social. So, for example, Roland Barthes, the French semiologist, posits the existence of elements of non-ideological consciousness (denotative signs), as forms free from social consciousness in their constitution as a kind of realm of pure meaning (see Chapter 5). It may be hard for some to accept readily that even the most elementary elements of consciousness, "denotative" signs, are, in some way, reflections of the (past or present) conditions of social practice. However, just because a sociological etymology may seem a difficult project, it does not mean that our principle is wrong. Everyday words come to have meanings so accepted that it is hard to imagine them having origins in social practice. As Marx continually emphasized, products always conceal the labour and circumstances which disappeared in their making. Having said this, however, it does seem necessary to distinguish in some way between simple elements (e.g. an image) and complex elements (e.g. a treatise) of social consciousness.

As a result of these considerations, I propose to use the term *ideology* to refer to the basic or simple elements (the ideas, images, impressions, notions, etc.) of any form of social consciousness, and the term *ideological formation* to refer to an element of any form of social consciousness which is a complex connected admixture, serialization or systematization of ideologies (e.g. a theory, a discourse, a complex idea, an item of social morality, a law, a theology).[1] These usages, although perhaps idiosyncratic at the moment, seem eminently appropriate in the light of the above discussions. They may be at odds with those of Marx, but they are not at odds with his theoretical principles.

What is an ideology in itself? The internal form of an ideology is that of a sign: it is a signification.[2] An ideology is a sign of something other than itself, an outcome and element of social practice which reflects and designates the world of that practice within the consciousness of human beings. It is a child of social parents whose first home is in the mind of an individual but whose subsequent residence varies promiscuously through a whole range of material phenomena. It is an element of social consciousness and, as such, a real thing with finite (although rarely precise) boundaries. It is one of the determinants of the products of social practice (since it is an element within such practice) and thus is a structuring element in the design of many phenomena, such as cars, paintings, architecture, laws, new social relations, forms of food, etc.

What is a sign? Following Saussure (1974) and others, I define a sign as a composition of signifying unit and signified meaning in relation. The signifier could be a word, a pictorial image, a sound or a material form (e.g. a statue, a road sign). The signified meaning could take the form of a mental image, concept or impression. Thus the word 'cup' designates the image(s) of a cup. Saussure argued that the relation between a signifier and a signified was not usually one of natural resemblance (the word 'cup' does not look like any cup), nor one of causality ('smoke' does not mean fire) (see Culler, 1975, p. 16). He thought that the relation was one of arbitrariness: each unit in a signifying system acted merely as an arbitrary function of the total structure. The relation between 'cup' and an image of a cup was thus given by the total signifying system of language of which 'cup' is a part. On the basis of my arguments, this cannot be the case and I would argue that the relation between the signifier and the signified emerges out of social practice or co-operation. As Marx put it, "language *is* practical real consciousness that exists for other men as well, . . . (it) only arises from the need, the necessity of intercourse with other men" (Marx and Engels, 1976a, p. 44). The linguistic sign 'cup' and its relation to a specific meaning thus emerge from *social* intercourse. The meaning of a linguistic term is in no way arbitrary or a function of some magical, ahistorical, linguistic system; although, no doubt, its relation to other linguistic terms required (and constantly requires) demarcation. In short, the relation between the signifier and signified is a social or historical relation.[3]

An ideology is a sign and, therefore, an ideological formation is a cluster or series of signs. And, given our basic principles, we can say that the relations linking the signs within an ideological formation are also social or historical relations. Like the relation between a signifier and a signified, the relations between signs are reflections of social conditions of existence. The connections between the signs 'cup', 'competition', 'sport' and 'victory' are no arbitrary concoction but the outcome of definite social practices in the historical development of a specific social formation.

Ideologies and ideological formations exist within people's heads (their first homes) and determine the way that those people live out their social relations. Certainly people make choices but only under the ideological, economic and political conditions of their time and place. The notion of free will is a false understanding of subjectivity which reflects bourgeois social relations.

Ideologies and their formations do not *just* exist in consciousness. Certainly, they are the elements of spontaneous and philosophical consciousness, but precisely because of that they are also something else. They also exist embodied within the material products of social practice. As determining elements within social practice, they help to shape the product. High-rise flats, motorways and parks are obvious examples of material form which, structured by ideologies and their formations, in turn act as material elements structuring our social practice. Laws are perhaps classic examples of ideology's active character. As the (passive) reflections of certain social relations, ideologies can become embodied in laws which, when applied, involve their intrinsic ideologies as (active) determinants of other social relations. The legal process also admirably illustrates the theoretical point that, once embodied, ideologies do not *necessarily* (re-)structure our practice; sometimes they need reinforcement to make them effective. The reinforcement of our ideology can, of course, occur outside the legal process and can take different forms. For example, the social relations of national news production result in most of the population being rarely exposed to some ideologies and overexposed to others, the latter being reinforced accordingly: ownership and/or control of property gives ideological, as well as economic and political, power. Ideologies also exist in the embodied forms of language, film and painting. It is a platitude that the latter two forms can (re-)structure our practice. Language, however, has long been taken for granted as 'natural': its *social* nature has only recently been rediscovered ('socio-linguistics'). But, as an embodiment of ideology, linguistic forms or units structure our perception of the world: words are not just words. Perhaps the use of words in a specific way reinforces ideology as much as sheer force. Considered in the same context as legal force and skyscrapers, one realizes how understated is the need to develop the sociology of language: at least, in terms of describing the (re-)structuring effects of ideology.

Ideology is thus both mental and concrete, a creation and creator of social practice and produce. Ideologies in this way are inhabitants of the social world and not creations of the human mind. Their origins, forms of existence, level of effectivity and effects are all purely social matters. 'Man' does not create them in any sense. What sometimes appears as an 'invention', the creation of new relations of signification by an individual, is just the same as the use of existing relations of signification: a practice of signification by an individual in a social position within definite social relationships and conditions.

New ideologies, new uses of old ideologies, old ideologies—all are thoroughly social products. I reject any theory of the human or biological origin of ideology. Moreover, I would reject any psychological approach which believes that ideologies only exist within the mind, whether it be an idealistic one where social reality results from 'man's psychology', or a behaviouristic one where concrete forms are causes which are not credited with ideological content. Matter, meaning and social relations do not just interact, they also interpenetrate.

Clearly, the phenomenal forms of ideology, whether in the mind (ideas, impressions, feelings) or embodied (language, architecture, action) are many and varied. What must be said is that these forms are not pure expressions of an essence. They *never* exist in a direct one-to-one relationship with the ideology they contain. This is an important point of theoretical principle. An ideology-in-itself is one thing, discrete and real, and its phenomenal form, equally real and much more discreet, is another. The phenomenal form, that which presents itself to the sense, has to be produced before it can exist and, therefore, the conditions, contexts and structure of that production will be the immediate determinations of the phenomenal form. In considering the appearance of an ideology we must therefore always pay full attention to both the conditions of existence of an ideology and its conditions of appearance. Things, including ideologies, are rarely what they seem to be. It is curious that modern students of ideology seem more interested in its inner nature than in its phenomenal form and manner of appearance. If some ideologies serve to maintain the hegemony of the ruling class, then it is also true that their forms and contexts of appearance serve the same function. An ideology's forms of appearance are often discreet and shy: it is often too modest to reveal its true self. Its contexts of appearance often ensure the easy belief in that non-appearance: they can be the water which allows the pill of ideology to slide down the throat without catching the mind's attention. We need to pay more attention to the social functions of the forms and contexts of appearance of ideology. The latter are real and determinant, just as much as the ideology itself. Is not the legal form and the legal machinery for imposing it just as socially important and interesting as the ideology embodied in it? Essentialist approaches to ideology which study the content of the book without considering the nature and effect of the book-form are exposed by analogy when we look at law and discover that a key question for modern state officials is whether to impose an ideology through a series of speeches, a national debate, a television broadcast or a law.

Vološinov claims that he does not draw on Marx for his conception of ideology as sign. For what it matters, I think that the conception is not only consistent with Marx but that it can enhance the Marxian analysis in *Capital*. I shall attempt to demonstrate this and thus develop the conception of ideology further in Chapter 7. In that chapter, I shall attempt to specify the causal mechanism for any ideology and the general conditions determining ideological transformations. Without anticipating that discussion too much, I want to make two final remarks before moving on to discuss Althusser and the social nature of ideology.

Firstly, it is easy to grasp the notion of sign and misuse it in a disastrous way. The common error is to say that everything is a sign of something else. This view leads to the idea that the world is only inhabited by signs or ideologies, and then we are right back to a fully fledged idealism. All else—practice, matter, social relations—disappears out of the window. What must be remembered, in order to avoid this tendency, is that something only becomes significant when its appearance in social practice is signified in terms of a signifying unit (e.g. a word) in the mind of an observer. Neither the object nor its observed appearance is a sign in itself. Signs are not constituted statically by objects or their outward forms, rather, they are the results of a practical process of socially contextualized signification. Nothing is thought of as a sign of anything else without social intercourse. Law is not taken to be a sign of civilization unless someone, or some class, designates it as such in social practice and ensures widespread acceptance of that designation.

Secondly, following on naturally from the first point, it must be emphasized that the relation between an ideology or sign and the 'reality' designated is a purely social one and has no necessary, *a priori* truth or falsity. The attribution of sign X to social occurrence M may be the result of stupid thinking or deliberate deception. Alternatively, A's designation of M in terms of sign X may be comprehensible to a sympathetic observer of the designation because the signified image within X can be shown by A to capture some of M's apparent character. Or, again, A may designate M in terms of signs X, Y and

Z and be able to convince many people that these signs capture in thought-form all the aspects of M's apparent and latent character. The theory of ideology is by no means purely a theory of false consciousness or deceptive designation. Far more interesting and important is the grey area of comprehensible designations: these are the signs that can live long and serve well the cause of class hegemony.

I want now to discuss the work of Althusser on ideology in order to illustrate the specificity of my own position and to place ideology within the totality of a society or a social formation.

Ideology in the Social Formation: a Critique of Althusser

How are we to locate ideologies and the forms of social conscious-ness within the total social formation? Are we to rely on the classic formulations of the "1859 Preface" (Marx and Engels, 1973), which seem to suggest that ideology is part of a political and cultural superstructure erected upon an economic base? Do those formula-tions betray Marx's conception of consciousness as a vital element of all social practice? How are we to understand ideology as a socially located phenomenon?

I want to explore these questions through a discussion of Althus-ser's observations on ideology and formulate a preliminary, but basic, position which will be developed in the course of the subse-quent chapters. This is not a critique of Althusser for its own sake, but for the purpose of developing a line of investigation.[4] Althusser's work is pointed in a similar direction to my own and therefore aids this purpose: moreover, I think that his approach is closer to that of Marx and to the rub of the matter than that of more phenomenologi-cal efforts, such as those of Habermas.

Louis Althusser is a Marxist philosopher and a theoretician of the French Communist Party. His work over the last fifteen years is now known world-wide.[5] He is concerned with restoring the original Marxian doctrine and with elucidating the epistemological basis of Marx's work. His concerns are not founded on the basis of the need for doctrinal purity, but are a reflection of the past failures of Marxism and the need within the French Communist Party for a developed modern-day analysis. Past errors and modern problems

stem from two political-theoretical deviations: Stalinism and humanism. Althusser is a critic of the former (although not unequivocally),
but directs most of his attention to the latter. Stalinism had reduced
Marxist theory to dogma and thus stunted its practical relevance.
This reduction was of an economistic kind whereby the economic
base was all powerful and the superstructure merely a compliant
effect. Althusser's work struggles with these Stalinist effects. Primarily, however, it is an intervention against the rising tide of humanism
in Marxist theory and practice. Althusser sees humanism as the great
philosophy of the rising bourgeoisie who established humanist ideas
and legal concepts in concordance with the new capitalist social
relations of production which separated men from each other into
individual units free from feudal restrictions. Humanism thus celebrates the autonomy and choice of the free individual, whilst
forgetting that freedom for the working class means freedom to be
exploited by those who own the means of production. It is thus, in
Althusser's view, a voluntaristic philosophy which forgets that men
only exist in the moulds prepared for them by the history of social
relations. In its purest form, he says, it tends to see all social
manifestations as the expression of a fundamental essence: the nature
of Man.

In Marxism, humanism has had the effect of reducing the social
formation to an expression of a basic essence: the capital-labour
dialectic. It is thus similar to Stalinist economism. Fighting against
both deviations, Althusser has attempted to maintain and clarify
Marx's dialectical use of structural determination whilst recognizing
and developing the relevance of ideology to the movement and
nature of capitalist social formations. He sails between Scylla and
Charibdis and lands on the shores of Scylla; however, it's an
interesting and rewarding journey to observe.

Marx and Engels could be said to have sketched out the answer to
the question of this chapter in *The German Ideology* (Marx and
Engels, 1976a). Various statements could be quoted to the effect that
ideology is a sublimation of "the material life-process", that "consciousness is a social product", "conceptions" are produced by men
active at a definite level of productive development, etc., etc. But, for
Althusser, Marx only began to break with humanism in 1845 and so
The German Ideology must be treated as one of the first works of
a major "epistemological break" (Althusser, 1969, pp. 21–40). These

works do not represent a complete rupture with Hegel's idealistic evolutionism or Feuerbach's sensuous materialism. For Althusser, therefore, they present "delicate problems of interpretation" because they still contain the humanist conception of the individual as the "subject" of history. Thus when Marx and Engels talk of ideologies as "reflexes and echoes" of the "life-process", we must not interpret this to mean that ideologies are an automatic, mechanical spin-off from the capital-labour dialectic or that they are the crude creations of the thinking, concrete individual subject. Such interpretations are clearly false says Althusser, since Marx's later work tells us that (1) levels other than the economic have "relative autonomy" and are also determinants of ideologies, and (2) that men are not the subjects of history but that history is a process, "*a development considered in the totality of its real conditions*",[6] without a subject. The later Marx, argues Althusser, develops the concept of the social formation which denotes a complex totality comprising economic, political-legal and ideological practices interrelated in a developing structure dominated by the economic, "in that it determines which of the instances of the social structure occupies the determinant place" at a particular time (Althusser and Balibar, 1970, p. 224). It is this movement of social formations that is, for the later Marx, the process that constitutes history. I agree with Althusser that it is to this concept of the social formation in movement that we must attend, in our attempt to locate ideology as a reflection of the life-process.

Paul Hirst has stated that, for Marx, forms of social consciousness are only "effects of the structure of the social formation" (Hirst, 1975a, pp. 211, 212). This seems to me to be a faulty formulation. In neatly paraphrasing Althusser's Marxism he has provided a sharp illustration of one of Althusser's weaknesses. At several points in his work, Althusser's attempt to smash humanism leads him to imply that ideology is not a determinant, and never can be, of the nature and movement of a social formation, but simply an effect of it. Althusser's formulations usually carry the notion of ideology as a mirror reflection or effect of the social process. For example, in an essay on Brecht and Bertolozzi, he says:

> But what, concretely, is this uncriticized ideology if not simply the "familiar", "well-known", transparent myths in which society or an age can recognise itself (but not know itself), the mirror it looks into for self-recognition, precisely the mirror it

must break if it is to know itself? What is the ideology of a society or a period if it is not that society's or period's consciousness of itself, that is, an immediate material which spontaneously implies, looks for and naturally finds its forms in the image of a consciousness of self living the totality of its world in the transparency of its own myths? (Althusser, 1969, p. 144).

An abstract, almost Durkheimian relation between ideology and the social formation is thus posed, and is then conceived within the basic concept of reflection in *The German Ideology*—as a mechanical, automatic, photographic replication.[7] "Society" gives off ideology just as steam rises from boiling water and thus the "agents" of social life cannot see through the stratosphere of ideology (or "mist" as Marx calls it) since it is the condition of their vision. Not only is this a unilateral, undialectical conception of a falsely posed relation (ideology is *part* of society), but also Althusser has only metaphorically described the rise of ideology. At first glance, it would seem that in *For Marx* (Althusser, 1969) he has not provided the precise concepts with which we can think ideology's emergence or effects.

In *Reading Capital* Althusser argues that ideology

> . . . bends to the interest of the times, but without any apparent movement, being content to *reflect* the historical changes which it is its mission to assimilate and master by some imperceptible modification of its peculiar internal relations . . . It is the immobile motion which, as Hegel said of philosophy itself, reflects and expresses what happens in history without ever running ahead of its own time, since it is merely that time *caught* in the trap of a mirror reflection, precisely so that men will be *caught* in it too. (Althusser and Balibar, 1970, p. 142)

Again, ideology is seen to reflect the social process in such a way that people are the "agents" of that process, captured and trapped in the circularity of their time-bound vision. Ideology here, however, is only seen as *dominant* ideology: there is no sense of a clear-sighted proletarian ideology with a vision of the future. The temporal fog of social life is the only sight for men caught in the vice-like grip of the dominant ideology of their period. Thus, for Althusser, it is no use humanist Marxists claiming that all we need for revolution is for the proletariat to get off its comfortable sofa and engage in revolutionary praxis, because social praxis merely acts upon and reproduces the clouded vision of a society's dominant ideology. However, there is something crucial in the above passage from *Reading Capital* that is an advance on the formulations of *For Marx*. Let us look at the nature of this advance in some detail.

For Marx contains an admixture of concepts of ideology. At first, when talking about theoretical ideology, Althusser clearly says in a remarkably humanistic, Feuerbachian way, that ideology has an "author", "a concrete individual" (1969, p. 63). That author, it is true, reflects history, and the meaning of his ideology depends on existing ideologies, social problems and the social structure—but, examining these points carefully only reveals that Feuerbach said no more and no less. At another point, Althusser proclaims vaguely, quoting *The German Ideology*, that "real history explains" the "formations", "deformations" and "reconstructions" of ideology, and that ideology thus has no history (p. 83n). In the later discussion of the levels of social practice he specifies the existence of "ideological practice" in conjunction with economic and political practice, urging us to take ideology "seriously as an existing practice", and then says that to recognize ideology *as a practice* is "an indispensable prior condition for any theory of ideology" (p. 167). This passage perhaps does not owe much to Feuerbachian humanism but it certainly conflates ideology with ideological practice. Althusser until this point had taken ideology to be an element of consciousness and practice to be a process of transformation of determinate raw material, through the agency of human labour and determinate means of production, into a social product. Thus, when he talks of ideological practice (he gives as examples: religion, politics, law, art), he is talking about that transformation process which has ideology as its object and instruments of production. Therefore to refer to ideology in itself as a practice is like defining coal as coal-mining or meat as butchery. Ideology may be the object and instrument of ideological practice but it does not itself constitute the practice—it merely is an important element within that practice. In my analysis, he is failing to distinguish ideology from the philosophical mode of consciousness and cultural practices. He continues throughout *For Marx* with this conflation, and at another point argues that ideology is "one of the basic practices essential to the existence of the social whole" (p. 191). Finally, later in the book, we are left with another confusion involving a conflation. This time ideology is limited to being a product of philosophical consciousness. Thus ideology is defined as:

> . . . a system (with its own logic and rigour) of representations
> (images, myths, ideas or concepts, depending on the case)
> endowed with a historical existence and role within a given
> society" (1969, p. 231).

Despite this problem that he is still using the Napoleonic
bourgeois concept of ideology as "the doctrine of the ideologues"
(Napoleon's phrase: see Williams, 1976, p. 126),[8] this last passage
does emphasize the possibility of ideology as an important determinant within the social formation. Althusser has thus, by the end of *For
Marx*, developed further than his earlier German Ideology formulations and, at this point, is beginning to see ideology as more than just
an effect, as an element in social formations which has determining
power, and which, under certain economic conditions, may, in its
compound forms, be the key element of a social formation.

That is one useful development. There is, however, a second
development of significance in *For Marx*. Following the passage
discussed above, Althusser ventures:

> Without embarking on the problem of the relations between a
> science and its (ideological) past, we can say that ideology, as a
> system of representations, is distinguished from science in that in
> it the practico-social function is more important than the
> theoretical function (function as knowledge). (1969, p. 231)

Ignoring the ideology/science distinction since it does not concern us
here, it is clear that Althusser is alluding to a concept of the close
links between ideology and social practice. The concept is forged by
the subsequent argument that ideology is "an organic part of every
social totality", including any future Communist society. He continues to confuse spontaneous ideology with its compounded,
theoretical forms in arguing that ideology *only* exists in "specific
formations" (p. 232), but, most importantly, he advocates the view
that ideology is largely unconscious and is "a matter of the *lived*
relation between men and their world" (p. 233). Ideology *is itself*
"the lived relation between men and their world". This would lead
one to think that ideology was *at the same time* "a system of
representations" and a "lived relation". Clearly ideology cannot be
both chicken *and* egg. In other words, ideology cannot be at the same
time an unconscious thought-element and a practical relation, for the
two are different things. He is confusing the issue by turning
unconscious signs into practical relations and vice versa. Althusser

does not recognize this confusion and inadvertently solves the problem by continuing as follows:

> Ideology, then, is the expression of the relation between men and their "world", that is, the (overdetermined) unity of the real relation and the imaginary relation between them and their real conditions of existence. (1969, pp. 233, 234)

Social ideology, then, in Althusser's furthest development in *For Marx*, is a system of representations (largely unconscious) whose determinations are: (1) the relation between their agents and the social conditions in which those agents exist, and (2) the "imaginary" view of that relation contained within the consciousness (again largely unconscious) of those agents.

As I have said, Althusser need not argue that ideology is always found in formations, structures or systems. They are merely the forms it takes as "humanism" (a theoretical, ideological formation), the target of Althusser's work. With that reservation, we can say that Althusser has forged, albeit in highly indecisive fashion, a new concept of social ideology, a concept which breaks from the 'auteur' theory of his Feuerbachian formulations from *The German Ideology* and from the confusions in *For Marx* which argue that ideology is a practice. This new concept specifies social ideology, albeit unclearly and uncertainly, as: mental representations produced out of the unity of men's social relations and their representations of those relations. Such a concept is obviously not satisfactory as a concept of ideology itself since it raises the problem: how can ideology be part of the determinations that produce it? how can ideology and social relations equal ideology? Thus, the concept is insufficient. Althusser's expression of it makes this more than clear:

> It is in this overdetermination of the real by the imaginary and of the imaginary by the real that ideology is *active* in principle, that it reinforces or modifies the relation between men and their conditions of existence, in the imaginary rèlation itself. It follows that this action can never be purely *instrumental*; the men who would use an ideology purely as a means of action, as a tool, find that they have been caught by it, implicated by it, just when they are using it and believe themselves to be absolute masters of it. (1969, p. 234)

Although he hereby abandons the Napoleonic conception of ideology, he only replaces it with a highly confused and condensed notion which lacks a distinction between the signs emerging spontaneously from mundane social practice and the sign-formations produced, on the basis of spontaneous ideology, within societally institutionalized philosophic or cultural practices. Both simple and compound ideologies reflect social relations and so the distinction could consistently be used by Althusser, but he fails to do so. However, what we must not lose sight of is the fact that in his efforts, Althusser has emphasized the importance of ideology as a social phenomenon and has conceptually tied ideology to the social relations within which men live. This was an important development and the take-off point for the statement in *Reading Capital*.

In the passage from *Reading Capital* quoted earlier (on p. 28), Althusser makes a further advance. He conceived of ideology as being closely and rigidly connected to social relations and that the rigidity of the connection forces ideology into amorphous, adaptive and flexible forms. Ideology is "the immobile motion" that reflects the events of history. It is "immobile" in that it *never* leaves its master's side. It is "motion" in that its form is adaptive and moulds itself to its ever-active master. How can this be? How can ideology be immobile yet mobile? It is because the master *always* has a servant, otherwise he would not be a master. Master and servant are two sides of the same relation. Moreover, they interpenetrate. Their relationship is dialectical. The master is a determination of the servant and the servant is a determination of the master. That is, the master is a part or aspect of the servant and vice versa. Similarly, *ideology and social relations exist in dialectical interconnection within social practice*. That is why ideology is mobile and immobile at the same time. It is always moving because of its immobility as an element of social practice, one of whose other permanent aspects is movement or action. Previous Marxist conceptions have often seen ideology as external to social practice, or as superstructure separate from a base, or as an image reflected in a mirror. Thus they have created a false understanding of reflection.[9] Too often they have reduced ideology's social existence by limiting its location to the superstructural practices and by limiting its origins to the economic practices. When this mechanical and economistic notion of reflection is replaced by the notion of ideology as a reflection of social relations, it is immediately obvious that ideologies can originate within superstructural as well as economic practices and can exist, in principle, within any social practice (whether the practice of origin or not).

Althusser's formulations in *Reading Capital* therefore contain, in unrecognized form, a key development: the concept of ideology as an element of practice. Until recently, orthodox Marxism has continuously failed to recognize this fact and has persisted in making the Positivist separation between 'materiality' and ideology. What I have done here is to bring out a concept, latent in Althusser, which confronts the traditional formulations of orthodox Marxism which, in false and Positivist fashion, have made ideology the reflection of materiality or economic practice. It is true that practice is a determination of its interior ideology, but it is also true, and this is my main point, that ideology is a determination of all practice. This latter determination has been concealed from some Marxist theory in its own metaphor of the reflection of the economic infrastructure in the superstructure of ideology. Reflection has not been interpreted in its full dialectical sense as a relation between interpenetrating opposites. Thus the correct Marxian position, that ideology exists in all practices and that practice only works through ideology, has been ignored with inevitably economistic effects: ideology has become the plaything of economic forces and its determining force has been lost to debates over the falling rate of profit.

Althusser had only unconsciously and incompletely produced this dialectical concept of social ideology in *For Marx*. In *Reading Capital* he threw a little more light on it but at no time did he ever explicitly develop the concept in the text. For example, during his critique of Gramsci's notion that science is part of the superstructure, he states:

> Science can no more be ranged within the category "superstructure" than can language, which as Stalin showed escapes it. To make science a superstructure is to think of it as one of those "organic" ideologies which form such a close "bloc" with the structure that they have the same "history" as it does! (Althusser and Balibar, 1970, p. 133)

Not only does Althusser seem to see language and science as neutral, non-social forms, but he also reduces ideology to a limpet of the economy and represses any conception of ideology as a determining element of social practices of all kinds. The nearest he gets to an explicit account of our concept in *Reading Capital* is during the discussion of legal and political social relations. Here it is pointed out that certain relations of production presuppose as a condition of their existence a certain type of law, politics and ideology. Althusser elaborates the effects of the concept of the dialectical relation between economic relations and superstructural practices, it means that:

> . . . they [relations of production—C.S.] relate to the superstructural forms they call for as so many conditions of their own existence. The relations of production cannot therefore be thought in their concept while abstracting from their specific superstructural conditions of existence. To take only one example, it is quite clear that the analysis of the buying and selling of labour power in which capitalist relations of production *exist* (the separation between the owners of the means of production on the one hand and the wage-workers on the other), directly presupposes, for an understanding of its object, a consideration of the *formal legal relations* which establish the buyer (the capitalist) as much as the seller (the wage-labourer) as legal subjects—as well as a whole political and ideological superstructure which maintains and contains the economic agents in the distribution of roles, which makes a minority of exploiters the owners of the means of production, and the majority of the population producers of surplus-value. The whole superstructure of the society considered is thus implicit and present in a specific way in the relations of production, i.e. in the fixed structure of the distribution of means of production and economic functions between determinate categories of production agents. (Althusser and Balibar, 1970, pp. 177, 178)

Briefly, the point he is making about the social totality here is that the relations of production are represented in the superstructure, and that the products of superstructural practice (e.g. laws, policies, propaganda) are effective within the production process: ". . . the whole superstructure . . . is thus implicit and present . . . in the relations of production". This specification of a dialectical relation between the infrastructure (economy) and the superstructure (law, politics and the cultural practices), a relation dominated by the infrastructure, is a conception we require. Unfortunately, Althusser did not continue this discussion and develop its ramifications for the Marxist theory of ideology. Moreover, he fails to see that not all superstructural forms are present within economic practice. Some laws, for example, may be products of purely political or cultural problems and may bear only a slight connection with the economy. More importantly, Althusser still fails to distinguish clearly between spontaneous forms of power and ideology present within economic practice and the institutionalization of these forms within political and cultural practice; consequently, he neglects the class struggles involved in those processes of institutionalization.

Basically, then, the concept of the ideology–social formation link as a connection between externals is a false one. Any attempted link between ideology and society presupposes that ideology is external to society. Clearly that is a metaphysical, religious conception. Yet orthodox Marxism, in its misplaced, Positivist materialism, has ironically been guilty of propagating this mystical notion that ideology is an "effect" of the social formation. Ideology, however, is not a thought-mirror of the social formation but an active aspect of social practice and hence an integral, determinant part of the social formation at various levels. At this juncture I must enter the caveat that the position I am developing here is *not* a humanist Marxist one. Ideology is not part of practice because of the essentially and eternally creative nature of men. Ideology became an active part of practice when, through the development of social relations, animal or "instinctive" (Marx's term), practice was transformed into social practice involving the means of social relation, language. Once language had developed, ideology could be realized concretely, and it was only when ideology materialized itself that it became an effective part of practice; at that point, instinctive labour became purposive, social labour. Men were not born "essentially purposive"—that facility developed historically. Moreover, the nature and effects of an ideology will vary with the society, and the level of practice considered. In some historical conjunctures, for example, the structure of the social formation may be such as to make the dominant ideology a minimally effective element in it; in others, dominant ideology may be very effective. No doubt the latter conjunctures give rise to the impression that choice, purpose, creativity or human agency in general is the key element in social life. But that would be to take the transitional as eternal.

Reflection, like all the other optical metaphors used by Marx to describe the dialectical relation, has often been adopted by Marxists as a one-sided notion incapable of comprehending the two-sided nature of any relation. It has been a major obstacle in the development of the Marxist theory of ideology in that it helped to conceal the interiority of ideology throughout the social formation. Althusser's failure to remove it in his two major texts has enabled critics to level charges of determinism against him. Many complained of his denial of the role of ideology in class conflict and the consequent absence of some policy on the role of ideology in revolutionary political practice and an adequate theory of ideological domination. From my analysis, we can see that they found a weak spot. Althusser's frequent reduction of ideology to an effect of society or the economy merely reinforced tendencies in humanism to support concepts of Free Will, Praxis and Creativity. It did not encourage the solution of the problem of ideology within historical materialism.

My reading of Althusser's theoretical discourse so far indicates that Althusser had not yet 'discovered' the concept of the integral existence of ideology in practice as a reflection of social relations. He had produced it, just as much as he had produced (but, in this case, discovered as well), the concept of the effectivity of law in economic practices; but he had not discovered it. This precise absence is the key structuring mechanism in the essay considered next. The concept seems to appear in the essay but, in fact, the terms Althusser uses are actually referring to another concept, the one he explicitly develops in the text. It is necessary to explicate my reading before commenting further.

In "Ideology and Ideological State Apparatuses" (1971), Althusser is attempting to put ideology back into orthodox Marxist theory. He notes its woeful absence and requires amends to be made; but amends which escape the Positivist formulations of Marx and Engels in *The German Ideology*.

> In *The German Ideology* . . . Ideology is conceived as a pure illusion, a pure dream, i.e. as nothingness. All its reality is external to it. (Althusser, 1971, p. 150)

The way Althusser chooses to conduct the rescue operation is *via the theory of the state*. Ideology, as an effective reality, is inserted back into society—and that is a development in Marxism which all anti-Positivists can only celebrate, along with the defeat of the old, materiality/ideology reflection debate—but, through the state, and not through its proper channel, social practice, Althusser *does* eventually place ideology within practice, but that re-location specifies an ideology produced by the state fulfilling the functions demanded by the economic structure. As a result, his account is one-sided and functionalist in nature. This is illustrated by the fact that the ideology of the subordinate social classes is forgotten until the postscript.

Althusser makes it clear from the beginning that he believes that the infrastructure/superstructure dichotomy is still valuable, although descriptive (1971, pp. 129, 130). What is of interest to him is to describe the relevance of the superstructure for the base or, as he puts it, "the functioning of the Superstructure and its mode of intervention in the Infrastructure" (1971, p. 170). His basic argument is that this description must be thought from the point of view of the reproduction of the relations of production. Hence, ideology is an aspect of the *reproduction* process:

> . . . the reproduction of labour power requires not only a reproduction of its skills, but also, at the same time, a reproduction of its submission to the rules of the established order, i.e. a reproduction of submission to the ruling ideology for the workers, and a reproduction of the ability to manipulate the ruling ideology correctly for the agents of exploitation and repression, so that they, too, will provide for the domination of the ruling class "in words". (Althusser, 1971, pp. 127, 128)

Having said this, of course, following classical Marxist theory, Althusser must turn to the state, which is held to be the machine by which the ruling class of a society maintains its political and economic supremacy. And this is the conceptual nexus for Althusser's emphatic reintroduction of ideology into the social formation.

Althusser proceeds to argue that the view that the state is just a repressive institution is simplistic and purely "descriptive". State apparatuses have ideological as well as repressive functions but, most importantly, Althusser says that Ideological State Apparatuses (ISAs) exist which appear as private institutions, e.g. the Church, the legal system, the Media, the Trade Unions, the Schools, the Political Parties. These 'private' institutions are part of the public state because they function for the state in reproducing ruling class power (and because the private/public distinction is interior to bourgeois law which the state is above) and they are called ideological because they function primarily by ideology (Althusser, 1971, pp. 137, 138). The function of the ISAs is described by Althusser as follows:

> . . . [the ISAs—C.S.] largely secure the reproduction specifically of the relations of production, behind a "shield" provided by the repressive State apparatus. (Althusser, 1971, p. 142)

The ISAs can function like this because they are the strongholds of ruling class ideology (this ideology ensures a harmony between the various ISAs and between the ISAs and the repressive state apparatus) and because they subject the dominated classes to their ideology. This subjection is uncontested and the proletariat are the playthings of this multiple propaganda symphony of ruling class ideology orchestrated by the ISAs.[10] Talking about education, Althusser argues:

> But it is by an apprenticeship in a variety of know-how wrapped up in the massive inculcation of the ideology of the ruling-class that the *relations of production* in a capitalist social formation, i.e. the relations of exploited to exploiters and exploiters to exploited, are largely reproduced. (1971, p. 148)

The only time in this essay, before the postscript, that there is any suggestion that the ruling class cannot just implant its ideology on the subordinate classes at will is when Althusser mentions in passing that the former ruling classes and the proletarians "occasionally disturb" the concert of subjection.

Thus, from our discussion of Althusser's developments from *For Marx* up to this point, we can see that Althusser has not really escaped from the one-sided or unilateral concept of reflection, he has merely made that conception more sophisticated. The economic structure gives state power to the ruling class who control the ISAs and transmit ("cram") their ideology directly to the willing receivers, into the empty brains of the subordinates. Equipped with the right messages, the labour-force is fit for its role in the economy. Thus ideology is a reflection of the economic structure which travels via the state into the workers' brains. The concept can be represented diagrammatically:

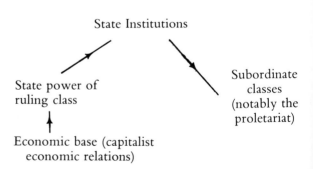

The travels of ideology in the process of reproduction

State Institutions

State power of ruling class

Economic base (capitalist economic relations)

Subordinate classes (notably the proletariat)

It is as though the position of having state power enables the ruling class to bounce ideology off the state institutions into the subordinate classes just as a radio transmitter can bounce images off a satellite to a receiver in another part of the globe. This is Althusser's 'satellite' concept of ideological transmission. It is highly mechanical and reminiscent of cybernetic models of information systems (see Chapter 3). What is disturbing is that Althusser seems to be employing structural-functionalist thought to develop the Marxist theory of ideology; it does look as though this system-function has been ascribed to these institutions simply because it appears to exist at the moment (because the French proletariat is not yet free from its domination by bourgeois thought). Certainly Althusser presents a very one-sided theory of ideological transmission, up to this point.

It has been necessary to register these deficiencies strongly because otherwise they would be concealed by the stealth of Althusser's subsequent formulations. He continues by arguing, despite his initial pronouncements, that ideology is merely a "pale, empty and inverted reflection of real history" (1971, p. 151)—thus taking the Marx of 1846 at his word. But how do these "phantoms", as Marx called them, find their way so easily into the empty heads of the masses? Firstly, Althusser says, each ISA involves a realization of a "regional ideology" (e.g. religious, legal, ethical, aesthetic) in its constituent practices. He then makes a crucial statement:

> . . . an ideology always exists in an apparatus, and its practice, or practices. (1971, p. 156)

Remembering that all the ISAs realize ruling class ideology, we can see that all regional ideology, bar those "occasional interruptions", is ruling class ideology.[11] This is clearly a remarkable implication: remarkable for its one-sidedness and thus for its exclusion of the possibility of existence of working class and petit-bourgeois ideologies supported by proletarian and petit-bourgeois practices and institutions. He ventures, now, to argue that all the people live within ruling ideology because they participate in the regularized, ritual practices of the ISAs. Thus he implies two things: (1) there is no non-economic practice except within an Ideological State Apparatus and (2) that people participating in the practices of the ISAs are automatically doomed to ideological subjection by the ruling class. These implications in turn, beg three questions:

1. Are there not non-economic practices outside the ISAs? Is the French Communist Party an ISA?
2. Are the practices which Althusser defines as elements of the ISAs necessarily so? Is not the definition of the ISAs so wide that it leaves no space for any other kind of practice (functional for the ruling class or not)?
3. How within this map of the territory of social practices can revolutionary, critical, liberal or mediated (mixed) ideologies arise except from thin air? (This particular absence leaves a wide-open space for humanists to insert such ideologies into the map as the products of 'human' response to oppression.)

It is clear that the one-sided concept of ideological reflection has produced a view of ideological domination which is one of transmission and implantation from above, and that, to enable his argument for the role of the state as the agent of ideological domination, Althusser has had to deny any contradictions or practices which may give rise to non-ruling class ideologies. This is so far, then, a non-dialectical analysis of ideological domination, with structural functionalist underpinnings.

However, despite this (or because of it) we must recognize that Althusser does advance the proposition that:

> . . . there is no practice except by and in an ideology . . . (1971, p. 159)

This does not mean that he has discovered the concept of the integral nature of ideology in all social practice at this stage, or the notion that contradictory social relations produce contradictory ideological formations, and contradictory classes to live them out. For what he is arguing is that all non-economic practices belong to the ISAs and therefore, since economic practices already have ruling class ideology inscribed in them, there cannot be any practice at all without ruling class ideology. However, the terminology is the right terminology for my conception. Thus I am bound to say that Althusser has produced the terms of our conception but not the conception itself. He makes a second important proposition:

> . . . there is no ideology except by the subject and for subjects. (1971, p. 159)

This proposition expresses his subsequent description of the mechanism of intervention of ruling class ideology in the everyday practice of the ISAs. That description is constituted by two premises: (1) ideology "constitutes concrete individuals as subjects" and (2) concrete individuals are "subjected to the Subject". And so the "duplicate mirror-structure of ideology" ensures:

> . . . the mutual recognition of subjects and Subject, the subjects' recognition of each other, and finally the subject's recognition of himself . . . (1971, p. 168)

Althusser is arguing that "all ideology is *centred*" by the notion of the "Absolute Subject" predicated by capitalist economic relations and that, consequently, bearing in mind that everyone participates in the practice of the ISAs with their deadly effects, men live in "the trap of a mirror reflection" centred on themselves as "subjects".[12] Ideological domination of the masses by the ruling class is thus achieved through two mechanisms:

1. The involvement of people in the practices and ideology of the ISAs.
2. People's recognition of themselves, as "subjects", in ideology which is centred on the absolute power of the Subject.

Men are caught in the spider's web of the ideology of the subject inscribed in the practices of the state's ubiquitous ideological apparatuses:

> Result: caught in this quadruple system of interpellation as subjects, of subjection to the subject, of universal recognition and of absolute guarantee, the subjects "work", they "work by themselves" in the vast majority of cases, with the exception of the "bad subjects" who on occasion provoke the intervention of one of the detachments of the (repressive) State apparatus. But the vast majority of (good) subjects work all right "all by themselves", i.e. by ideology (whose concrete forms are realized in the Ideological State Apparatuses). They are inserted into practices governed by the rituals of the ISAs (Althusser, 1971, p. 169).

The above passage illustrates the one-sided nature of this concept of ideological domination through the state and encapsulates its mechanism.[13] But where do the "bad subjects" come from? Althusser's whole argument is merely a sophisticated re-statement of the classic, mechanical materialist position that ideologies originate in the mode of production and are made effective by the state. The proletariat are thus caught in a vicious circle and class conflict has no conceivable explanation.

At the end of his essay Althusser adds a passage written one year later. In it he faces "several important unanswered problems", or, I would say, he tries to correct two of his great mistakes. Firstly, he brings himself into line with Marx and states that the reproduction of the relations of economic production is only realized within the economic production and circulation process itself. Thus, reminding himself of the fact that his colleague, Balibar, had argued this same point in *Reading Capital*:

> The concept of reproduction is thus not only the "consistency" of the structure, but also the concept of the necessary determination of the movement of production by the permanence of that structure; it is the concept of the permanence of the initial elements in the very functioning of the system, hence the concept of the necessary conditions of production, conditions which are precisely *not created by it.* This is what Marx calls the *eternity* of the mode of production . . . (Althusser and Balibar, 1970, p. 272)

In other words, the dialectical concept, which Althusser and Balibar had developed in *Reading Capital*, of *the necessary but relatively autonomous conditions of existence of a mode of production* had been omitted in the essay on ideology. This was a key omission because it prevented Althusser from determining the "mode of intervention" of specific ideologies in the mode of production. The omission had left Althusser with a concept of the production process as simply a means of producing commodities, and a concept of the ISAs as a means for reproducing the relations of production of commodities. Such a sociological conception, of course, is alien to Marxian theory which locates the reproduction of the relations of production within the production sphere itself. If he had remembered his earlier notion (it seems I was right in concluding that it was very underdeveloped), he would have realized straight away that, of course, some ideologies, laws, politics, etc., all "intervene" directly in the mode of production and that, therefore, their function in production is not an effect from without. That is, "intervene" is the wrong word and implies a Positivistic infrastructure/superstructure notion. Instead, we should say that determinate political, legal and ideological relations are elements of (or, are inscribed in) the social practices of economic production, just as the social relations of production are inscribed in those same political, legal and ideological formations and procedures. Some superstructurally elaborated forms orginate and live within the infrastructure as organic elements. The infrastructure/superstructure metaphor is just that, a metaphor, but it lived on in Althusser's discourse in this essay in a more than metaphoric manner. Having corrected himself in the postscript, he is now able to conclude correctly that the reproduction of the economic structure must be a matter of class struggle (fought out, I would say, within the economic, political, legal and ideological forms organic within a specific mode of production).

Having corrected this error, a door opens reminding him of the class divisions within production and hence the class conflict necessarily involved in that sphere. Once that is apparent, the weighty importance of class conflict in ideology is felt (emphases in italics by C.S.):

> In fact, the State and its Apparatuses only have meaning from the point of view of the class struggle, as an apparatus of class struggle, ensuring class oppression and *guaranteeing* the conditions of exploitation and its reproduction. *But there is no class struggle without antagonistic classes. Whoever says class struggle of the ruling class says resistance, revolt and class struggle of the ruled class.* (Althusser, 1971, pp. 171, 172)

The use of the dialectical materialist concept of "the necessary conditions of existence", in order to think the superstructural forms which are integral, yet separately organized and produced, aspects of a mode of production, has enabled Althusser to return the sadly neglected 'other side' to his exposition—the side of oppositional and class ideologies. He now goes on to realize that the installation of the ISAs and the dominance of ruling class ideology within them, "guaranteeing" the reproduction of the classes, is itself only possible through class struggle within the ISAs (e.g. within the legal and educational institutions).[14] Unfortunately, in restoring social contradictions to his analysis, Althusser reduces ideologies to class ideologies and the complex variation of ideological formations is thus lost to analysis. Consequently, intra-class conflict is still absent in Althusser's theory of ideology. Althusser admits his biggest error when he admits that:

> . . . ideologies are not "born" in the ISAs but from the social classes at grips in the class struggle: from their conditions of existence, their practices, their experiences of the struggle, etc. (1971, p. 173)

Ideologies are thus no longer in general the resource of the ISAs, the elaboration of the Absolute Subject or the weapons of class domination. They may be all of these things in specific instances, but Althusser now clearly recognizes the integral existence of ideology in general within all social practice and, thus, can theorize the existence of "class ideologies". Ideology, in general, is thus an element of social practice, reflecting its interiority, i.e. its structure and other elements. Ideologies, therefore, exist outside the ISAs in practices located outside the ISAs: they are not "effects" of a social formation but determinant elements of its composition.

The publication of Althusser's *Essays in Self-Criticism* (1976) in English could have been embarrassing to earlier drafts of this chapter. In fact, these essays tend to sustain my account of the changes within Althusser's theory of ideology. The 1971 essay on the ISAs had represented ideology as an imaginary reflection of the relations of production, sited in the ISAs, centred on the concept of the free subject and securing the reproduction of the economic structure. Only in the postscript did ideology become one of the weapons used on either side of the class struggle and a reflection of social practice of all kinds. This development is continued in Althusser's self-criticisms. Rebuking himself for not locating ideology within the class struggle in *For Marx* and *Reading Capital*, he emphasizes that within the different regions of ideology there are "antagonistic class tendencies which run through them, divide them, regroup them and bring them into opposition" (Althusser, 1976, p. 141). Class struggle, therefore, is the central theoretical site for the analysis of ideologies, as it was in the famous "postscript":

> Ideologies are not pure illusions (Error), but bodies of representations existing in institutions and practices: they figure in the superstructure, and are rooted in the class struggle. (1976, p. 155)

Class struggle, as before, is the process of overt economic, political, legal or ideological conflict between classes which results in the secured reproduction of the social relations of economic production (or in their overthrow).

In these latest *Essays*, Althusser develops his view of ideology in ways that correspond to my own earlier formulations, e.g ideologies are, emphatically, not necessarily mere illusions, they exist within practices and ensembles of practices (institutions) (1976, p. 155), they contain partial truths (p. 122), and they exist in both "practical" and "theoretical" forms (pp. 151, 155 *et seq.*). However, there are still several criticisms I would make of his position. The most fundamental point is that Althusser is really only developing his 'satellite' conception of ideology elaborated in the essay on the ISAs. Ideologies may now be rooted in class practices and struggles but they are still essentially products of economic practice which are extended and systematized in the practices of the superstructure. In short, Althusser's analysis is only concerned with those ideologies organic within the social division of economic labour. Because of this concern, he fails to grant relevance to two other major types of ideology: (1) those ideologies originating within the superstructural practices themselves (e.g. the ideology of "Law" developed in the legal institutions), and (2) those ideologies originating within the 'technical' division of economic labour (e.g. ideologies of the "status" of different occupational positions). In relation to superstructural ideologies, Althusser has only ever been concerned with those features of the superstructure that act as "necessary conditions of existence" of the economic base, so the new *Essays* mark no change there.[15] In relation to intra-class ideological differences emerging from the technical division of labour (in any form of social practice), Althusser has already explicitly asserted that technical divisions are merely masks for class divisions (Althusser, 1971, p. 171) and thus makes no change there either. The net result is that throughout his work Althusser fails to develop the concepts which can begin to deal with the ideologies of sexism, law, 'culture' (in the sense of 'high culture'), racism and scientism, the ideologies arising from political practice, and those ideologies arising from the technical division of economic labour.

In this light, it is true to say that Althusser is always guilty, in his theories of ideology, of (1) class reductionism and (2) economism. Class reductionism, in the theory of ideology, is a tendency which limits the social relevance of ideology to its class forms and its place in the class struggle. Economism is a theoretical tendency which limits the relevance of the relative autonomy of the superstructure and its intrinsic ideologies. These tendencies, and their fusion in his work, greatly limit the value of Althusser's formulations on the question of ideology. This limitation has the effect of theoretically restraining Althusser, and Althusserians, from beginning concrete studies of ideological differences which divide classes or cut across classes.[16] In modern Europe (and perhaps the Third World, e.g. 'tribal', nationalist and inverted racist ideologies), it is precisely these ideologies which are of the greatest political relevance to Marxists.

At this juncture, there are two further points to make about the *Essays* (Althusser, 1976). The first would not normally concern us because it relates to mere hints, rather than arguments, made in the *Essays*. However, it relates to law. Because Althusser rescinds his view that ruling ideology directly reproduces the social relations of economic production, he was, I think, inclined to rethink the view that all ideology was centred on the concept of the Subject as Origin. His new view, that all ideologies are the outcome of class practices and struggles in the economy, takes him away from the assertion of one single base ideology, that of the Subject, reflecting "the" major feature of capitalist social relations. It leads him into a realm of ideology which lies at the centre of class struggle in shaping its forms and outcomes: the realm of legal signification. Legal ideology, for Althusser, thus becomes the new "centre" of bourgeois ideology. The whole search is ridden with theoretical flaws. The biggest error he makes is to miss the point that the similarity of bourgeois ideological formations is due to their use of several basic, simple signs rooted in the economic, political and cultural practices of society as experienced by the bourgeoisie. These simple ideologies form the core vocabulary and conceptions of many ideological formations, not just those structuring legal discourse. If legal ideologies are those complex ideologies which most systematically elaborate the basic signs of bourgeois ideology in general, then we want to know why; we do not conclude that legal ideology is the pure form of bourgeois ideology in general. In short, legal ideology in capitalism is not the "centre" of bourgeois ideology, but, rather, a refined and developed form of the practical or spontaneous ideologies of the bourgeoisie mediated in the course of legal practice by their confrontation with historically situated social conflicts. I shall develop this provisional formulation later, but, for the moment, let me say that it carries no implication that all the ideologies embodied in legal discourse are simply the results of the economic practices of capitalists; the bourgeoisie engage in more than economic practice, and the practical ideologies intrinsic to their political and cultural practice can also become embodied in legal forms. More positively, I do imply that, although changes in legal ideology are partially determined by extant legal ideology and procedure, such changes are founded in transformations in social relations and their corresponding shifts in spontaneous bourgeois ideology.

My second additional point about Althusser's *Essays* is that, whilst he continues to recognize that people "live out" their lives through ideologies, he does not really emphasize the consequence of this recognition for his conception of people as "agents" of social practice. He does clarify his earlier positions in saying that he called people "agents" rather than "authors" of social practice because capitalist social relations of all kinds reduce people to "functions" or "bearers" of these relations. In capitalism, he says, we are all branded with economic functions, political roles, legal rights and statuses and ideological forms. Yet, having made this clear, he also makes it apparent that he believes that subordinate classes can mediate or fight against their oppression. But, if "ideological social relations" are only part of the oppression, where do the ideologies of resistance come from? Put another way, how does "proletarian ideology" come about when the proletariat are captured and branded as functionaries of bourgeois social relations? Althusser has no explicit answer to these questions and leaves the impression that he is operating a kind of stimulus–response model of proletarian resistance. He thus leaves a gap into which humanist ideas of 'human nature' could be inserted. Althusser has, however, implicitly provided an answer, but not developed it. Since he recognizes more clearly than ever, in these *Essays*, the centrality of contradiction in social life, he ought to be able to say that proletarian ideology in general comprises the spontaneous and philosophical ideologies of the proletariat which have emerged out of their experience of bourgeois social relations. That is, proletarian ideology is a reflection of social relations just as much as bourgeois ideology, but a reflection from one pole of those relations, a reflection of the class position and conditions of the proletariat within the overall structure and conditions of a capitalist social formation.

Althusser's previous use of terms like "agents" and "bearers" is thus compromised by his new, implicit views on ideology. As a political animal, he now rightly recognizes the reality and possibility of subordinate class resistance: can he then say that these classes are "agents" of social relations, mere functionaries of the structure? In my view, we must recognize the historically and structurally located nature of human individuals and see that, in some places and at certain times, people are merely functions of the system, whereas in other places and at other times they can make the system a function of their efforts. We cannot generalize a concept of people as agents from the nature of the capitalist economy. Having taught a course on *Capital* and seen students arrive at Althusser's view, I am more convinced than ever that Marx was at fault in his great work in not clearly specifying the economic effects of politics and ideology. This is not a fault with Marx's work in general because at many other points he indicates the general possibility of the superstructural practices changing the current forms of the economy (although not its "iron laws"). It is a fault of *Capital* that Marx fails to spell out a general position on the role of politics and ideology and thus leaves an impression of economic evolution which I am sure he would not welcome. His positions in the "Theses on Feuerbach" of 1845 became submerged in the great research task of elaborating the basic mechanism of capitalist economies.

Let us remind ourselves of two of his statements in those "Theses":

> The materialist doctrine that men are products of circumstances and upbringing, and that, therefore, changed men are products of other circumstances and changed upbringing, forgets that it is men who change circumstances and that the educator must himself be educated. (Marx and Engels, 1976a, p. 7)

> But the essence of man is no abstraction inherent in each single individual. In its reality it is the ensemble of social relations. (ibid.)

Marx impresses on us here that (1) there is no such thing as 'the essence of man', and that (2) people are neither always 'agents' nor always 'authors' of practice. There is no such thing as the essential character of human individuality. This is true even for a specific epoch, the history of the capitalist mode of production, for example, because it is the "ensemble" of social relations that determines the social nature of individuals as it differentially affects them. Political, legal and cultural relations, as well as economic relations, are determinants of the social character of individuals. For example, whilst an individual may be a mere functionary at work, in his political associations and leisure activities he or she can, in association, attempt to inaugurate new social relations. Moreover, collective action by workers may attempt to inaugurate new social relations at work. Such attempts are, of course, dependent for their success on the stage of development of the existing pertinent social relations. But, equally, the efforts of the capitalist economy to reduce working people to mere functionaries of its operation depend for their success on the stage of development of the political organization and general attitudes of the work force.

Althusser's attempt to establish a theoretical anti-humanism, therefore, goes too far and loses a sense of the dialectical interpenetration of economic structure, political organization and ideological differences. The state of consciousness of an individual or class is one of the practical determinants of social forms. That is one of the few correct statements that a Marxist can make about 'humanity in general'. One of the incorrect statements he can make is that we are all, eternally, "bearers" of social relations: such a statement, as I have attempted to demonstrate, is merely humanism in reverse. In forming the philosophy of historical materialism, Marx did not simply negate humanism; by forming an anti-humanism he transcended it in the classic sense of "aufhebung"—it conserves what it transcends but in a new and higher form. Both humanism and anti-humanism, I venture to suggest, existed in raw contradiction in Feuerbach's work—Marx's work represents the supercession of that contradiction. Althusser merely takes one side of Feuerbach and Marxifies it. Marx's position is that people in general are neither eternal agents nor eternal authors. Rather, class character and social individuality are historically and structurally constituted by the social relations of a social formation in movement. The ideological forms typical to a class (or individual) are one constituent element of that class's (or his/her) historical or social character: the others being economic function and form of political organization. In sum, we must no longer talk in terms of agents *or* authors. Instead we should begin to understand: (1) the political, legal and ideological conditions under which the tendency of the capitalist economy to reduce workers to system-functions is mitigated (i.e. the superstructural counter-tendencies limiting the operation of the "laws" of capital); (2) the political, legal and ideological conditions under which such a reduction is facilitated (i.e. the superstructural tendencies aiding and abetting the economic); and (3) the economic conditions under which real political and ideological (or cultural) 'pluralism' (or 'natural development') is possible. Agency and authorship, as modes of social being, should be examined, in an historical materialist perspective, as features of determinate social practices and historical moments.

This apparent digression has developed further my conception of the integral nature of ideology in social practice and emphasized the importance of recognizing the interiority of ideology as a determining force and reflection of any social formation in movement. That was the purpose of my review of Althusser's work and the latter has served me well in achieving that purpose. A summary of the changes and features of Althusser's theory of ideology can thus be dispensed with. Other things are more important, namely a clear, concluding statement of the rub of the positions on ideology I am adopting.

Conclusions

The mode of production "reveals the secret" of any social formation (Marx, 1972, p. 791). A knowledge of the economic structure does indeed disclose the most important and general features of a society's political organization and ideological character. But this is not true in any Positivist, cause and effect sense. A mode of production does necessitate specific political, legal and ideological forms, but these forms are not only relatively autonomous social entities elaborated within distinct superstructural practices, they also act as organic elements within the dynamic of that mode of production. Moreover, political, legal and ideological forms exist which are not necessitated by a current mode of production. Such forms can affect the movement of an economy and, in turn, the economy can affect their movement. Some ideologies move as the structure of production moves, whereas others may remain the same. This uneven development of a social formation means that contradictions may arise between its elements (e.g. between an organic and non-organic ideology). Also, contradictions within a social formation may arise because of the relative autonomy of superstructural practices. For example, the law of contract may remain static whilst the economic structure develops (even though such law is organic to economic practice) because legal practice is relatively autonomous and may involve principles or procedures which prevent the law moving in step with its economic partner.

When a newly established mode of production becomes established, it does bring into line the political, legal and ideological forms necessary to its stability. This will usually mean that such forms antithetical to its existence will eventually be incorporated or abolished. Thus, the establishment of capitalism in a Third World country will gradually involve the incorporation and effective extinction of the customary laws of people living within a subordinate mode of production. These processes of the establishment of a political, legal and ideological unity (in the forms of the state, the legal code and the dominant ideology) have, of course, occurred in the history of long-established capitalist societies. Such processes involve conflicts and struggles between classes, nations, races and other social groups. No new mode of production is established without social conflict. Nor is it maintained without conflict. Just as the economic masters are challenged in the economic sphere, so too do they find their political, legal and ideological supremacy threatened also. These conflicts represent the contradictions in the social formation and are fought out within the opposed economic, political, legal and ideological forms reflecting those contradictions.

Every mode of production, once settled and established, gradually extends its tentacles into every sphere of social practice. Social relations necessitated by a prior mode of production are transformed into the manner of the new relations. This does not negate uneven development or relative autonomy, but it does explain why the mode of production is the innermost secret of a society. For example, as British capitalism developed, the social relations of legal practice were transformed into commercial relations. Lawyers were no longer mere political functionaries of the state but had to rely for a living upon the successful sale of their wares to a wider clientele. This subsequently involved the expansion of their market through the conversion of social problems into legal problems, the formation of a profession with limited membership, the development of large firms of lawyers, and the devaluation of law in the lives of the poor because of its increased cost. In the same way, the notably feudal social relations within various organized sports gradually became transformed into commodity relations (upon which capitalism hinges as a mode of production) and, today, we watch the logical extension of this process as various sports (as industries or businesses) become swallowed up by the sharks of monopoly capital. For the cultural practices, those practices that specifically produce new ideologies or develop old ones (e.g. teaching, art, news dissemination, writing), capitalism also meant great changes. Such practices became geared to the systematic and profitable production of commodities and, correspondingly, their forces of production were greatly developed: mass communications came into being. Ownership of the means of ideological production and distribution, like all forms of capitalist ownership, became centralized and concentrated in the course of capitalist development. The practical ideologies of the non-owning majority are now daily bombarded (opposed, mediated or reinforced) by a stream of practical and philosophical ideology from the powerful devices of the owners and controllers, the big and small bourgeoisie.

An ideology is a sign and involves a signification of the world of the social practitioner in the terms of already available signifying units. Ideologies can become compounded, serialized or clustered in ideological formations such as conversational discourse, theory, law, theology and popular images. Both ideologies and ideological formations exist within the two main forms of social consciousness: practical (or spontaneous) and philosophical (or developed). These two forms sprang into life with the division of mental and manual labour and, in capitalist social formations, their distinction is extensively socially institutionalized through the extensive development of the cultural practices. All social practices, however, contain ideology in all its forms and every social practice contains ideologies integral to its nature as reflections of its structure or inner relations. Ideology then is integral to all social practices and, therefore, integral to the movement of the total social formation.

All hitherto social formations have contained modes of production which have divided people into economic classes. Moreover, these classes themselves have often been divided, again according to the social relations of production of the day. These economic divisions

2. IDEOLOGY AND SOCIAL PRACTICE   53

have entailed divisions within politics and culture. The economically dominant classes have been able to make their power and ideology the dominant features of the society's superstructure. Despite the qualification that there have always been ideological differences within and across classes, reflecting their subdivision within social practice and the national and international extensions of the social structure, this is the most general form of ideological patterning in a class society. Because of the differences within and across classes arising from the development of the social formation, ideologies are usually also patterned along lines of sex, race, nationality, area of residence and technical function in the economy.

Ideologies of a simple or compounded form reflect the social relations from which they arise. The links between a signifier and a signified in a simple ideology, and between signs within a complex ideological formation, are reflections of the relations between people concerning the means of production (economic, political or cultural). Social relations of signification reflect practical social relations. Because practical relations are experienced by opposed classes and groups, we find that opposed ideologies exist which nevertheless contain similarities. Thus, whilst capitalist social relations generally give rise to ideologies of Freedom, these ideologies can take opposed forms within different classes or groups: freedom for the bourgeoisie usually means something different to freedom for the workers. However, because the dominant economic class usually exerts control within the political and cultural realms, it can effect the overdetermination of its own ideological positions. These positions take economic, political and cultural forms, and act in triplicated co-ordination to assist the perpetuation of hegemony. Ideological reflection is never a single process, but always a process of multiple, combined determinations. Exactly how far ruling class ideologies permeate subordinate class consciousness in any given conjucture is a question which depends on the economic, political and cultural conditions of the day.

In a capitalist society, with a myriad of developed contradictions, many different kinds of ideology can exist but it is a central tenet of the Marxist position that these ideologies are fundamentally grouped around the class axis. For example, feminist ideologies are not simply a set of ideologies about women, but a set of ideologies about women that are differentiated along class lines. Thus, without reducing the matter to the fact of class division, it is essential to realize that class division is fundamental. In addition, since class divisions can erupt into class struggles within economic, political or cultural practice, it is vital to recognize that it is not just the naked structures of society which produce its overall ideological pattern. That pattern is changed by class struggle; the latter is the dynamo that precipitates major changes in the societal map of ideology. But, in order that new spontaneous ideologies can make any major impact, they have to be made effective in practice. Such practice, in a class society, usually gives rise to some degree of class struggle (since it will affect all the participants in a situation and since all classes exist by definition in a state of structured opposition of interest and perspective). The very process and the actual result of this struggle determine the concrete magnitude and form of an ideological shift. Class struggles are thus a vital key to understanding major changes in societal ideology. This is doubly the case when one realizes that class conflicts also determine the extent of a change in social relations, which are the ultimate foundations of ideological change.

Changes in the social structure are only realized through the conflict of different classes and groups carrying specific forms of power and ideology. In other words, ideology is a component in the dialectics of structural change. So, whilst a mode of production may have attained a new stage of development, this major change of economic structure will only be realized concretely in a manner circumscribed by the results of the political and ideological conflicts that it generates. If the class struggle is the major mechanism precipitating large changes in societal ideology, it is also true that extant ideological forms are an important determinant of the form and result of class struggles.

Notes

1. Throughout the general discussions within this text, I shall use 'ideology' to refer to both simple and complex forms of signification for the sake of clarity and style, except where indicated otherwise.
2. Vološinov put forward a similar definition in 1930 (see 1973, Chapter 1).
3. The descriptive history of such relations has been called "historical semantics" (Williams, 1976, p. 20).

4. Other critiques of Althusser include Callinicos (1976), Geras (1971, 1972), Glucksmann (1972), Glucksmann (1974), Hirst (1976a), Lewis (1972), McLennan *et al.* (1977), Rancière (1974), Rusher (1974) and Walton and Gamble (1972). I have found none of these critiques very satisfactory.

5. His own introduction and summary of his own work is as accurate as any, although it does tend to shade over his errors (see Althusser, 1976, Chapter 3). In this essay I shall only consider his major works in English (Althusser, 1969, 1971, 1972, 1976; Althusser and Balibar, 1970).

6. From Marx, *Le Capital* T.1 (1948, p. 181n. Editions Sociales, Paris), quoted by Althusser (1972, p. 185).

7. Durkheim (1964) continually concerned himself with, and talked of, a supposed relation between the conscience collective and the social division of labour. Althusser's notion of a relation between ideology and society is of a similar kind. Both pose ideology as separate from social structure in a totally reified way. See also Vološinov (1973) who poses a relation between the "sociopolitical order" and ideology. What is faulty with these positions is that ideology and structure are held separate without the recognition that they interpenetrate in the process of social practice.

8. This conception bears heavily the connotation that ideology is concocted from denotative signs by the politically motivated consciousness. This connotation is not incompatible with the notion of ideology as "unconscious" which Althusser later develops. The Napoleonic concept depends on a humanistic philosophy and thus, to be consistent with his aim to set up a "theoretical anti-humanism", Althusser should reject this concept of ideology—which he does in *Reading Capital* and at the end of *For Marx*, although only implicitly.

9. Thus, for example, Jameson defends Sartre for arguing that the superstructure "must be seen as a reaction" to the situation constituted by the infrastructure: "The economic base is therefore inert matter which is transformed by human action . . . this rearticulation of the reflection model into two consecutive moments, into situation and freely invented response . . ." (Jameson, 1971, pp. 290, 291). Jameson and Sartre display a humanist view of the links between a falsely posed dichotomy of economy/ideological superstructure: yet, Sartre himself is clearly aware of the active existence of ideologies within economic practice.

10. For examples of Althusser's notion of easy subjection, see p. 146 in Althusser (1971).

11. Althusser constantly defines ideology in this essay as·a representation of the "imaginary relationship of individuals to the relations of production and the relations that derive from them" (p. 155), thus reiterating the definition developed in *For Marx*. I have already observed that this definition presupposes a concept of ideology already within itself, indicated by the term "imaginary" (*see* pp. 30, 31).

12. In *Capital*, Marx makes it abundantly clear that the formation of capitalist economic relations separated people out from the feudal estates ordained by God and constituted them as 'free individuals'. They are free to starve if they refuse to work for the owners of the means of production, but nevertheless an illusion of freedom was produced. Upon this basic illusion arises the ideological formation of the choosing Subject (e.g. in law, philosophy and social theory) which is possibly the most dominant of all bourgeois ideologies. Althusser's fervent theoretical anti-humanism leads him to make this ideology the basic structure of all ideologies in bourgeois society in classic structuralist fashion (see Chapter 4).

13. In my view, Althusser completely overestimates the success of dominant ideology. For example, in every factory I have worked in, the workers do not "work by themselves": they need considerable supervision and control if they are going to produce any surplus value at all for the capitalist. On the other hand, I think that Althusser underestimates the effects of economic practices (e.g. piece-work) in persuading the workers to work.

14. This question has been neglected by many more than Althusser. Surprisingly little research has been done on the class struggles *establishing* the state as a *multiply*-armed machine of ruling class domination. These struggles and processes are of special relevance today in the Third World.

15. All they indicate which is new is a greater readiness to accept superstructural practices as highly relevant to the course of the "class struggle" (see Althusser, 1976, pp. 203, 204).

16. Thus, Hirst (1975a) refuses to give the sociology of deviance a Marxist theoretical object which will enable it to analyse the way certain legal and cultural practices divide up the subordinate classes into certain ideological categories (e.g. the mad, bad, delinquent, disturbed, Utopian, hippy, promiscuous and sick) and thus study the concrete processes of "divide and rule" political practice.

Part Two

Methods of Reading Ideology

3 Content Analysis: Speculation Disguised as Science and Art

The Need to Discuss Method

In the previous chapter, I outlined a general theory of ideology and its location within a social formation. General theory may be lifeless to some, and for others it may seem to be an end in itself, but it is indispensable to the production of any concrete knowledge. Every researcher works on the basis of general concepts and assumptions. Whether it is acknowledged or not, this is an eternal fact of research practice. It is therefore better that these concepts and assumptions are clearly specified and organized so that they are openly available to scrutiny, enabling the limitations of the produced knowledge to be clearly identified. With no indication of the researcher's theoretical perspective, it is also difficult to determine the full meaning of a thesis and the adequacy of its evidence. Facts never speak for themselves, they have to be produced on the basis of concepts, assumptions, methods and available evidence.

Theory on its own, however, does not produce concrete knowledge. It requires a consistent extension in research practice, i.e. method. Research requires a theorized objective *and* a theorized method of attaining it. Method is, therefore, not simply raw technique but a combination of technique and general theory. In answering the question "how do we locate our object?", we must state our practical procedures, our modes of utilizing technique to a given theoretical end—our method. Any discussion of method should, consequently, be a discussion of the way a researcher operates a given theory in practice. A discussion of raw techniques is not a debate about method; in fact, it often tends to be a means of avoiding talking about method. In my view, then, the two main features of a method, therefore, are the theory it embodies, and the action it entails. This view will colour the present section of the book.

Method, in this sense, is rarely openly described in accounts of social research. In Positivist analysis, we hear of techniques and results. In Marxist analysis, we hear of general theory and results. In neither do we often see an open description of method. All researches involve method and, as with theory, if that method is described, the concrete knowledges produced can be more satisfactorily scrutinized as attempts to grasp the totality of a phenomenon. The absence of explicit theory and method within a study does not, of course, necessarily make the produced concrete knowledge any less possible or any less valuable. Implicit assumptions and procedures can 'work', in principle, just as well as explicit ones. However, in practice, they usually do not. As any decent social scientist will confirm, studies that fail to make theory and method as available to scrutiny as possible are usually studies which actually do not have any clear, logical direction. Such studies are usually derogated as speculative, journalistic or incoherent. Marxists are often the first to apply such labels yet, in the study of ideologies, their record on the question of method is little better than that of anyone else.

We need to consider our methods of reading ideology since research practice indicates to many that there is an enormous gap between general theory and complex data. But can we theorize a method in the abstract, before doing an actual analysis? Not to a great extent. Given a general theory one *can* outline a general mode of procedure for concrete research, which is what I shall do later on, but *only* when one realizes the problems faced by such a theory in the actual practice of research. The chapters in this section of the book represent an attempt to clarify the problems involved in the reading of ideologies through the device of a critique of the major, existing methods of reading ideologies. Having defined these problems a number of conceptual developments from the general theory become necessary before a satisfactory mode of reading ideology can be established. Those developments and a proposed method are discussed in Chapter 7 before we examine the reading of ideologies in legal discourse in Chapter 8.

The problems of method, and the theoretical developments they demand, are the subject matter of the rest of the book. They do in fact arise from the practice of a particular research project. In 1973, I engaged in the task of investigating the ideologies present within the national press news reports of political demonstrations. I took all the relevant cuttings from one month's newspapers and analysed many of them. In all, 570 cuttings were taken (or 'found' according to certain criteria), and around 200 of them were studied in extreme detail. This task was arduous and the cutting, filing and analysis took 6 months of full-time work. The results of the analysis were interesting, and no doubt of great polemical value, but the work raised so many problems of method that I could not justify publishing the actual findings. These problems centred on the highly impressionistic nature of existing reading methods: methods which, with their scant attention to history and social structure, seemed flimsy in their foundations. This experience of the difficulties involved in the actual practice of reading ideologies, in a specific form and context of appearance (news discourse), was an unusually intensive one. Whether I have learnt well from it can be judged from what follows, but it is enough to say here that without this experience I would not have appreciated the magnitude and the extent of the problems of reading ideologies. These problems apply as much in the analysis of legal discourse as in the analysis of newspaper reports. Of course, the reading of ideologies in legal discourse will have peculiar problems of its own and these will be dealt with when we come to them at the end of the book.

The development of a Marxist method of reading ideologies is, then, a vital necessity for the Marxist science of ideologies. Methods are relatively autonomous practices and, of themselves, partly determine the knowledge produced in research. Therefore, one cannot just start with a Marxist theory and tack on any old method just because it is fashionable or the only one in existence. A non-Marxist method will be in opposition to the theory employed and that contradiction will be reflected in the results of the research. To establish a method consistent with a given theory, it is first necessary to examine the existing methods. Whether such methods are presented as Marxist or not is irrelevant. As Marxists we must look to what these methods are rather than what their users say they are. This examination of existing methods must operate in the light of specific problems raised in research practice. In this case, my research on ideologies in news reports raised three questions in particular:

1. How does a method of reading ideology determine the absence or presence of an ideology within a discourse? This question raises the issues of the conception of ideology at work within a method. It also requires a discussion of the procedures adopted by that method.
2. How does a method of reading ideology 'think' the mode of existence of an ideology within a discourse? This question raises issues such as: Is an ideology embodied in the discourse? Does it show itself on the surface? or, Does it 'lie behind' the discourse?
3. How does a method of reading ideology justify its results? On what grounds is the reading said to be valid and possible?

These three questions will be put to all the methods examined in this section and will therefore determine our method of criticizing them. More than that, these questions in themselves are partly determinant of the selection of the particular methods to be examined. The latter provide us with a good working-ground for the development of our own answers to the questions. They are chosen partly on that basis; they are also chosen because they seem to be the most developed methods of reading ideology.

The problems operative in our interrogation of existing methods cluster around the classic epistemological question: how do we know? That question is not conceived here in a rationalist manner. That is, I am not searching for the purely logical grounds upon which truth can be constituted. What I am concerned with are the actual conditions of production of a concrete knowledge. "How do you know?" here means "Upon what theory, method and evidence do we produce our conclusions? And in what social circumstances is such a mode of knowledge production rooted?" 'Knowledge' here is seen as the product of a practice with definite means of production conducted within specific social circumstances. 'Truth' is not given any transcendental meaning but is seen as the product of the truth criteria at work within a socially situated mode of knowledge production. In this sense, my ensuing interrogations are generated by the basic questions of historical materialist epistemology. In order to produce a conception of the methods required for a Marxist knowledge of ideologies, I shall describe and criticize some of the existing methods of reading ideology. This does not involve a reading of their logic matched against some transcendental logic, nor a description of their meaning for either their practitioners or the social formations in which they exist (their political effects, for example). It is an attempt to describe their actual inner structures, their modes of working, and to evaluate them in terms of the theory outlined in the previous chapter. In this way, we can produce a method consistent with our professed theory.

The questions to be put to these methods also entail a concern with the question: what is it to 'read' something? Reading is a practice which we usually take for granted. We read newspapers, books, people and situations all the time. Sometimes, we even reflect on our readings to see if they are justifiable in the light of the evidence. Usually, however, we assume that reading is a physical act and that any ambiguity lies in the object of the reading. Social science is fundamentally concerned with reading the social world and is, nowadays, extremely sensitive to the fact that different modes of reading exist. How often do social science teachers reach exasperation at the novice's apparent inability to read the meanings of a situation or discourse? But what is it to read? Some definition is required before we examine reading methods. I am using "reading" here to refer to the practice of recognizing/misrecognizing/failing to recognize the significance of a social phenomenon. Put another way, reading is a practice within which we become aware of significance or meaning in social phenomena. *It involves an attempt to determine the signified meanings of a series of signifying units.* This reasonably precise definition makes it clear that to read is not to explain or to describe. Reading does of course depend on explanations and descriptions, but in itself it does not explain why a signifier relates to a signified nor does it describe that relation. Marxist work on ideology, thus far, has tended to move from an explanation of an ideology to the description of its existence within a discourse or practice. The intermediary step of the reading or identification of that ideology within that discourse has gone unnoticed and untheorized. As in other fields of study, social scientists are now more concerned than ever with the nature of this intermediate practice of identification or reading. What I am interested in here is the method by which one identifies an ideology within its discursive forms of appearance.

Having said this, two possible objections to my own procedure can be pre-empted. Firstly, it is not in any way true that the following discussion of reading methods, as they are applied in the reading of newspapers, television output and literature, is irrelevant to the reading of legal discourse. Law indeed has its own peculiarities, but the process of reading its discourse is exactly the same in general terms. Therefore, let us establish a general position first before dealing with a specific form such as law. To this end, the present section of the book can be seen as a review of recent developments in reading methods within the sociology of culture. Law is a major cultural form. Our knowledge of law can thus be enhanced by placing it within the general study of culture. In fact, this kind of comparative study, which contrasts several kinds of discursive forms of appearance of ideology, is probably far better than that which never leaves the realm of legal discourse. The comparisons should allow us insights which we could not have otherwise reached. This is especially true with law where professional modes of reading legal discourse are long established and where legal scholars may not easily be able to see beyond them.

Secondly, it may be observed that the actual presence of an ideology within an object or discourse is amazingly obvious. I shall not reply to this in a facile manner by crying "empiricism", although such a response would be justifiable. Anyone who has done any kind of reading knows that sometimes the meaning of a signifier is totally obvious, without any deep reflection on the matter. And, from the experience of a detailed study of press discourse on politics, I can confirm that the existence of even a complex political ideology, within news reports of various lengths and types, becomes compellingly obvious after the analysis of only 30 or 40 reports. This phenomenon cannot be readily dismissed and is of great intrinsic interest in itself. In fact, it is of so much interest that when the science of ideologies is more developed we should direct our attention to the compulsion which ideology impresses upon us. This fact must be explained. However, not all ideologies are obvious, nor are obvious ideologies readily observed by all people, therefore we do need to elaborate a clear method for identifying all ideologies. Compulsive obviousness is something to explain with a developed theory of ideology, not something which should prevent that development.

What is *ultimately* at stake here is not academic pedantry on my part but the politics of consciousness. Readings of social life and discourse need to be more sensitive to the relations of signification that reflect existing social relations of exploitation and domination. I am convinced that a sharper and better method will greatly enhance the sensitivity of readings of ideology, not hinder it. Concrete studies using sound method need to be done to render more ideologies more obvious to more people.

During the next few chapters I shall be dealing with methods not authors. The writers I refer to are not a comprehensive selection of the leading analysts of ideology. I am not capable of producing such an overview of the leading figures. Writers such as Lukacs, Sartre, Goldmann, Foucault, the Frankfurt Marxists and the ethnomethodologists are not dealt with. However, in so far as I correctly understand their work, their methods of reading do seem to fall under the categories of method dealt with here. How far my observations apply to their work must be for more expert commentators to judge.

Finally, the particular methods dealt with in this particular chapter are those which claim to derive the meaning of ideology from "the content" or significant units of a discourse. The methods dealt with in Chapters 4, 5 and 6 claim to derive the meaning of ideology from the forms or relations of signification within a discourse. This distinction between the methods is not water-tight and overlaps do occur. However, it is sufficiently viable to act as the principle organizing the following discussions into a sequence of sections.

Content Analysis—A Case of Pragmatic Empiricism

Berelson, in a much-quoted essay, defines what is called "content analysis" in communication studies as follows:

> Content analysis is a research technique for the objective, systematic and quantitative description of the manifest content of communication. (Berelson, 1966, p. 263)

The "technique" is said to involve the invention of a set of analytic categories which should be applicable without any problem of interpretation (this is said to constitute its objectivity) and which can be used on the whole of the analysed item (e.g. a news report) to produce results of general application (this is said to constitute its systematicity). Once the categories have been created, *the key operation* in content analysis takes place: the numerical quantification of "the *extent* to which the analytic categories appear in the content" (Berelson, 1966). For example, to prove that a politician has an ideology, content analysis might count the number of times he used the words freedom and order in his election speeches. If we investigate the definitions of the terms and look closely at the assumptions inscribed in the method, we shall find that content analysis is as it appears: superficial, limited in value, and dubiously founded.

Content analysis, says Berelson, is concerned with what is communicated, not the intentions of the communicator (1966, p. 262). So, what is the object of content analysis? According to Berelson, the answer is a body of meanings. But, apparently, not all meanings are relevant. Only those meanings which are *shared* between the communicator, his audience and the analyst are to be investigated. Content analysis concerns itself with "denotative" rather than "connotative" signifiers, with the aspects of the discourse which are part of a "common universe of discourse" (Berelson, 1966, pp. 264, 265). But what are the grounds for this supposed distinction between denotative and connotative communications? Berelson replies that communications can be placed on a continuum of universal comprehensibility. At one end we find denotative materials which are understood by all, and, at the other, connotative materials intelligible to some groups or individuals but not to others; and there are various gradations in between. Only denotative signifiers should be dealt with by content analysis and, even then, the quantification of this supposed class of signifiers should only take place when the frequency of occurrence is thought to be "an important factor in the communication process".

What is to be deduced from the findings of the count? Berelson declared that content analysis was a technique to enable description and did not say anything about its explanatory value. So nothing is to be deduced, but wait! It appears (Berelson, 1966, p. 264) that the knowledge of the denotative content can legitimately support inferences about the intentions of the communicators! But Berelson had forewarned us that he was only interested in the "what" of communication, not the "why", on the grounds that any content analysis which took its object as the motives and intentions of the communicator had "low validity" (without direct data on the communicators), "low reliability" (owing to the likelihood of inter-coder differences in interpretation) and "circularity" (deducing cause from effect would be followed by inducing effect from cause) (1966, pp. 262, 263). From this contradiction I conclude that content analysis is not simply a 'neutral technique' of description but also a device for producing a particular, practically useful knowledge about communicators' consciousness where the analyst cannot or does not wish to study it directly.[1] The *real* object of the theory involved in this method is not the "manifest content" of the communication but the intended message of the communicator. It is thus an implicit notion in the practice of content analysis that communication is achieved by and through an individual human subject and that the true meaning of what he or she says is an outcome of his or her intentions. To illustrate the strength of my critical explication, let us note Berelson's words:

> Content analysis is often done to reveal the purposes, motives, and other characteristics of the communicators as they are (presumably) "reflected" in the content . . . (1966, p. 264)

Having drawn out the nature of the theory or ideology involved in the practice of content analysis, the next task is to examine the relation between the ideology and the action involved in the practice. My thesis here is that this relation involves a severe contradiction, which in many writings is often antagonistic. Fundamentally, content analysis is a research practice whose action is in contradiction with the object of its integral ideology. Why is this so? Because the action only becomes technically feasible on the condition that it is directed towards a "shared universe of discourse", and, therefore, its products can *only* tell its practitioners something about the nature of that "universe of discourse"; they can provide no information about the "purposes, motives and other characteristics of the communicators". The necessary object of the action of content analysis is *denotative discourse*, but the necessary object of the ideology of content analysis is the *communicator's consciousness*.[2] The research action of the practice of content analysis gives a knowledge of an object different to the object of its implicit ideology!

However, I do not think that we can leave the matter there. The contradiction between the object of the communications theory and the object of the action within the practice of content analysis has *as a necessary condition of its existence* the concept of the significance of a repeated denotative sign. This concept is the site of the expression of that contradiction in as much as its function is to mediate between its opposing components. For how can one use a method aimed at denotative meanings to produce a knowledge of the communicator's "ideological" consciousness *unless* the repetition of denotative signs is thought to signify something about that consciousness? Thus the notion of the significance of repeated denotative materials lies in dialectical relation to the contradiction between the object of the action and the object of the ideology in which the practice operates. The contradiction necessitates the concept of the significance of repetition as the vital cohesive function which enables the practice to continue with a degree of coherence: that is why the quantitative aspect of content analysis is seen by commentators as its most distinctive feature—this aspect *is* in fact crucial to the coherence of the practice. As soon as content analysts begin to search for a qualitative method, the existing practice of content analysis must begin to fall apart at the seams.[3]

We can now deal with the questions posed in our introduction. The absence or presence of ideology for content analysis, as we have seen, lies in the consciousness of the communicator, and the frequency of appearance of selected denotative signs is taken to signify the presence or absence of some kind of ideological consciousness in the communicator.[4] In consequence the absence or presence of an ideology is detected in content analysis by counting (or, in some cases, by a rough estimation of quantitative extent) the appearances of these denotative categories—a procedure justified for the analyst by the allegedly shared, universal nature of denotative signification.

Having laid bare the main aspects and interrelations constituting the structure of the practice, it is possible to make a critique of content analysis. The central argument must be the nonsensicality of the key notion of the significance of repetition. However much a message is repeated, if the receiver cannot give it a meaning then it is not communicated to him. Repetition itself is insignificant (literally). Significance, however, *is* significant and if repeated would undoubtedly raise some kind of attention from its receiver. It is not the significance of repetition that is important but rather the repetition of significance. In which case the first question to answer concerns significance and perhaps then there can be some counting. But content analysis has no theory of significance. It merely assumes the significant existence (or existence-as-significance) of what it counts. It may be counting illusions or a fragmentary part of a real significance, but without a theory of significance it would not *know*: its concept of the significance of repetition gives it no knowledge of the significance of what is being repeated. The absence of a theory of signs, signification and significance renders content analysis absurd because its key concept is left unsupported and that concept gives it no knowledge of its avowed object, the content! The concept that holds content analysis together, the significance of repetition, is in itself a nonsense. In fact, therefore, content analysis is an incorrect label: 'repetition speculation' would be more accurate, since its practitioners are merely speculating about the significance of repetition.

Aaron Cicourel arrives at the same criticism from a different theoretical perspective:

> Any field researcher is confronted with the task of deciding how meanings are assigned to events. But in content analysis the project cannot get off the ground without some preliminary specification of the linguistic problems involved and of the cultural definitions presupposed in each analysis. (1964, p. 150)

Cicourel agrees that a theory of signs is required. Unfortunately, Cicourel's critique is immersed in a "differential"[5] concept of culture, which involves a view of society or culture as the product of the empirical interaction of a mass of psyches. Consequently he is more concerned with the definitions of the categories in content analysis than the stupidity of counting their repetition:

> Since the content analyst is dealing exclusively in meanings of verbal communications, the categories used obviously presuppose rules which define the provinces of meanings under which elements in communication are to be assumed. The assumption that a quantitative description of communication content in terms of the frequency of occurrence of some defined characteristics is possible requires that the categories employed stand in some specifiable correspondence with the characteristics, and that equivalence classes exist among the characteristics thereby

permitting counting to take place. But Berelson does not explicate the theoretical assumptions and methodological procedures for generating equivalence classes. (1964, p. 150)

In addition, Cicourel is more interested in the "normative rules governing communicator, audience and analyst interpretations of the meanings of one another's communications" (1964, p. 151) than the social relations governing the production and consumption of mass messages which structure the normative rules of interpretation held by communicators and receivers.

My second, more peripheral, criticism of content analysis is short and simple. It is a research practice founded on empiricist epistemology. The analytic categories, which it employs as elements of significance worth counting, are said to be *intrinsic* to the discourse, yet they are really the practical arm of the undeveloped concept of denotation. Content analysis holds that its concept of denotation is by nature at one with, or in correspondence to, the real object, the selected signs of the discourse, when, I would suggest, the concept is in fact an element of content analysis's ideology, "communications theory", which holds ideology, or connotative significance, to be a 'distorted, sectional discourse' or a 'perversion of the truth'. This communications theory claims that what is denotative or universal, and what is connotative or sectional ideology, is obvious or pre-given to the naked eye. No justification is ever given for this claim: an insidious one, too, since it enables its proponents to convert their political and cultural assumptions into 'the true meaning' of discourse and those of their opponents into partial and disputable interpretations of that true meaning. The concept of denotation becomes particularly insidious when operational in a research practice which is commonly granted scientific status and is effected forgetful of its unclarified, undeveloped, theoretical support and practical origin in the political conjuncture of the Cold War. The 'truth' of the theory (that is, its concepts of denotation and ideology) becomes transformed into 'neutral, objective technique' and the analytic categories are thus selected from the discursive material as obviously significant, obviously denotative units. What begins as a vague concept of ideology, as a distortion of truth or genuine discourse, finally ends its life as a method of arbitrary selection. The ideology inscribed in the practice of content analysis is thus embodied in the method of category selection and disappears, so enabling the conclusion that the method or practice is objective or scientific. Clearly, with no theory of significance, the method is *arbitrary* and *unsystematic*, and could not be anything else. Content analysis is based on empiricist thinking which provides that the truth is self-evident and visible—a provision which conceals the operation of its own highly political concept of ideology.

This brings us right back to Berelson's definition of content analysis as a "research technique". He can see it as such since its corresponding ideology of ideology disappears in its practice and renders that consequent practice a simple matter of efficacious technique and arduous labour. Content analysis can thus be presented as a scientific, neutral, objective, technical device for the analysis of content when in fact it is a ritualized, superficial practice, based on a contradictory and unclarified structure of ideas, logically only enabling the description of repetition. Thus grasped as "a technique for studying content", content analysis can act as a shield behind which the real activity of slandering the invented motives of the enemy can proceed.[6] Content analysis is social science's war method.

The third criticism is that content analysis contains a "communications theory" and therefore reflects the weaknesses of that theory. It is the peculiarity of communications theories that they are theories of communication. This concept usually refers to a process whereby one human being emits a message which is received and comprehended in its intended meaning by another human being. Communication is thus seen purely as an interpersonal, interactional process where meaning is transmitted, negotiated or modified: meanings are held to be created and affirmed by reciprocal, conscious, interpretive subjects. And this is the whole problem. As a consequence of "communications theory", the question of ideology production is reduced to the question of conscious/unconscious bias by prejudiced, 'communicating subjects' and, therefore, to the identification of frequent themes which reflect that bias. I would prefer a view which held that the emergence of a particular ideology is an outcome of a structured social practice. Individuals do not invent ideologies or prejudices. Such signs and corresponding psychological states are rooted in history and social structure. Socially located communicators may use and purvey certain ideologies with intent but they, themselves, do not invent those ideologies or their corresponding psychological states. Moreover, the existence of such social locations is no individual invention but a result of historical development in a social formation. This is not to say that the people involved in 'mass communications' are irrelevant machines, far from it. It is to say that they have an important role in that they carry and use a range of social ideologies, but that the precise selection and effectivity of the ideologies they employ in the process of mass communications production is determined by the structure of that production and its place in the social formation. Hence, in my view, personal bias and its alleged quantitative indicators are merely superficial points of focus: more consequential and fundamental are the social relations, which produce particular forms of ideology and consequent biases, and the hierarchies of class power which govern the publicity and effectivity of particular ideologies.

Because of the human communications theory within its method, content analysis can only locate ideology in a shallow way as the existence of a personal bias. It is not a method which is founded upon a social and historical analysis of the roots and functions of specific ideologies. It cannot, therefore, specify the inner nature and limits of any unit of significance, for the latter is a social, not a psychological, product. The fundamental problem with the view of ideology as the product of intentional consciousness is the fact that all this view declares is that a person's beliefs, as discerned in the discourse, are a product of a person's beliefs. Ideology *is* motivated consciousness in communications theory, but how can it be its own product? Again we find ourselves back to an earlier point: content analysis has no theory of signs or significance. It merely asserts signification and symbol as existing bits of psychological reality. The absence of a developed social theory of the sign constitutes its most damaging deficiency. For unless a theory of significance exists it is impossible to have a rational method for the detection of signs. When the impossible is attempted, as one would expect, the result is a non-rational and superficial method based on an everyday or commonsense ideology of ideology where the socially significant is an asocial product of the peculiarity of the individual psyche. And, alongside the *Homo economicus* of political economy and *Homo sapiens* of social anthropology, emerges the *Homo significans* of communications theory. He is ultimately the hidden hero and creator in content analysis: the human essence (albeit in its evil, demonic form) becomes the ultimate source of ideology.

Content analysis exists in a theoretical vacuum created by the absence of a theory of significance.[7] Hence we must look elsewhere to discover a theoretically valid method for the reading of ideology. But before we do that, it is necessary to make one thing clear. My objections to content analysis are not objections to the technique of counting itself. If a social theory of significance is used which presents a rational and convincing explanation of why certain signifiers should exist within a discourse, there is no reason why it should not count the appearances of those signifiers in order to illustrate its point. The extensive appearance of certain signifiers in a discourse does not indicate their significance, but, given a theory of that significance, there seems to be no objection to the researcher counting the appearances of those signifiers which, according to the theory, stand for the signified meanings expected. In that case, the quantification would indicate the strength of the theory. Here, the theory establishes the significance of the signifiers within a specific social practice and the count merely illustrates the theory (or requires its reconstruction).

The work of Halloran et al. (1970) is a pioneering effort in the direction of a theoretically grounded, quantitative, content analysis. Although it is not systematic and far too slender, Halloran et al. (1970) do develop a theory of the professional ideologies of news reporting which structures their content analysis of the significance of the news reports. They suggest that the structure of the news industry in Britain is such as to make certain ideologies a necessary part of being a journalist. It is this structure which is said to account for journalists' use of two major ideological formations, the "news angles" of "negativity" and "personality", which result in the signification of "events" (selected as 'news') in terms of violence, danger, damage, conflict, individual character and unusual action. Although made only partially clear by the authors, the concept of news itself is the over-arching ideological formation within news production, bathing all other ideologies in its colours and ranking their influence. Because of this theory, the categories of discourse selected by Halloran et al. (1970) for observation are those which, in the context of the news reports in question (those of the 1968 Grosvenor Square demonstration against the American presence in Vietnam), are demanded by the news angles of negativity and personality. These categories include violence, external influences, splits and boycotts, LSE, personality aspects, aims and objectives, and ban (Halloran *et al.*, 1970, p. 104). Certain signifiers within the news discourse are taken to refer to meanings contained within these categories, and thus the appearance of these meanings is identified and quantified. On this basis, and by using other methods such as interviewing, the authors conclude that "the underlying frame of mind" (1970, p. 26) of the reporters, reflecting their occupational position within a particular production process, was an important determinant of their accounts of this political event. Although it is not stressed, Halloran *et al.* clearly thought that these accounts were fairly reactionary, unbalanced, trivializing and uninformative.

The work of Halloran *et al.* (1970) is a major step forward away from content analysis as conceived by Berelson (1966). Although the authors still use the phrase to describe their quantification procedures, their method is crucially different from content analysis in that it does not use the count to indicate the significance of the discursive signs. A theory of significance precedes and structures the count, thus openly rendering the latter as the plain and simple technique of illustration it always was underneath the mystifying cloak of the tautologous 'communications theory' of content analysis. Having said this, the work of Halloran *et al.* (1970) suffers from three major faults:

1. Their theory of the social or practical basis of the professional ideologies of newsmen is so undeveloped that it is unclear which of these ideologies (and which of their fused constituent elements) reflect the structure of news production in general, which of them reflect the structure of capitalist news production, and which of them reflect social structures outside news production. No doubt, ideologies from various sources cohere and fuse within the practices of news production, but they need to be distinguished in analysis and their ranking elaborated. One would suspect that the ideology of 'news' itself and the ideologies of news in capitalism are dominant ideologies within modern news production, but what form these ideologies take is surely determined by non-professional ideologies (ideologies deriving, for example, from the class background of the reporter) and also by the very appearances of social reality observed in the process of 'news-

gathering'. Perhaps following communications theory, Halloran *et al.* have tended to see the communicator as *Homo significans*, constrained only by the organization within which he does his signifying. To say merely that preconceived ideas of news are operative in news reporting is to repeat an old platitude. Not even a journalist would deny that newsmen have operative ideologies of the news. To reach beyond platitudes about imbalance, sensationalism and trivialization, Halloran *et al.* had to demonstrate that the forms taken by the ideologies of news were influenced by wider, social ideologies reflecting the interests and experiences of classes and groups constituted by the dominant social relations. But their theory of the social origins of ideologies in the news was too narrow for that. Their theory was basically focused on the cultural relations between newsmen and resulted in the view that news ideologies arose from "professional socialization". This limited application of structural determination pays little attention to the social relations of production and control which govern the cultural intercourse between newsmen and the consequent forms of news ideology. It should be noted, however, that two of the authors have moved on considerably and have developed a more comprehensive conception of news organizations (see Murdock and Golding, 1973, 1977; Elliott, 1977).

2. There is a lack of clarity on some of the details of their method. This is, no doubt, partly because of the last-minute nature of the decision to do the research, and partly due to the lack of an existing, satisfactory method. In part, however, it is because of the lack of a developed theory of ideology (and its reading) in their work. Halloran *et al.* (1970) create big problems when they fail to tell us, for example, why negativity and personality are the only news angles given much attention. Were not any others in operation? Are these the only news angles in capitalist news production? Also, they do not tell us how they induce certain content categories, such as "external influences", from the fundamental news angles. Why would the activity of foreign, student activists count as an "external influence" from the point of view of negativity? In other words, why are foreigners seen as external and in a negative light? These connections need explicating. Halloran *et al.* simply take the connections for granted, yet these significant connections are surely the expression of a dominant

ideology, about the causation and nature of social problems, which needs to be brought to light. Without a developed theory of the role of 'non-professional' ideologies in news reporting, Halloran *et al.* were often blind to the profound operations of such ideologies in the reports under survey. The links between funda-mental news angles, content categories and specific significant items of news discourse cannot be left unexplicated because they are constituted in the terms of the non-professional ideologies at work. An adequate theory of significance must be able to specify the *necessary* links between these 'levels' of signification.

Similarly, Halloran *et al.* (1970, pp. 92–96) do not make clear exactly which signifiers were taken in practice as instances of a particular content category. Again, they no doubt used rules of classification based upon a rough hypothesis about the nature of the non-professional ideologies at work. Thus, the signifier 'arrest' was probably not taken as an instance of the content category of "violence"—because the ideologies at work in the reporting would see the police work as good and directed towards order. But these assumptions must be made explicit for together they constitute a theory of the non-professional ideologies at work in the news reporting of political demonstrations, and it is on the basis of such a theory that the research method (in part) proceeds. In short, the lack of clarity about their procedure indicates that Halloran *et al.* (1970) only had a limited theory of the ideologies in the news and the connections between them. Such a limited theory becomes particularly damaging when the readings of news consumers are examined, for it becomes very difficult to explain how the consumers came to particular conclusions about the significance of the news reports. Moreover, the consumers' readings of the wider, non-professional ideologies embedded in news discourse are crucial to an understanding of the political role played by the agencies of news production. Unless the researcher can identify those ideologies and consequently their mode of consumption, he cannot get beyond a narrow 'communications' study and into the realms of the analysis of class hegemony.

3. Finally, and this is a complex point which can only be developed gradually throughout this book, Halloran *et al.* (1970) do not investigate the social form of appearance of the demonstrations reported in the mass media of 1968. It is certainly true that, more

than any of the more recent writers on the subject, they make it clear that there was a particular reality to be reported. Modern research often gives the impression that discourse is entirely a function of the ideologies of the communicators. Content analysis gives the same impression. As yet, however, no students of ideology, to my knowledge have developed an explicit distinction between the ideologies of the communicator and the forms of appearance of the reported reality. It is my contention that discourses always refer themselves to the appearances of reality and, therefore, that the ideological configuration within a discourse is a fused concentration of the ideologies of the communicator and the forms of appearance of social reality (both being reflections of their constituent social relations). Traditionally, social science and the humanities have been divided into two basic schools: that school which sees discourse as the natural reflection of social reality (Empiricism) and that school which sees it as the natural reflection of the observer's ideas (Relativism). In my view, Marxism entails a conception of discourse which welds these two positions into a new form—discourse as a reflection, under determinate social relations, of both observing ideologies and observed appearances. This conception also holds that the professional fusion of ideology and appearance is a distinct cultural practice conducted within definite social relations. Thus it is that we need to develop the distinction between ideology and appearance and the concept of *the social relations of cultural production*. I shall attempt these developments later on. Suffice it to say here that both developments are way beyond the conceptions of content analysis.

Information Theory[8]

Like content analysis, information theory blossomed from wartime. It is an approach to communications studies deriving from physics and electronic engineering. Its proponents are rightly ambivalent about the transfer of a theory from one field to another, but that does not deter them. To explicate and illustrate the structure of information theory, let us look at Brian Winston's *Image of the Media* (1973). Like other information theory supporters, Winston admits that:

> . . . it is dangerous to extend a theory from pure physics into less
> discrete areas . . . (1973, p. 82)

But nevertheless he goes on to claim that:

> It is because of this substantial extension to the mathematics that
> it is possible to see in information theory a classic attempt by
> Western man to find a system of interpreting the universe. Such
> systems are all now in jeopardy. Information theory and its
> child, cybernetics, possess perhaps more validity than some
> older universal keys because they are part of the theoretic basis
> of those machines which are most destroying our old categoriza-
> tions and conceptual frames. (Winston, 1973, p. 93)

This amazing claim alternates with more sober statements which
suggest that, combined with sociological work, information
theory could be very powerful. More specifically, the use of
information theory is said to enable us to:

> . . . analyse on a statistical basis the *words* in the various *codes*
> used by the media, note the differences that occur from society
> to society and gauge more accurately than by other means the
> relative informational content of different messages. (Winston,
> 1973, p. 98)

These claims collapse when we realize that information theory in
the communications field is simply the use of an analogy. What in
fact happens is that the concepts of electronic engineering are taken as
applicable, on the grounds of insightful analogy, to what are seen as
'human' communication processes. The problem lies in the fairly
unmediated transformation of the concepts from one field into the
concepts of the other without regard to their use as analogy.
Consequently there is an absence of argument as to why these
concepts are appropriate: the metaphor becomes the reality. Thus,
although information theory in engineering is concerned with the
quantity of "information" that can pass through a particular channel,
the reduction of interference ("noise") and the use of "feedback"
devices to control the strength of the input, information theory in
communications studies implicitly equates "information" (the "reduction of incertitude") with meaning (whilst explicitly denying that it
does so), "noise" with misunderstanding, and "feedback" with learn-
ing.[9] Consequently Winston is able to construct his statements about
the ability of information theory to "quantify the content of the mes-

sage"; and we are able to see this theory as a form of content analysis.

But is this analogy insightful? No. The use of information, in the engineering sense, is inadequate for a theory of reading ideology. Why? Because the notion that any piece of discourse contains a certain number of "bits" of information is based on several mechanical and untenable assumptions: that the whole system is static and stable, that each bit of information is equal in strength, that there is a universal sharing of the significant code constituted by the bits, that the communications system is totally autonomous and has no external conditions of existence, that the relation between the communicator and receiver is non-antagonistic and non-contradictory, and that this latter relation functions and therefore was created to that end. This mechanical, systems theory of communication is more suited to electrical processes than social processes and has many absent concepts, but, notably, it lacks a concept of significance. The "reduction of incertitude" is assumed to occur without the receiver actively reading the code which is said to structure the message and thus dictate the meaning. Certainty is alleged to be intrinsic to the message whatever the mode of its production or the class of its consumer. Certainty is not seen as a product of class relations of production and consumption of mass messages over time, but as the intrinsic property of the message. The electrical engineer's concepts of redundancy, noise and feedback cannot be used as analogies unless there is some theory of significance. How could a message have a definite, large redundancy score unless we assume that the receiver automatically receives the non-redundant bits of information? It is logically impossible for it to be otherwise. Hence a consensus of meaning is always assumed to be simply and automatically extant. Similarly it is logically impossible to have fixed redundancy scores if it is the case that specific historical changes in the signifiers of meaning can also change their interrelations. (Consequently I would suggest that the concepts of information theory are compatible with structural linguistics and structuralist anthropology which also tend to assume that changes in relations are independent of changes in the units of the structure.)[10] The significant units (or signifiers) of the code are fixed in information theory. All round, the latter is very much an ahistorical, static, consensual, structural functionalism.

In conclusion, lacking a theory of ideology, information theory is unable to discern the absence or presence of ideology, or its mode of existence in discourse. Nor does it offer us any reasons as to why its adherents should be able to read ideology.

Speculative Criticism

Like content analysis and information theory, speculative criticism is a method of reading ideology which derives its significance (or signified meanings) from the apparent signifiers of the discourse. Unlike those two methods it carries no pretence to science, preferring to rest its case on the aesthetic and/or political value of its readings. Speculative criticism (my term, incidentally) is usually avowedly subjective, qualitative and unsystematic. It is thus the reverse of content analysis, whilst still being a form of content analysis in general. Literary criticism of the classic Leavisian type is a good example of speculative criticism to begin with.

Traditional literary criticism has many variants, but has two basic ideological elements dominating its practice. Firstly it involves a notion of the text as self-sufficient or self-enclosed. That is, the text is seen as intrinsically separate from its reading and its properties are to be found on the surface, readily available to a sensitive reader. Secondly, the reader must be thorough, sensitive and critical. He must give himself to the discourse in all its richness. No model or method is adequate because a method could not deal with the complexity of the text in all its variable wonder. We are reminded of the similarity to content analysis; Berelson's remarks illustrate the link:

> Since the content represents the means through which one person or group communicates with another, it is important for communication research that it be described with accuracy and interpreted with insight. Communication content is so rich with human experience and its causes and effects so varied, that no single system of substantive categories can be devised to describe it. (Berelson, 1966, p. 260)

This view is more than shared by many literary critics. It represents the atheist position in regard to the contention that a theoretical science of ideologies is possible. It is also a classically Positivist position in taking the observable as the only reality. The notion of the text's richness of meaning is symptomatic of the communications theory which corresponds to the Positivist epistemology, the theory which views the message as the chosen effect of the antecedent condition, the author. Both speculative criticism and content analysis share this theory which specifies the text as the simple concretization of a complex of intended meanings; in other words, as a simple but complex 'human communication'. Consequently both methods of reading spend their time attempting to discover what the communicator 'really' intended to say. In content analysis this activity is speculative in form and pragmatic in content: speculative in that its counting is based on a shot in the dark—that repetition expresses ideological intent—and pragmatic in that it counts what it can—denotative signs. It is the same in speculative criticism. The form of its operation is speculation over 'the real meaning' of the text; an activity which produces a narcissistic esotericism in critics regarding the quantities of literary sensitivity they possess, and a contemptuous hypercriticism which functions as a display of the alleged magnitude of those quantities. Literary criticism is classically the reading of texts in a speculative, empiricist manner which produces a type of criticism as its corresponding mode of discourse. The substance of the operation of speculative criticism, its criticism, is pragmatic in that the speculation seems to focus randomly on the text, having renounced any possibility of method. Consequently any systematicity or coherence achieved by speculative criticism is a mysterious one with apparently untheorized foundations. And this is, of course, why I describe the mode of reading as speculative. It cannot be anything else without an explicit theory of ideology and its reading.

Speculative criticism, then, involves a critical reading of texts without any explicit theory or method of reading. It is this mode of reading discourse that is characteristic of studies of press reports in the sociology of deviance. The operation of this mode can be well illustrated by Cohen and Young's book, *The Manufacture of News: Deviance, Social Problems and the Mass Media* (1973). The text is very much an outcome of the Marcusian libertarian socialism of the late 1960s. In itself, it is a political attack on the manufacturers of the images of "one-dimensional man". It is worth close attention on that basis and because it is widely read. In producing a reading of this text, let us look firstly at the effects of the implicit theory within the method of speculative criticism on the book as a whole. Only one article in the book consciously focuses on the question of the discernibility/transparency of ideology in its effects and that one is heavily edited.[11] The other articles that involve a reading are all critical and are thoroughly devoid of any systematic method of reading ideology. Next, we can also note that the linking sections between the readings also effect the method's theoretical position. The introduction is classic in its terminology and its absences (emphases in italics by C.S.):

> The second part (of the book) is the largest and consists of separate case studies—*using diverse sources and methods*—*on the modes of presentation* and *underlying models* of deviance and social problems *employed* in the media. (Cohen and Young, 1973, p. 11)

Part Two is entitled "Modes and Models". In the preface to that part (emphases by C.S.), the editors comment that:

> The first set of readings describes the content of the *images presented* to the public by the mass media, contrasting this, where possible with evidence from alternative sources. (Cohen and Young, 1973, pp. 97, 98)

The transparency of the "models" expressed by the significant content is given and thus unproblematic: they are assumed to be immediately readable. This concept of the immediate readability of signifiers is coupled with a political concern for the content of the models which, without its corresponding theory, exists as naked protest, a kind of Hobsbawmian "primitive rebellion" at the level of research practice. Like all anarcho-syndicalists in a period of militant dissent, Cohen and Young take mere symbols very seriously (see Williams, 1975).

Let us listen to the editors' own words, bearing in mind our comments on communication and literature studies:

> To stress the creative nature of journalism and the way it moulds events into particular world views is to narrow the distinction between fiction and non-fiction. From this point of view, neither form of writing is inherently "superior": our critical evaluations do not relate to the actual use of an interpretative paradigm—this is inevitable—but to the content of the models and world views which shape such interpretations, whether by journalist, film producer or novelist. (Cohen and Young, 1973, p. 97)

This passage illustrates the implicit theory of speculative criticism very well. Its illustrative elements can be broken down into seven sections as follows:

1. "the creative nature of journalism",
2. "it moulds events into particular world views",
3. "an interpretative paradigm—this is inevitable",
4. "the models and world views which shape such interpretations".

These four pieces of discourse reflect the basic element of the communications studies problematic: the authorship of meaning lies in the *human* nature of the agents of communication. Cohen and Young are, in the classic manner of speculative criticism, arguing that subjectivity in journalists' discourse is unavoidable and that therefore it cannot be criticized in itself. It is unavoidable because of the characteristic of journalism as an occupation which is necessarily carried out by human agents who can only act and think subjectively. All ideology is thus essentially a product of human agency. Thus all practices producing a discourse are equivalent in this view:

5. "to narrow the distinction between fiction and non-fiction",
6. "neither form of writing is inherently superior",
7. "whether by journalist, film producer or novelist".

These last three examples illustrate the continuity within communications studies grounded in their intrinsic view of the origin of all communication in its intentional author. Working within this humanist perspective, Cohen and Young can only *protest* against the content of the communicator's interpretations: speculative critics of ideology can only be critical, they can only make "critical evaluations" or subjective comments. Operating strictly within such a perspective, analysts are forbidden a scientific knowledge of the discourse by their own premises; science for them is merely the pretence of human communicators under definite social pressures.

In Cohen and Young's view of the fundamentally human nature of communication, bias in press reports is "inevitable". As in content analysis, *Homo significans* is congenitally a purveyor of ideology, the form of which is governed by his purposes. However, unlike content analysis proper, our speculative critics develop a theory of the social circumstances influencing the choice of purposes. Like Halloran *et al.* (1970), they see news, sociologically, as a product of the social organizations that produce newspapers, not as the simple necessity of a communicator's evil intent. News is still seen as a product of journalists' subjective interpretations, but those interpretations are a linear effect of the requirements of organizations for the production of newspapers. Journalists' interpretations are the result of a prior cause:

> News, rather, is manufactured by journalists through interpreting and selecting events to fit pre-existing categories, themselves a product of the bureaucratic exigencies of news organizations and the particular concentration of media control and ownership ... distortion is not limited to the heavy hand of direct censorship but is a less obvious process—often unconscious and unstated—of interpreting the event in terms of an acceptable world view. (Cohen and Young, 1973, p. 97)

Thus, as in the work of Halloran *et al.* (1970), a sociological, linear cause-effect determinism is added to the ideology of human communications intrinsic to content analysis. Despite the fact that their position marks progress away from the absurdities of classic content analysis in locating the *social* nature of subjective intentions. Cohen and Young reduce ideologies in news reports to the effects of news production processes. They fail to allow for the influx of ideologies from other social processes and thus produce a picture of *Homo significans* in a prison. They fail to capture the dialectical tension between the whole range of ideologies in journalists' heads and the structure of news production.

Part Two of Cohen and Young's text consequently consists largely of readings which illustrate speculative criticism and do not repudiate the method of content analysis. In fact some of the readings contain classic content analyses.[12] Most of the other readings whisk their findings out of thin air. Well suited to political protest, but lacking in clear direction and rigour, they make no attempt to justify themselves: the content of the analysed discourses speaks for itself.

Part Three of the text is devoted to readings by Cohen and Young supporting their own theory of social deviance which argues that images of deviance disseminated by the media fall into a narrow range around a "consensual image of society" and that the consumers can "rarely escape" the boundaries of these images of deviance. Consumers are highly segregated into "normative ghettoes" and, therefore, know little about the nature of social deviance. So, it is said, the media (the institutions of cultural practice, in more theorized terms) reinforce the "consensual image of society" already present in the consumer brain (Cohen and Young, 1973, pp. 337–349). Such shallow theorization of the effects of mass media discourse is typical of literary criticism (and speculative criticism in general) which tends to tack on bits of superficial analysis to an essentially moral, aesthetic or political evaluation. Now, let there be no mistake, moral, aesthetic and political evaluations are necessary, but, in my view, they should be made on the basis of thorough and reflexive explanatory studies of the discourse in question. Indeed, I would argue that, whether we like it or not, evaluation, description and explanation are inseparably linked in intellectual work (as philosophical consciousness it cannot escape its constant companion—spontaneous consciousness). Therefore, ignoring the need for thorough explanation, in favour of militant protest, does not make it go away. Speculative criticism uses shallow speculations rather than explanations of some depth and consequently I would argue that even its avowed speciality—criticism or evaluation—will only rarely achieve any great insight. The best literary critics are thus those who can explain their object, for evaluation requires recognition and recognition requires knowledge [see, for example, James' analysis of the changing forms and styles of cricket in the light of Arnoldian values, capitalist development and imperialist domination (James, 1963)].

The fourth part of Cohen and Young's book is entitled "Do-it-yourself Media Sociology", implying that reading ideology requires no theory or method and is a pursuit Anyman and Everyman can take up. It is simply a matter of application and imagination—just like putting up shelves. And, as any one who has put up shelves will know, application and imagination only produce frail attempts. Thus, it is not in the spirit of elitism when I say that reading ideology requires conscious theory and method to guide Anyman and Everyman to success. Cohen and Young's approach reflects the libertarian-anarchist spontaneism of their political conjuncture. Under the heading "Suggested Projects", Cohen and Young give the following handy advice (emphasis by C.S.):

> The project you pick depends on how ambitious you are. You might want to limit yourself to one form of mass media—for example, the press—and to one form of deviance—for example, vandalism—*and you might want to confine yourself to a simple*

description of the dominant imagery through which this phenomenon is reported. (Cohen and Young, 1973, p. 373)

"Simple description" only occurs as an effect of an empiricist epistemology, a position common to all forms of content analysis. Further on, our would-be, do-it-yourself, empiricist, speculative critic is advised to learn "something about content analysis and other techniques of collecting and classifying and coding your material" (p. 377). Any old "technique" (note the use of the term) will do—as long as it works—it's only 'a way in' to the data. Coding categories. are not theoretical issues—merely arbitrary instruments in the handiwork: base them on the data, dress them up as explanatory and present as confirmation of your theory.

In conclusion, *The Manufacture of News* (Cohen and Young, 1973) is a good illustration of speculative criticism. The transparency of ideology in its signifiers is given. The nature of the absence/presence of ideology, and the grounds enabling a reading of ideology are not seen as issues. Thus the book speculates with a criticism of the consensualism and conservatism of media products. But the critique is undermined by its nudity of theory (and consequent status as primitive protest) and the pragmatism of the abstraction formed lazily upon it. Again there is a gaping absence of an elaborated, adequate theory of ideology. Nowhere is this more evident than in this fourth part of the book. Here, theory and method are treated with contempt and as long as the approach is critical, any kind of speculation on the nature of the discourse is permissible. Nowhere is it clearer that the subjectivist view of communications is simply prepared to take the truth of its sense-impressions on trust.

Young's essay in the book, "The myth of the drug taker in the mass media", is an excellent example of speculative reading in full flow (see pp. 314–322). Without any hesitation or doubt, Young immediately moves into a reading of "the media". He fails to specify which medium exactly, or precisely how many media he bases his reading on: a methodological anarchism typical of speculative criticism. Young soon suggests that news is not just information and that "facts do not speak for themselves". He argues that the mass media offer "a consistent world view", "an amazingly systematic frame of reference". It is interesting to note that he immediately assumes that the fact of this media world view speaks for itself and can be observed by anyone who cares to look. He continues with a series of speculations which state that media myths are "grounded in a particular view of society". This world-view contains contradictions and the media's myths are an attempted resolution of these contradictions. He gives no reasons why this should be the case. He cannot do that because he is simply speculating: a practice indexed by the regular use of the phrase "I wish to suggest". The essay continues with an imaginative (literally) description of the alleged consensualist world-view of the media and its contradictions which the myths attempt to solve. Young concludes the essay by making a final, vague speculation:

> . . . the mass media portrayal of the drug taker is not a function of random ignorance but a coherent part of a consensual mythology. (Young, 1973, p. 322)

This totally speculative account of a specific ideology in the media illustrates perfectly the practice I have explained in this section. The method is purely imaginative, containing not the slightest bit of explicit theoretical guidance. Of course, we must register the fact that Young's practice in this article is also critical. Implicitly he rejects the hypocrisy of those who propagate and support propaganda about 'deviants':

> For by fanning up moral panics over drug use, it [the mass media—C.S.] contributes enormously to public hostility to the drug taker and precludes any rational approach to the problem. (Young, 1973, p. 322)

Explicitly, he criticizes the media for helping to make deviants the scapegoat for the problems of contemporary British capitalism. Both these criticisms are surely to be welcomed by anyone concerned with liberating people from the oppression of capitalist societies. But, as they are, Young's arguments and comments are only counter-propaganda. As such they are valuable to a degree, but, without a basis in a precise, theoretical grasp of the practical grounding of ideologies of drug abuse and the practical grounding of news discourse, his comments only have the status of political polemic.

"World Views" and the Possibility of a Science of Ideology

The subjectivist ideology within speculative criticism raises in a sharp form the central issue of the possibility of a scientific knowledge of ideological discourse. I shall now discuss this issue. It is a discussion which follows naturally all that has gone before and naturally precedes all that comes later: it is not a digression.

The key concept in speculative criticism, behind which all its other concepts throw their weight, is that of the world-view. There is a great difference between the world-view of a subjectivist-empiricist perspective and the concepts of ideological formation and ideology within a Marxist theory.

Firstly, a world-view is defined as a *total* way of looking at the world. It is a "model" or a "paradigm" which produces "interpretations". It is an overall philosophy which structures and ranks all the other mental forms in an individual's head. This conception also exists in content analysis, to a certain extent, in the form of the conception of the ideology of the politically motivated actor. It is clearly implicit in the notion of a world-view that human subjects carry a total vision to all their practices which assimilates every new impression into its grand pattern. The first point, then, is that the world-view is a highly undifferentiated concept which, in Marxism, is superceded by a number of concepts and premises: ideology, ideological formation, spontaneous consciousness, philosophical consciousness, and the connections between an ideology and practical social relations. It is not at all clear whether a world-view is easily conceived in these terms. On balance, I think that Marxism could accept the possibility of a linked set of ideological formations dominating an individual's practical and philosophical consciousness: the linking being done in philosophical practice. However, it would be necessary to qualify this by insisting on the primacy of social practice and its consequent continual re-structuring of the overall philosophy. This re-structuring could mean that the overall philosophy is highly contradictory and fragmented at some junctures. One would, secondly, need to say that overall philosophies are not congenital properties of human beings and that it would be necessary to know the social conditions in which their development was hindered or helped. All this is to be more than fair to the concept of the world-view. In practice, speculative critics rarely see the matter in such a differentiated and qualified manner. More often than not, the concept stands for a view of ideology as the totalizing bias of a human being which is peculiar to that person and not readily affected by social relations. In fact, the world-view is usually much more of a determinant than a result of practice: its origins are not usually clearly specified. What is normally argued is that the world-view is moulded by social "influences" and exists as an unchanging unity through which the adult eyes see. There is little of the Marxist emphasis on the contradictory nature of ideologies within the mind of an individual living out a wide range of contradictory social relations.

The subjectivist concept of the world-view thus tends to posit a unity within an individual's ideologies which has been constituted mysteriously by the brain under social influences. This tendency involves the danger of seeing that unity as a human, rather than a social, product. The work of the brain is easily separated from the social preconditions of that labour, in this perspective. As a consequence, the dialectical interpenetration of individual thought and social structure within the activities of social practice is often lost and one is left with the dualist conception of man versus society. In this conception, the relation is one of interaction between two external things, and it entails an uneasy mixture of a humanist emphasis on human authorship and a Positivistic sociological emphasis on societal influences. Dualism often results in the existence of a particular world-view being explained by certain social conditions, which in fact could only account for its formation or fusion and fail to explain the existence of its components. It is at this point, in particular, that the lack of differentiation within the conception of a world-view begins to produce effects of shallowness. Marxism always separates out the origins of a simple ideology from the origins of a complex ideological formation.

The second area of difference between the subjectivist (or humanist) conception and the more differentiated Marxian conception concerns science. One world-view is said to be as good as another because they are both equally the effects of human subjectivity. Humanist notions of man are thus brought to the fore here. For Marx, as I read him in this difficult area, although all ideologies are reflections of social relations, they are by no means all equally adequate approximations of their real referents. The social term 'science' has many meanings; however, Marx did use it. It seems to me that Marx saw science as a serialized discourse of signs and ideological formations which grasped in thought the range and nature of the forms of appearance of a thing and the inner or hidden structure of that thing which gave it those forms of appearance. All sciences were of this nature: a science, for Marx, explains why things appear as they do and thoroughly describes those appearances. Of course, Marx recognized that a science would not necessarily be seen as such, either by its proponent or by others. But the forms of appearance of a science or its differential perception by social classes were not for him the criteria of its existence. An explanation, in his conception, specified the latent causal mechanism and its necessary, perceptible effects. As such, it was capable of being tested in the light of the carefully established effects it supposed. Unexpected appearances did not automatically disprove the science; however, if it could not logically develop to encompass their existence and form, its validity was limited. In short, Marx thought that it was possible for things to be knowable and that science was the conscious, discursive explication of that knowledge. He thus rejected the humanist conception of the equality of world-views. Marxists, therefore, rightly posit the possibility of a science of ideologies and reject the notion that observations on ideology must be restricted to political, moral and aesthetic evaluations of their effects. One can go further than that and attempt to describe the inner structures and conditions of existence of ideology which necessitate certain identifiable consequences.

This thesis is too important to be left unsupported by evidence and further argument, so I shall briefly consider the operations of Marx in *Capital* which, more than any of his other works, he clearly saw as a text containing a scientific discourse. To begin with, it is evident that Marx did not expect the ruling class, or even many of the rest of the population, to accept immediately that his analysis was a very close approximation to the workings of the capitalist mode of production. Indeed, the analysis in *Capital* itself suggests two reasons (at least) why this should not be the case:

1. Because the capitalist mode of production resulted in the political and cultural supremacy of the bourgeoisie which they used to suppress views, scientific or otherwise, which they saw as subversive to their world.

2. Because the capitalist mode of production necessarily presented itself in practice in ways which concealed its constituent relations. This would always be true to some extent and only when the socialist movement had attained some degree of hegemony within the proletariat and allied subordinate classes, could these "mystical veils" begin to be shredded in practice. Only then would his scientific analysis begin to carry weight amongst a sizeable sector of the population. At that point, it was foreseeable (although not perhaps foreseen by Marx) that the veracity of his science would emerge from the shadows and become, itself, one of the things at stake in the class struggles within a thoroughly international capitalism.

In *Capital*, Marx develops a theory of value which specifies its inner nature or latent aspects, which elaborates its conditions of existence and transformation, and which specifies its outer characteristics or forms of appearance. This theory, therefore, also explains how value tends to be signified spontaneously in economic practice and thus theorized (philosophically) in superstructural practice. That tendency is to see value in its forms of appearance: thus value is seen in practice as exchange-value inherent in a given commodity. Commodities are seen spontaneously as having intrinsic worth, and in economic theory this is translated into a concern with prices and market forces. The fact that value is produced by labour and that its quantity in a given product is determined by the average amount of social labour time necessary to make that product, is a fact that is imperceptible to the senses. Scientific statements about economic practice for Marx thus (1) explain why its elements take particular forms of appearance, and (2) generate propositions about the manner in which they will tend to be signified in practice. Like any science, Marxian theory explains why things appear as they do. Such explanations, therefore, are not radically different from ideologies. Indeed, they depend for their existence on significations of appearances (albeit accurate ones). The latter are *necessary* conditions of existence of a science. The *sufficient* condition for a science is a philosophical consciousness which accurately signifies the abstractions, or latent realities, which are necessarily connected to the concrete or outer realities. These abstractions, like the descriptions of the apparent, are reflections of existing social relations. As Marx pointed out, Aristotle could not conceive of value in the abstract as the product of all human labour because the social relations in which he lived (master–slave relations) did not enable him to imagine the existence of the equality of all human labour, "the secret of the expression of value" (1974, p. 65). Therefore, all the components of a scientific discourse are merely significations reflecting social relations, i.e. ideologies, except for one thing, their relation to the real object. Science, then, for Marx, is accurate ideology or, more precisely, a series of ideologies which adequately approximate to their real referent in all its aspects. It is distinguished from ordinary ideology in that (1) it must take a conscious, discursive form, (2) it approximates adequately to all aspects of the phenomenon studied, and (3) it contains a description of the mechanism which causes the inner aspects to be connected to the outer aspects of that phenomenon.

This position on science distinguishes Marx from several other thinkers, notably:

1. Those who see science as truth and ideology as falsehood.
2. Those who see science as the knowledge of latent reality and ideology as the description of apparent reality.
3. Those who see science as a result of careful method and ideology as received commonsense.

Although Marx thought that what is socially termed as scientific knowledge often contained truth and a knowledge of latent reality as a result of careful method, it did not always have these characteristics and, more importantly, these features were often contained in what is socially termed as ideology. In other words, he saw the science/ideology distinction as an inadequate one for the characterization of modes of signification. The logic of his position in *Capital* is that such a distinction is very much a political one (disliked ideas are ideological) and, indeed, he himself often used it in a political manner. His usage of the terms and the way he thought out the problem were, in fact, consistent yet apparently contradictory. But it was precisely because he thought of the distinction as a political one that he could use it as such. Science for him was really only a rather special type of ideological formation (or complex signification) rooted in social practice, and as such it lost the reified and mysterious character granted to it by bourgeois social relations which set it on high apart from everyday practice and the common man. Thus, the distinction for him would not be between ideology and science, but between levels of approximation to an object and its mechanism. Although not in these terms, he frequently evaluated statements or theories as: (1) so shallow and limited that they were undeserving of the term "approximation", e.g. lies, stupid remarks, platitudes; (2) as shallow and limited approximations lacking a logical theory of the object's movement; (3) as accurate approximations of some extent which laid out the nature of the object, but which failed to grasp its internal logic; or (4) as extensive and profound approximations to both nature and internal logic. Clearly, such a scale of evaluations cannot be adequately conceived within the framework of the political distinction between science and ideology, which we must abandon for our scientific purposes.

Some observers wish to read the Marx of *Capital* to say that his account of "commodity fetishism" is the basis of a theory of ideology (see Marx, 1974, pp. 76–87). It is necessary at this point to dispute that view. Crudely, the theory of "commodity fetishism" states that people in economic practice will tend to be misled by the fact that commodities appear to have intrinsic exchange-values and see the relations between commodity values as relations between things rather than as relations between people in different productive practices. Thus, it is said, ideology equals the mystificatory appearance of things and science is necessary to uncover the real relations. Modes of appearance, in general, are thus seen as illusory or ideological, and hidden relations as the truth of the matter. There are statements and phrases in *Capital* which support this reading. Marx talks of "the fantastic form" (1974, p. 77), "the mist through which the social character of labour appears to us" (1974, p. 79) and, of course, argues generally that Political Economy failed to reach the correct theory of value because it remained deluded by the mystical form of commodities.

It seems to me, however, that Marx does not mean to say that all appearances, in whatever practice, are deceptive. For example, Marx frequently pointed out that feudal social relations did not present themselves in a deceptive way, even though they were not seen for what they were. Moreover, I do not think that Marx saw deceptive appearances as necessarily illusory or unreal. Forms of appearance are, for Marx, merely the visible side of a phenomenon as it is observed from the standpoint of a specific social practice. Thus, value within capitalist economic relations only reveals as much of itself as can actually be seen in capitalist economic practice. It is from the standpoint of such practice, Marx says, that social relations between producers present themselves to the senses as social relations between commodities. For in that situation, that is "what they really are" (1974, p. 78):

> . . . this fact appears to the producers . . . to be just as real and final, as the fact, that, after the discovery by science of the component gases of air, the atmosphere itself remains unaltered. (Marx, 1974, p. 79)

Even the discovery of the laws of value, says Marx, will not alter their working and their consequent forms of appearance in practice. Commodities are "social things whose qualities are at the same time perceptible and imperceptible by the senses" (Marx, 1974, p. 77). Forms of appearance are thus not conceived by Marx as illusions but as the aspects of a phenomenon as it appears within the social relations of a particular practice. These appearances are real manifestations, they are "perceptible by the senses". It is precisely because they are real that they tend to be observed regularly and signified as the realities of the matter. But, the point is that they are not their own significations. The basis of signification is the social structure within which people signify appearances and that structure is not necessarily identical in its conditions of existence to the structure of the appearances. Things, apparent or imperceptible, have to be signified to become signs and the processes of signification can be subject to different determinations to the processes generating the things to be signified. Thus, feudal social relations were not absolutely identical with the conditions underlying their mystificatory signification in religious ideology.

It is true that some appearances of the capitalist economy do conceal its essential features. For example, the appearance of contractual agreement between employer and employee does not of itself reveal the fact that the employee is actually forced into work to survive because of his lack of means of production. But this argument is only true on the basis of Marx's analysis in *Capital* and that analysis is only put forward on certain theoretical conditions. The most important of these conditions, for our purposes, is that the analysis of Marx is intentionally, and in fact, merely, an analysis of the "economic formation of society" (Marx, 1974, p. 21). People are only dealt with in as much as they are "personifications of economic categories, embodiments of particular class-relations and class-interests" (ibid., p. 21). Moreover, this analysis always assumes that all other things are equal. "All other things being equal" could be described as the principle, theoretical condition of *Capital* and indicates that he is merely analysing the abstract, inner logic of the capitalist economy. He is not explaining world history or the English economy or a particular social conjuncture. Marx is analysing in the abstract the economic formation of capitalism. Because of the theoretical conditions which presuppose the theory of the capitalist economic formation, when Marx deals with its forms of appearance he is positing that capitalist social relations present specific apparent features to the senses of people in economic practice, all other things being equal. In short, that is not a theory of ideology, but a theory of the forms presented for view within capitalist economic relations. It can not be a theory of how those forms are actually signified for several reasons:

1. Modes of appearance are different from modes of signification. The latter are distinct phenomena with their own distinct conditions and mechanisms and are by no means determined only by the economic structure of society. Political and cultural practices are vitally important as social resources of ideology. So, too, is the level of development of the productive forces (notably abstract scientific theory), for, although determined by the economic structure, such forces are distinct and act, positively and negatively, as preconditions for the emergence of forms of ideology. The modes of appearance dealt with by Marx are in themselves purely features of the economic structure or relations.

2. As Marx pointed out many times, the internal logic of capitalism, which he had discovered, necessitated conflict and struggles between a number of social classes, notably the bourgeoisie and the proletariat. Even in its purely economic form, class struggle renders the mechanism of the capitalist economy more and more transparent. That is, even if we ignore the superstructure, the veils of the economy become less mystical the more that its internal structure heightens the conflict of the classes. Modern capitalists

can no longer totally rely on the economy to conceal its inner nature—political and cultural apparatuses and ideologies need to be manufactured and developed in order to justify its existence. In any case, it is doubtful that capitalism ever relied for its continuation upon its own self-concealment; political repression and cultural division of workers' movements has been one of its recurrent requirements.

3. Apart from the superstructural developments consequential upon class conflict, the purely economic development of the system has resulted in a form of capitalism (international and monopolistic), totally predicted by Marx, which presents itself in ways which are more transparent than those of previous forms. Capitalism today more openly depends on social relations between the different branches of production. Does the price of oil present itself as an effect of the commodity's intrinsic nature or as an effect of relations between different sets of producers? In the capital-intensive industries of today, the need for continuous exploitation of labour-power becomes more and more apparent as each big strike brings those industries to a greater and greater crisis: so apparent that intrinsic class divisions are openly recognized and mitigated by that recognition in its expression in higher status for workers, worker participation in management, systematic "industrial relations", inflation-linked pay rises and factory-based welfare services. It would be dangerous to overstretch the point, but nevertheless as capital develops it does reveal more and more of its total nature to the naked eye: and one can say this without a word about crises of overproduction, unemployment, bankruptcy and inflation.

4. Apart from the effects of class conflict, the logic of the capitalist economy necessitates, of itself, the high development of technical and general education geared to capitalist production, *and* the development of the means of communication. The establishment of institutions of education and communication has, of itself, I would argue, resulted paradoxically in greater proportions of the population being able to see straight through to the heart of capitalist production. Of course, whilst enabling this, these institutions have also provided new justifications for the system. But nevertheless it has made more of its functionaries more capable of seeing beyond their noses than ever before.

In short, all other things are never equal and the very logic of capitalism has opened up its skeleton to view and enabled many to see through its fleshy exterior. The capitalist economic formation has changed its forms of appearance and has also necessitated developments which render the relative autonomy of modes of signification more and more important. Perhaps these are the real conditions which enable me to say emphatically that the distinction between forms of appearance and modes of signification is a vital one. In any case, it was always there in *Capital*, albeit in an implicit way. Forms of appearance are *not* ideologies. They merely act as one of the components fused with others in the formation of an ideology. Therefore, the theory of commodity fetishism is only a theory of the social appearance of commodities and no more than a contribution to the theory of the signification of commodities in social practice. Appearances may encourage the mystification of their observers but they do not necessitate it. Modern conditions make it more and more clear that it takes a lot more than a surface mask to conceal capitalist social structures. Correspondingly, it now needs more than a scientific theory of the economy to reveal the nature of capitalist social formations; it needs a scientific theory of the social emergence and production of ideology. Marx thought that such a science was in principle possible; it is the task of modern Marxism to develop it.

To conclude, the concept of the world-view is markedly different from the Marxian concept of ideology. The concept of the world-view is founded upon a conventionalist epistemology (see Keat and Urry, 1975) which refuses to accept the existence of a real world beyond that designated in the observer's mind. It thus cannot accept the Marxian view that the real world is a determination within the formation of an ideology in that its forms of appearance offer themselves for signification. In Marxism, signs are never simply unilateral products of the observer's existing conceptions. The real world is doubly determinant of the forms of ideology because it offers appearances for signification and also structures the practices within which people signify. Conventionalist epistemology is only prepared to accept the latter type of social determination of ideology. It thus refuses to accept that ideologies vary in their degree of approximation to, and depth of understanding of, the apparent world and its inner mechanisms. The fact that some approximations and understandings can be shown to be more adequate than others in practice is alien to the concept of the world-view because of its one-sidedness as the concept of the expression of the socially situated human being.

A scientific knowledge of ideology is possible, but not through the subjectivist theories of pragmatic content analysis and speculative criticism. Such theories are superficial: they are themselves the victims of ideology's deceptive form of appearance in that they only see it as an expression of a motivated human consciousness. Just as value only appears *in* utilities and *as* exchange-value, and is thus often seen in practice as exchange-value intrinsic to a utility, so too ideology is only concretized *through* human individuals in social practice and *as* a chosen viewpoint, and is thus often spontaneously seen in practice as a systematic prejudice invented by a capricious human being. The historical conditions which relate signifier to signified to form an ideology are hidden from view when that ideology is regularly expressed in social practice. All the theories contained in the methods discussed in this chapter are blind to the full historicity of social relations of signification and repress them in favour of studying the apparent prejudices of contemporary individuals and groups. They are thus of limited value as approximations to the full nature of ideology. To read only the signifiers of a discourse and attribute their speculated meaning to the intentions of the communicators is superficial indeed. It might suffice for reading a newspaper over breakfast but it is insufficient for scientific analysis.

Conclusion

The methods dealt with in this chapter are superficial. They are geared to ideology's immediate, concrete appearance as a series of signifiers expressed by an individual or group. Even the addition of sociological theory to them does not alter that fact: these methods are limited. Their limitations centre around their lack of a theory of significance, of how meaning is constituted, of the social relations of signification which give signifying units their signified, social meanings. In content analysis, these relations are taken as given and meaning is inferred automatically from the signifiers. Its practitioners often become conscious of this deficiency (see especially De Sola Pool, 1959). Those who use classical content analysis today feel the need to supplement it with imaginative use of other data in order to provide insight into the meaning of the discourse. Information theorists are sensitive to the precariousness of the analogy founding their method. Speculative critics formally abandon method and submit themselves to the task of being eternally insightful and imaginative. This burden reduces many of them to the insecurity of contention, taste and polemic. From the plaintive remarks in their texts, it seems that the practitioners of content analysis in general do not bear its oppressive weight without some discomfort. This makes a nice dialectical contrast to the extravagant exuberance of the explorers of form to whom we now turn.

Notes

1. This conclusion is supported by the fact that content analysis developed rapidly in World War II and in the USA in the McCarthy period, and by the fact that many of the studies using content analysis attempt to demonstrate to the communication-receivers that the message is "biased" and that the communicators intend to deceive the receivers. In other words, the social conjuncture of its development required an apparently scientific method which enabled the legitimacy and the transmission of the message: "Take no notice of them. They are not objective. They are trying to subvert you". As Lasswell noted:

> . . . it may be pointed out that quantitative ways of describing attention may serve many practical, as well as scientific, purposes. *Anticipating the enemy* is one of the most crucial and tantalizing problems in the conduct of war. The intelligence branch of every staff or operations agency is matching wits with the enemy. The job is to out-guess the enemy, to foretell his military, diplomatic, economic and propaganda moves before he makes them, and to estimate where attack would do him the most harm. A principal source of information is what the enemy disseminates in his media of communication. (Lasswell, 1966, p. 253)

2. Whether this research practice is adequate to its *political* function of "*detecting political propaganda*" (as Lasswell puts it, 1966, p. 254) is another matter. At the political level of the social formation, power is more important than internal logic. The products of the practice can be declared scientific, and used to support the theory that they reflect the consciousness of the communicators, simply by fiat from a position of power. Thus it is that "propaganda" is "detected" from the findings of a method which can only technically produce knowledge about the frequency of appearance of units of universally shared meaning! In fact then, the detection of propaganda disguises the production of prop-

aganda: a nice piece of ideological inversion.

3. This search and this consequence seem to be taking place in De Sola Pool's collection of papers from a 1955 conference on content analysis (1959).

4. Whether ideology is said to be conscious (e.g. "prejudice") or unconscious (e.g. "unwitting bias") varies with the version of "communications theory" employed in the practice of content analysis. The method itself is totally capable of carrying a strong Freudian theory of the significance of repeated utterances.

5. Bauman's term, see Bauman (1973a).

6. For examples of this, see Leites and Lasswell (1940) and the titles in the bibliography of Berelson and Janowitz (1966).

7. All the developments in De Sola Pool (1959), however tentative, do seem to revolve around a growing awareness of the need for a theory of significance.

8. This will not be dealt with in great depth since its influence and value at this time remains limited.

9. Equations which, unsurprisingly, given the lack of a theory of signs or ideology, fail to provide information theory with a method of analysis; mere speculations are the only consequence.

10. This seems to be supported by Smith's linking of information theory with the linguistics of Chomsky and the anthropology of Pike, and by Slater's combination of the work of Levi-Strauss with that of Shannon and Weaver. See Smith (1966) and Slater (1970).

11. Hall's paper "The determination of news photographs" in Cohen and Young (1973, pp. 176–190).

12. The articles by Berelson and Salter, Davis, Nunnally and Linsky.

4 The Analysis of Form: Structuralism

Structuralism in General

From the analysis of manifest content we have arrived at the exploration of inner form. The target of this method of reading ideology is the invisible, significant structure of things, the relations of signification which link the manifest content (the signifiers) with latent, signified meanings. Since these relations touch upon all objects within the ambit of social practice, the structuralist method is not restricted to discursive forms. Thus, structuralist research has been done on codes of fashion and food, as well as on myth and literature.[1]

Like all methods of reading ideology, structuralism is ultimately geared to discovering the social meaning of things. Not all its proponents recognize this however; some say that they merely wish to determine the universal structures of signification in order to understand the actual meanings derived from the text (or signifier) by its social audience (see Lane, 1970). The distinctiveness of structuralism is that, unlike content analysis, it deduces the social meaning of the sign from its structure rather than from its apparent, significant units. In fact, one needs to add that most structuralists argue that a signifier relates to a whole range of meanings and that to specify the meaning for a given group or individual one must study the interpretations of that group or individual and the context in which they are made. All most structuralists are concerned to do, in other words, is to identify the general structure at work and leave the matter of its exact significance for any particular person or group to sociological research. In general, the structuralist approach only finds things of interest as manifestations of invisible, basic structures: it is not usually concerned with authors' intentions or socially situated audience interpretations.

Structuralism is a term in wide use today. It has come to refer to various things in a derogatory way, such as abstract analysis and the belief in structural determination. Basically, it refers to the modern variant of the study of latent and long-lasting structures, a variant carried forward primarily by French intellectuals such as Levi-Strauss (in anthropology), Godelier (in economics), Althusser (in philosophy), Barthes (in literary criticism), Foucault (in the history of science), Lacan (in psychoanalysis) and Bourdieu (in sociology). However, the term is of wider value than as a specific reference to this modern, French, intellectual movement. It designates a method which examines phenomena as the outward expressions or concrete manifestations of their invisible, inner structures. In this sense, structuralism could be called the semiological method because it takes appearances as signs of the inner form or structure of a phenomenon. Semiology, in general, is the study of signs. However, despite what some writers say to the contrary (e.g. Culler, 1975, p. 6), I do not think that it is the same as structuralism. One could, in principle, have a non-structuralist semiology, although one cannot have a non-semiological structuralism.

In this chapter, I shall examine the structuralist method in general and in the next I shall look at the structuralist semiology of Roland Barthes. Althusser's *lecture symptomale* (symptomatic reading) will be held back until Chapter 6, despite its structuralist tendencies, because it is an especially complex mode of reading which can only be understood fully in the light of an extended discussion of the structuralist method.

Generally speaking, the structuralist method presents itself as full of promise (see Bauman, 1973b). It appears to reject the empiricist assumption of the immediate obviousness of ideology in discursive forms in favour of an emphasis on the distinction between the outward, transient, signifying appearances and the inner mechanism of the ideological structure. Unlike all forms of content analysis, the structuralist method is founded upon the view that the elements of signification do not of themselves reveal the meaning of the message. It is based on the premise that the possible meanings of a discourse (or other significant form) can only be derived from the structures of signification operative within that discourse. The significant structures set the parameters of the range of meanings which can be drawn from the significant form. Consequently, structuralism is geared to the discovery of the code within the message, in the same way that one might learn Morse code in order to read a message in Morse.

Because it is concerned to read the code which gives the message its possible meanings, structuralist method tends to result in the production of a series of binary oppositions (see Levi-Strauss, 1968; Slater, 1970). All codes involve a series of oppositions, e.g. 1/2/3/4/5/6, and, thus, when specifying any one significant item in a code, one must always be specifying its antithesis. The structuralist method aims to produce the series of oppositions (or relations between units) which constitute the code of the message and, therefore, establish its range of meanings. It is claimed that, in doing this, the researcher does not make any assumptions about the dominant *social* meanings of the signifiers, that is, about the intended or received meanings. All that is assumed is that the method extracts the code which makes possible all the actual meanings given to the sign. Let us look more closely now at the theoretical object of the structuralist method—the structure—to see what limitations and faults are involved in this approach.

The Concept of Structural Determination

Roland Barthes' definition of contemporary structuralism as a "mode of analysis of cultural artefacts which originates in the methods of contemporary linguistics" (Culler's paraphrase, 1975, p. 3) is a good one since it brings out the key point that linguistics has a central role in the structuralist perspective. Structuralism has drawn many analogies from the concepts of linguistics—not the least being that the structure of a discourse is a coded ideological *language*. As Barthes says,

> I have been engaged in a series of structural analyses which all
> aim at defining a number of non-linguistic "languages" (1964,
> quoted in Culler, 1975, p. 4)

I do not intend to investigate the technical weaknesses of the
linguistic analogy in structuralism. That would be beyond my
competence. However, there is one important thing to say: linguistics was already dominated by a structuralist approach; modern
structuralism did not just lift elements from linguistics and make
them its own. Language in general was already seen to be constituted
by a number of arbitrary units linked by a definitive structure (see
Lyons, 1973; Culler, 1973). Structuralism, in its recent attempts to
understand myths and other cultural artefacts, naturally applied the
concepts it had developed in the field of linguistics. Thus cultural
artefacts were seen as arbitrary signifiers governed by the language of
myth or ideology.

The concept of the language of myth (or ideology) can be better
understood if we look at language in linguistics (structuralist variant):

> What, then, is the central thesis of Saussurean structuralism as far
> as language is concerned? To put it first at its most general, it is
> this: that every language is cut to a unique pattern and that the
> units out of which utterances are composed—more carefully, the
> units which we identify (or postulate as theoretical constructs) in
> the analysis of utterances—can be identified only in the terms of
> their relationships with other units in the same language. We
> cannot first determine what these units are and then, at a
> subsequent stage of the investigation, inquire what structural
> relationships hold between them. Linguistic units derive both
> their existence and their essence from their interrelations. Every
> distinct language is a unique relational structure; and the units
> which we identify in describing a particular language—sounds,
> words, meanings, etc.—are but points in the structure, or
> network, of relations. (Lyons, 1973, p. 6)

Language, in both linguistics and cultural analysis, is from the point
of view of structuralism best seen in terms of units or functions and
relations between them. *The units of the system only get their
meaning and existence from their formal position, their location in
the structure.* This was the main thesis of Saussure, the founder of the
analysis of signs (semiology) and the founder of the structuralist
school of linguistics. It is the central premise of the structuralist

method. Thus, Saussure argued that language was a socially produced system, independent of the will of groups or individuals,
composed of relations which link signifiers and signifieds (Saussure,
1974). Imperceptible to the senses, these relations constituted the
linguistic code which enabled speech and communication. They
were the object of the Saussurean science of linguistics which was not
reducible to the study of individual utterances and variations.
Similarly, therefore, units of ideology, in modern structuralism,
"derive their existence and essence from their interrelations"—to
transpose Lyons' dictum. Units or signifiers exist and are meaningful
only because of the relations between them.

   Given this concept of the phenomenon, the structuralist method
has as its object the *structure*, the relations between the elements
which produce and define those elements. To focus on the elements
themselves without examining their internal relations is anathema,
since to do so would be to avoid the source of explanation and would
thus be to produce mere speculation or meaningless abstraction.
Structuralism therefore derides Positivism which sees the given
apparent element as the product of some outer external force and not
as a product of the relations between itself and the other elements of
the entity in question.

   The structure is so important for structuralism that we must grasp
precisely what is meant by it. It is absolutely wrong to think that, in
structuralism, the elements are anything but the creations of the
relations. This point can be expressed by drawing four lines as
follows:

| | | | |

By making these four marks, I have created five spaces on this
particular horizontal, which can be termed as follows:

A | B | C | D | E

Now, A, B, C, D and E are all internally 'blank'. They have been
created in "their essence and existence" by my act of imposing a
vertical structure of lines upon an undifferentiated horizontal space.
They only exist as moments of the relations between them, as
"points in the structure". It is vitally necessary to comprehend this
fact in order to understand the object of structuralism. The units of a

system are not determined within themselves for they only exist as places, locations or points in the structure. The structure is all. Elements are arbitrary: as Saussure said, the signifier is arbitrary in that it has no "natural connection" with a signified reference (1974, p. 69). Thus, in my example, the relations between A, B, C, D and E—the elements of our system—are purely arbitrary and so the existence and meaning of A, B, C, D and E are also purely arbitrary or "unmotivated" (to use Saussure's term).

The conception of structural determination inherent within the structuralist method is that of an arbitrary system of relations which constitutes a series of units or functions. This notion is applied to any entity, whether language, myth or novel. Such generous application indicates the colonization of other disciplines by the imperialistic use of the concepts of structural linguistics. All phenomena become reduced to languages; moreover, to languages as conceived in structuralist terms. In my view, no entity (not even language) can be adequately understood within the structuralist conception of structure: the method is open to many damning criticisms of its fundamental tenet.

A Critique of Structuralism in General

Having outlined the key concept of the structuralist method, I want to make several criticisms of that method. Like the critiques in the previous chapter, this critique involves developing the theory of reading ideology that Marxism requires. There are five points which must be made:

(1) Structuralism cannot logically deal with a structure in its historical aspect and, in practice, it frequently fails to. Structure is seen as a static system of relations. Burgelin sums the matter up correctly in saying that structuralist linguistics view language as:

> . . . a form not as a substance, that is to say, as a pure system of differences, in which what determines the value of each linguistic unity is not a relation of absolute character which may be maintained with some non-linguistic entity, but its situation within the system of language. (Burgelin, 1968, p. 154)

Structure is a form, a "pure system of differences", which produces the content. But how does a structure change and develop? And how did it emerge in the first place? Structuralist method contains no answer to these questions since its theory posits that elements have no lives in themselves (they have no internal determinations) and hence no independent movement. The relations themselves have no explicable movement either, for that would entail some causative factor outside the structure itself. Clearly, in structuralism, a structure cannot be the cause of its own movement because the relations constituting the structure have no internal determinations (just like the elements or units). The structure is simply a system of differences or relations between the elements or content, i.e. relations only exist as links between elements. Therefore, just as elements exist only as poles in the relations, and therefore lack internal determination, so, too, the relations exist only as links between the poles and also lack internal determination. All together, then, real movement is impossible within a system. Neither the elements nor the relations can change their nature—they are conjoined for ever in a static phenomenon.

In short, the theoretical assumptions of the structuralist method are, of themselves, incapable of explaining system changes. Some other theory and, therefore, some other method would be necessary to achieve that object. In itself, structuralism provides no certainty that any proclaimed systematic unity is merely an accidental conjuncture of elements with no socially rooted permanence. A social theory of the historically rooted permanence and unity of a system can of course be added to a structuralist method, and in practice usually is, but then what is being practised is not structuralism because the logic of the system is derived from social circumstances rather than from the discourse under analysis. In practice, therefore, structuralists are like content analysts and rely on sociological and political assumptions to produce statements about ideology: they do not practise what they preach. Discourses cannot speak for themselves however much the analyst tries to make them do so.

The absence of an in-built concept of movement or history is one which can easily be filled with metaphysical notions such as the Absolute Logos or the Absolute Telos. Some external body can be taken as the ultimate source or the ultimate goal, and hence as the cause of a posited movement. A good example of the realization of this possibility is provided by Levi-Strauss. He declares structuralist linguistics to be a science, because it has:

... reached beyond the superficial conscious and historical expression of linguistic phenomena to attain fundamental and objective realities, consisting of systems of relations which are the products of unconscious thought processes. (Levi-Strauss, 1972, p. 58)

In registering this point, he has partly provided an example of my criticism in that he actually praises structuralism for having got beyond the "historical expression of linguistic phenomena". He excludes from structuralist science the need for a knowledge of change. He provides full example of my criticism when he goes on to ask:

> Is it possible to effect a similar reduction in the analysis of other forms of social phenomena? If so, would this analysis lead to the same result? And if the answer to this last question is in the affirmative, can we conclude that all forms of social life are substantially of the same nature—that is, do they consist of systems of behaviour that represent the projection, on the level of conscious and socialized thought, of universal laws which regulate the unconscious activities of the mind? (Levi-Strauss, 1972, pp. 58, 59)

The exclusion of history goes hand in hand with the provision of an Absolute Logos, thus Levi-Strauss can attempt to locate or reduce all social phenomena to representations of the absolute laws regulating the operation of the unconscious mind. In structuralism, the comprehension of history reduces historical forms and events to mere variations on a theme—the Absolute Form or Structuring Structure. History, as a structuralist discipline, requires a knowledge of forms of appearance, as forms of the Absolute Telos or Logos, The Structure. Such teleological thinking is not a necessary adjunct to the structuralist method, but the method's limitations make it a common occurrence in structuralist work. Renouncing an explicit reliance on history and social structure, structuralists (like Positivist statisticians) need to import a social theory implicitly to make sense of a discourse. It is not a novelty to observe that backdoor introductions of theory often result in metaphysical theories with many unexamined assumptions.

(2) Structuralism involves functionalism. The method by the very nature of its internal concepts grants every relation of the structure a function or element. Everything is a function of the system and

caused by it. There is no sense of the uneven development of a phenomenon or set of phenomena, no conception that relations and elements exist within their own time and space, that each aspect of the phenomenon has its own integrity or internal determinations. Consequently there is no concept of relations existing in contradiction to elements, nor of the difference between antagonistic and non-antagonistic contradictions (see Mao Tse Tung, 1962, pp. 214–241, on this distinction). For example, structuralism could not allow for the possibility of an ideological formation, born within the structure of one social practice, being active within the structure of another social practice and losing its place within the original practice. In structuralist theory every element of the system has its functions within the system and that system is the life-blood of its functions: the two are inseparable. Relations and functions (or elements) exist simultaneously in structuralism in a state of mutual 'causation'. This explains why a structuralist can point to the conservative functionalism of Parsons' sociological theory as an example of structuralist thinking (see Burgelin, 1968). In Parsons' view of society as a functional system, all the roles, institutions and norms (the elements) have a function for that system and are thus harmoniously integrated (the relations). There is no sense of contradictory co-existence in structuralism. For example, structuralism could not explain that, within a system (the capitalist mode of production), two elements (the capitalist and proletarian classes) can exist in contradiction and conflict. Furthermore, it could not explain why the contradictory relation between those two classes could continue without the dissolution of the system. This is because it has no concept of the specificity of the conditions which maintain the system despite the antagonism of two of its main elements. These absences involve another central absence: the concept of the dominance of some relations and elements of the phenomenon at the expense of others. In a nutshell, the structuralist method will not allow us to discover the unevenness, the contradictions and the inequalities within a given system.

(3) Structuralism is an idealism. In any phenomenon, for structuralism, the concrete units are arbitrary and the relations between them are all important. Thus the concrete is ephemeral and transient and the abstract totally determinant. But if a system of units had a given object then surely certain units are necessary to that system? It is

impossible to build a brick wall without bricks. Thus, in some circumstances, we could argue, the elements are just as important as the relations within a phenomenon—and, in others, perhaps the elements may be more determinant than the relations between them. A passage from Culler illustrates my criticism:

> In separating the functional from the non-functional in order to reconstruct the underlying system, one is interested not so much in the properties of individual objects or actions as in the differences between them which the system employs and endows with significance. (Culler, 1975, pp. 10, 11)

In structuralism, intrinsic properties disappear and are replaced by system-functions. Apart from showing that the structuralist disposes of the "non-functional" aspects of a phenomenon (these aspects play no part in an adequate description or explanation of phenomena in this approach), the above passage shows that structuralism excludes the internal determinations of units from its systems (even if it recognizes that they could exist somehow) and thus leaves a causative residue of relations or structure. Clearly the internal qualities of bricks are not important for the structuralist's house-building practice—only the relations between the bricks. I prefer the Marxian view that the force of the elements is just as important as the force of a structure. It is pure idealism to ignore and reduce the materiality and effectivity of the apparent, however much it is merely a transitory manifestation of some more permanent structure. As Third World experience illustrates, the good life cannot be produced on the sole basis of equitable social relations, one also needs tractors. The structuralist method is blind to the nature and effects of individual objects.

(4) Structuralism is descriptive and not explanatory. Because of its intrinsic inability to talk of the movement, contradiction and properties of the elements, structuralism tends to produce descriptions of connections abstracted from their existence at a given moment in the elements of a discourse. As we have noted, the specificity of the content cannot be fully explained by its inner structure: a full explanation requires a knowledge of the historical movement and situation of the content and the forms which it adopts. Thus structuralism tends to produce abstract descriptions of one side of a phenomenon as it exists at a given point in time and remains blind to the other side and to the historical specificity of that time in the

development of the phenomenon. Descriptions of what may be accidental connections (at worst), and (at best) abstracted unsituated real connections are unsatisfactory if we are searching for explanations of the existence of specific instances. The assumptions within the structuralist method do not enable explanations of any depth as a consequence.

(5) Structuralism speaks of closed systems. This flows from all that I have said so far. However, it is worth emphasizing. Because of its central concept of immanent causation—the outward formation of a totality being an expression of its immanent organization or inner structure—it is impossible for structuralism to specify the effects of the location of a set of phenomena within a wider set for either the relations or elements of the narrow set. That is not to say that structuralists do not do such a thing. But it is to say that, logically, they cannot do it within the perspective embodied in the method. Each system, for structuralism, is closed unto itself as a totality and has no effectivity on the relations or elements of any other totality. It cannot provide for this effectivity because to say that a totality acts as a determining element in another set of totalities is impossible for structuralism since only the internal relations of a totality can determine its nature. Nor can it logically say that the elements of one system are constituted by the relations of another, or vice versa. Yet it would have to say these things if it placed one system (A) in its place within a system (B) of systems. In such a case, system A would have to be seen as an element constituted by the relations of system B. But that view would contradict the concept of the constitution of system A by the relations between its elements! And thus structuralism would have to speak of A as simply a random feature of B, or of B as an anarchic aggregate of subsystems A, C, D, E, F, etc. The first alternative, when applied to human history, would give a view of society which denied autonomy to its elements (e.g. industry, classes, ideology) and made them simple reflections of some master structure. Levi-Strauss tends to this alternative. The second alternative would give a view of society which denied any effectivity to the relations between the elements and which made the latter totally autonomous. No structuralist could hold such a view.

In short, structuralism cannot logically envisage a society as the conjoint existence of a set of related, autonomous systemic elements. So if we consider a number of systems together the structuralist method breaks down: it cannot conceive of a determinant system of systems. It can only deal with one system at a time, as a discrete entity.

Clearly the inability of the structuralist problematic to think of the social totality as a system with a structure and relatively autonomous elements is a very serious defect. Consequently some structuralists have imported ideological notions to cover the gap. The only way the structuralist can have a concept of the structure of structures (e.g. society) is to abandon immanent structural causation. The common standby is an Absolute Logos or an Absolute Telos. Hence, as we have seen, Levi-Strauss adopts the 'universal structure of the human mind' as the Absolute Logos riding through history. Levi-Strauss's mind-structure is the form of which all social life is the concrete manifestation: it is the absolute structure. Clearly this is a religious concept of social causation in that an external metaphysical thing is made responsible for social phenomena and their interconnections. Structuralism cannot think the internal determinations of the 'social', the conjoint existence of things. Zygmunt Bauman provides us with another example:

> Nothing but the formal universals of praxis, its "generative rules", constitutes the tough, invariant core of human history; and perhaps even this can be reasonably claimed only insofar as we deliberately confine vision to the life span of our species, which is, in itself, a historical event within a wider context. (Bauman, 1973a, p. 146)

> Human praxis, viewed in its most universal and general features, consists in turning chaos into order, or substituting one order for another—order being synonymous with the intelligible and meaningful (Bauman, 1973a, p. 119)[2]

For Bauman, the Absolute Logos of human history is the universal structure of Human Praxis and the Absolute Telos is Order, and thus all social phenomena are reduced to the concrete manifestations of this abstract, transcendental, innately human capacity to 'order' the world. To put the criticism of this in terms of my own concept of social practice: just because the formal aspect of social practice is constituted by its elements and relations does not mean that specific social practices and their specific products are immediately comprehended. To comprehend a social practice in its exact specificity we would need to know both its formal and its material aspects. We could not understand journalism simply by knowing that social practice in general requires raw materials, objects, labourers, non-labourers and relations of production, we would need to know what those formal aspects of journalism were in concrete actuality. That is, we would need to know what journalism's raw materials were, what its objects were, what were its relations of production, etc. One formal aspect of the human agency is that humans, physiologically speaking, have brains, but having a brain did not make a man into a Fascist or a Marxist. The exact forms of thought adopted by men can only be understood when we know the historic social relations within which these men act as elements of a definite social formation. Structuralism will often look for Universal Structures which are immanent in all phenomena considered in their conjoint existence since, because, in its very nature, it lacks a concept of the social, the mobile but conjoint existence of specific, propertied units. This tendency is a paradoxical effect of the very working principle of structuralism, immanent causation, and its inability to conceptualize a system of discrete systems.

Problems for Structuralist Readings of Ideology

I have argued that structuralism is seriously deficient and contains great limitations on its ability to generate a knowledge. I shall now turn to the consequences of these weaknesses for structuralist readings of ideology.

Significance, in structuralist thought, is given by the location of a unit of significance in a system of sign-units. A unit or sign only has any meaning or substance inasmuch as it is a point in the structure of signs, the system of significance. Thus to decipher a sign, the structuralist argues that the analyst must discover the code, or the relations of the sign-system which give the signs their meaning. Significance only arrives therefore with a system of differences or relations between signs and can only be created through the use of that system. Significance is only possible for those who understand the code behind the message.

The process of decoding signs involves an analysis of the empirical articulation of signs-in-conjunction which aims to bring out the logical interconnections within the discourse that are said to produce their significance. Immanent or structuralist analysis, of course, specifies that no outside elements are to be taken into account when determining the logical relations of significance. The analyst can only take into account the signs as they appear in the text or system of artefacts. Hence the structuralist analyst should ideally be a Trappist monk, avoiding all contact with his social world. As Barthes puts it:

> But when a myth reaches the entire community, it is from the latter that the mythologist must become estranged if he wants to liberate the myth. (Barthes, 1973, p. 157)

It seems to be the case that the absent concept of the social in structuralism leads structuralists to take shelter in an imaginary hermetic isolation to protect them from the feared, yet unknown, effects of their social existence. Burgelin provides an illustration of an explicitly asocial analysis:

> The essential moment of the linguistic work is, therefore, that of *immanent analysis* of language, in the course of which, one considers only the interior relations in the system, by excluding all that have to do with the relations of the system with men, culture, society, in short, with the outer world, where one makes efforts to establish a "code", only through analysis of the structure of the "message" without being guided by any other consideration whether it be physiologic, psychologic, sociologic or historic. (Burgelin, 1968, p. 154)

The concrete-historical content of the real-world appearance of the magic structure must be swept aside. All the structuralist wants in his analysis is a clear sight of the inner, purely logical relations which produce significance. There is no sense that the full specificity of a thing can only be grasped by viewing its inner structure in its specific content, a content which can only be understood, in itself, in its social and historical context. I think it is clear that the relations of signification sought by the structuralists in their analyses are purely transcendental, abstract, asocial and ahistorical. Structuralist idealism produces a structure which appears as magic and as if by magic. It has no history nor social existence, no physiological nor psychological determinations—nothing but itself in its purity as the "system of pure differences". Thus, to the critic of structuralist analysis it appears that the structure is magical in quality and is produced out of the analyst's hat by magic. Structuralism makes the structure appear by magic in its research technique since it exists as a magical form within its theory.

If we pose structuralist reading the question of the observation of the absence or presence of ideology, the answer is clear. Ideology, or (in structuralist thinking) the relations of signification, can be discerned immediately in its effects and, thus, the analyst must observe the effects and deduce the relations from them. Ideology for structuralism is a structure, code or system of relations of signification which produces the units of significance and is immanent in them. Ideology is therefore immediately readable in its elements or effects: *ideology is transparent in its effects*. Therefore all the structuralist analyst of ideology has to do is to read the content to see immediately that ideology's form of appearance. In other words, since the content is arbitrary and only constitutes the points of the structure with no internal determinations of its own, the structuralist reads ideology as if it exists on the surface, immediately present in its elements.

How could it be otherwise? The reader must not forget that structuralism has no concepts of history, sociality, the uneven development of elements or relations, the internal determinations of elements and relations, and of contradictions within phenomena. The apparent elements of a phenomenon are directly the product of its internal relations or structure. Therefore the structure is directly visible in its appearances: ideology is transparent in signifiers, providing that the analyst can exclude the influences of his or her socio-historical situation.

In structuralism it would appear that ideology, with one fell swoop of its assumed sharp blade, cuts through an assumed primeval continuum of insignificance and effects itself in its creation and creates itself in its effects. Thus, in this Garden of Eden concept of the emergence of ideology, the magical appearance of ideology in "its existence and essence" takes place in the "existence and essence" of its content. Just as God made man in his own image so does ideology make its effects in its own image. The absence of a theory of the genesis of forms in structuralism is filled by the presence of a magical, quasi-religious, original creation at the beginning of history. This notion is a condition of existence of Leach's account of signification:

> I postulate that the physical and social environment of a young child is perceived as a continuum. It does not contain any intrinsically separate "things". The child, in due course, is taught

to impose upon this environment a kind of discriminatory grid which serves to distinguish the world as being composed of a large number of separate things, each labelled with a name. The world is a representative of our language categories, not vice versa. Because my mother tongue is English, it seems self-evident that bushes and trees are different kinds of things. I would not think this unless I had been taught that it was the case. (Leach, 1972, p. 46)

I am immediately reminded of the *tabula rasa* journalist of Halloran *et al.* (1970) who learns ideology in his professional socialization and Parsons' concept of the emergence of norms in the interaction between the *tabula rasa* Ego and Alter! All three accounts share the same gap created by the absence of an adequate, social theory of the genesis of forms of ideology. All three fill that gap by viewing the emergence of the ideological form as the product of an act of creation by factors external to the human agents at the beginning of their relevant history. If the outside Creator is not posited as God, that is not important. The point is that the creation is external to the carriers of ideology and is the act of others whether they be teaching parents (Leach), guiding senior newsmen (Halloran *et al.*) or negotiating fellow interactors (Parsons). The emergence of certain relations of signification as widespread structures of meaning is not seen as an integral part (both active and passive) of people's experience of specific social relations within the conditions of determinate social practices. Structuralism cannot easily produce a structuralist social theory of the genesis of forms and has to import other kinds of theory. These imported theories often posit an external creator who creates ideology suddenly in its effects and effects it in its creation. The above passage from Leach illustrated this well. It also shows how structuralism grants form a dominance over content (a child only perceives things when it is carrying some knowledge of their forms—[*sic*]). Material reality is excluded from view until the structure of language is learned and applied. Classically, units of reality only appear as effects of ideological structures.

Our previous critique had made it abundantly clear, although always implicitly, that structuralism was incompatible with dialectical materialism. The present applied criticism shows how undialectical structuralism is since it demonstrates the one-sided determination of a content by form, and elides the determination of form by content. It also shows how empiricist the structuralist method is in assuming that the content (the effect of the form) is immediately visible outside any given social practice (literally). Reading ideology in its effects à la structuralism is hardly any different from the readings of the content analysts—the only difference is that, whereas ideology is external to the content in the work of the content analysts, for the structuralist reader ideology is immanent in its content. In content analysis, the ideology of the communicator produces repetitions of significance which are said to be an index of that ideology. In structuralism, ideology is intrinsic to the sign-system and not the external tool of an intentional communicator. In both modes of reading, however, ideology is immediately read from the apparent elements of the discourse.

What enables the analyst to read that transparency of ideology in its contents, according to structuralist theory? The usual answer given is that the ideological relations constituting meaning are universally recognizable (see Eco, 1967; Veron, 1971). As Burgelin points out:

> In short there is none exterior to a message which can tell us the significance of one of its elements. Thus we are forced to go back to the message itself and to admit that the only strict definition of the significance of an element of "vocabulary" of the mass media is the one involved in the context (or the "phrases"). (Burgelin, 1968, p. 157)

As in content analysis, the meanings of the text are obvious, they are easily and readily available to Anyman. Both the analysts of form and the analysts of content assume that the discourse of the ideology is obvious and readable at the surface level of the text. Content analysts embellish their assumption with a count of the allegedly significant repetitions and the structuralists embellish theirs with an emphasis on their rigorous extraction of the logic of the discourse. But, really, both only provide coverage for proceeding on the tenuous assumption that the true ideological discourse is spontaneously readable from a text or sign-system. This is reflected in an interesting fashion in Burgelin's article (1968) where he sees structuralist analysis and content analysis as different modes of tackling the same object. Content analysis is seen as the mode of reading "manifest content" (Berelson's phrase) and structuralist analysis as the mode of reading "latent content" (Berelson's phrase) or form, or "style" (as Burgelin calls it). Both forms of analysis have the same object, but they concentrate on different aspects of it: one takes its internal logical connections, the other examines its outer forms of appearance. The *it* is the same in both cases: the visible signs of the discourse. Both forms of analysis take as their object, ultimately, the *apparent ideology*: the ideology that is allegedly apparent in the spontaneous reading of a text. In this sense both content analysis and structuralism are thoroughly empiricist: reality is limited to the 'visible' ideology of a visible text. Neither method attempts to deal with aspects of the ideological discourse which are not immediately readable in their effects. Neither method, in my view, satisfactorily establishes that the apparent ideology of the discourse does in fact appear. Structuralism's 'discovered, logical' interconnections may be as contingent or imaginary as the 'significant' repetitions of content analysis. Both methods lack the grounding support of an adequate social theory of an ideology's historical specificity and forms of appearance. For all its apparently theoretical nature, then, structuralism belongs to an empiricist problematic just as much as content analysis. Each mode of reading ideology is a wing of another entity: the problematic of empiricist epistemology. This problematic has as its dominant aspect the concept of the immediate identifiability of the essence of a thing in its visible appearance. As one wing, structuralism thinks it can identify the essential structure of the ideology in its visible appearances, and on the other wing, content analysis thinks it can identify the essential substance of the ideology in its visible, consequent repetitions.

The structuralist reading of ideology is undisputedly non-dialectical, idealist and empiricist in nature. These deficiencies have several major consequences. They can be listed as follows:

1. Structuralism cannot comprehend the possibility of an ideological formation which is born within one social practice yet lives on in another practice (perhaps even a practice within a different mode of production). Within structuralist theory there can be no concept of the historical fragmentation, overlap, lag or prematurity of ideological formations: ideology for structuralism is a contemporaneous system of elements without a historical dimension. Similarly, structuralism cannot comprehend an ideological formation with internal discontinuity, fragmentation and looseness: all its ideologies are neat, fully functional, cybernetic systems.

2. Some relations of signification in a system may beget units which are repressed by other units or relations with whom they co-exist in contradiction. Such repressed units may therefore be absent on the surface text. Similarly, some units of significance (signifiers or signifieds) may be the products of historically prior relations of signification, thus the units may appear at the level of the text without their original constituent relations. In addition, an ideology's relations with another ideology may no longer be effective in new social conditions. Some units of significance may be more dominant in one period than another. Structuralism cannot allow for any of these possibilities within the strict terms of its theory. With its mode of reading ideology as a total system present at the level of the text, it cannot detect the absence or presence of these possibilities.

3. The social function of an ideological formation in a particular conjuncture may demand, of necessity, particular relations of signification or particular units of significance (terms or meanings). Particular units of significance, therefore, may be socially necessary conditions of a mode of production and yet their allegedly constitutive relations of signification may not yet exist; in fact, the relations in such a situation often seem to be produced after the units![3] In some social conditions, moreover, an ideological formation may find itself in rupture through no internal contradiction of its own, and its constituent signs may float apart. Structuralism's inability to conceptualize adequately the social determinations of ideology results in its neglect of the externally conditioned dissolution of an ideology and of the determining effect of specific significant units. Thus structuralism is weak in that it relegates units of significance to a passive, subordinate role. The task of investigating the relations between particular units of significance and particular social practices is one that structuralism has neglected.

4. Structuralist readings of ideology can only result in limited descriptions of apparent relations of signification and cannot help to explain the existence of changing, socially situated, ideological formations. This explanatory absence is built into its practice of reading which is a method for producing a description of the spontaneous impressions of a static form. Spontaneous impressions of a temporary, static form are, on their own, of little value

in the production of theoretical explanations of a moving content. Structuralist practice has no concept of the dialectic of significance and hence its significations have no dynamic nor any mechanism of development. In other words, structuralism lacks a concept of the mode of production of ideology and its essentially social and historical character.

Structuralism's emphasis on closed systems produces, in practice, ideologies which are discrete, isolated and asocial phenomena. Ironically, it is true to say that the structuralist method takes the sign out of the "heart of social life" and the society out of "the science that studies the life of signs within society" (Saussure's phrase). This crucial, absent concept of the social character of the significance of signs, in the heart of its science, leaves a space which is frequently occupied by concepts of the non-social origin. As we have seen, *Homo significans* and the Universal Mind have appeared in this manner. Structuralism has no tools to provide a reading of social and historical significance, merely the equipment for a reading of purely logical relations of signification, which have no theorized social roots and may be the entirely imaginary creations of an entirely imaginary creator.

5. In order to be able to deduce the logical connections between a series of signs one must know what they mean. Thus, one could begin to specify the elements of the Morse code given a certain number of Morse messages and their linguistic meanings. Structuralists can *only* produce discoveries of ideological codes because they examine a number of messages with in implicit knowledge or assumption of their meanings. These knowledges or assumptions must derive from the reader's participation in the social formation and his conclusions about what is going on, about who is doing what to whom. Despite its hermetic pretensions, structuralism can, therefore, only operate on the basis of some sociological and historical assumptions and theories. Those structuralists who keep quiet about these assumptions and theories are cheating on their readership. It is probably also true that the better developed the sociological and historical knowledge of the structuralist analyst, the more likely it is that the intrinsic weaknesses of the structuralist method are mitigated. But then, one must add, even the informed structuralist is required to cheat because his socio-historical knowledge will lead to the 'discovery' of connections

between signs which are not logical in themselves (but which have a social and historical logic). In short, hermetic structuralists conceal their socio-historical premises and informed structuralists conceal their technical manoeuvres. The structuralist method is an inadequately conceived method of reading ideology and its practitioners have to perform secret operations outside its boundaries in order to produce a worthwhile reading.

Structuralism at Work

The operation of structuralism in the practice of reading ideology can be illustrated by Melvyn Slater's excellent dissertation *Levi-Strauss in Fleet Street* (1970). This text is suitable for such an exercise since it is structuralist whilst not being concerned with developments in French semiology and since the reading it contains is of the English press reports of political demonstrations in the same period (September and October, 1968) as that used in *Demonstrations and Communication* by Halloran *et al.* (1970). I shall not make a direct comparison between Slater and Halloran *et al.* but will proceed straight away to an investigation of the effects of structuralist thought on Slater's reading practice.

Slater claims to show "that the structuralist method of myth analysis can potentially be used in the Marxian critique of ideology" (1970, Preface). His specific project is to demonstrate that the "Great Student Plot" of 1968 (elaborated in the mass media) is a myth in the sense that myth integrates langue (language or code) and parole (speech or message) into an inclusive totality. This intention immediately alerts us to a structuralist display of functionalism. The integrative functions of the relations of signification in the myth, and the theme of closed systems in the notion of the inclusive totality are classic aspects of the structuralist perspective.

He begins by applying structural linguistics and declares that the "surface meaning" of the myth is not "the" meaning of the myth. Instead, he argues, the meaning of a section or "episode" of the myth must be sought at a deeper level:

> Rather the episode should be thought of at first as a content-neutral (in a sense, mathematical) structure, the meaning of which is discovered by its relationship to other structures within

the same myth (or other myths in the same culture). (Slater, 1970, p. 20)

Thus it is that he outlines with clarity the basic principles of the structuralist reading of ideology. Content is neutered in favour of the overall structure.

Methodologically, the immanentist imperative is taken up in Levi-Straussian style. This requires the classification of the functions of the system, or in Levi-Straussian terms, the "gross constituent units", which, in the terms I am using, are groups or classes of significant elements. The grounds for classification are unclear, except that there are "similarities" among the units or functions of a class. Versions or variants of the myth must then be analysed to discover and declare the laws of their permutation, which lead to the discovery of the myth's "deep structure" or, again in my terms, the ideological formation at work. Classical structuralism this! The relations are read off from the units on the principle of transparency derived from the concept of immanent causation. The meaning or social significance of the units is assumed in order to put them into classes: an assumption presupposing a knowledge of the relations of the classifying code which the structuralist is supposed to be 'discovering'.

To his credit, Slater critically notes that the analyst must have some notion of the structure he is looking for from the beginning, otherwise he could not group functions or units (1970, pp. 33–36). He declares this to be a weakness of the structuralist method. From my analysis earlier, it is clear that the structuralist analysis of ideology grants no significance to the units outside their constituent relations and that historical, social or extra-systemic significance is an absent concept. Structuralist theory holds to a closed system with a functionalist concept of its nature and cannot, strictly speaking, recognize the social significance of the functions. Hence the methodological "flaws" (Slater) are a necessary aspect of the method in action—they are not simply a defect in its application. The method could work no other way. The analyses of Levi-Strauss and Slater could *not* be done without an imported "knowledge" of the *social* significance of the significant functions in the myth which enables the production of a social theory of the myth's relations of significa- tion. The knowledge of the socially significant functions is *ex cathedra*, unexplicated. The method of structuralism thus lapses into empiricism because it allows the social significance of the mythic or discursive functions a privileged position as given. Transcendence of the "flaws" in the "technique" is not the solution to structuralism's problems. Only the provision of a theory of reading which takes into account the social significance of the functions could be that: a provision that is impossible for a rigorous structuralism. Without such a theory we can only say that the social significance of the units, postulated *ex cathedra* by the structuralists, is spontaneously read and hence conceals the laws of the production of social significance in its visible impressions.[4]

In passing, we should note (since it later develops an importance) that Slater at least doubts Levi-Strauss's view that the structuralist analysis of myth (ideology) tells us something about the universal structures of the human mind. For Slater, "structural analysis" attempts

> . . . to discover the relation between the myth as an aspect of the superstructure of a society, and its material infrastructure. It is also concerned with mythic thought as a "relatively autonomous" superstructure, and thus with formal mythic structures, transformations, and various logical operations. (Slater, 1970, p. 68)

Marxist analysis of social structure seems to be combined with structuralist analysis in a somewhat unholy alliance. The dominant tendency is the structuralist one because the relation between base and superstructure in Slater's conception is somewhat direct and one-sided, involving a non-dialectical, immanent causation by the base. Thus the combination of structuralism with the "Marxist critique of ideology" only leads to a structuralist revision, rather than a development, of Marxism.[5] Consequently Slater's many passing references to the relation between myth and social practice fail to take any grip or bite in the actual analysis—his own discourse provides us with a good example of an antagonistic contradiction between relations of signification involving the repression of some significant functions!

When we arrive at Slater's analysis of the data, the scene is set by his announcement that he will amalgamate information theory, Lukacs' notion of the totality and structuralist analysis of myth. He wonders whether they are compatible and decides that the task of explicating the grounds for their compatibility would require a "philosophic, and necessarily massive debate" and is therefore outside the scope of his dissertation. Under the weight of that task, I am inclined to say that he was right to continue with the problem unsolved, because the three theories *are* compatible. Information theory involves a concept of a static system of relations and functions which means that significance is internal and automatic. The Lukacsian concept of the totality sees each part as an expression of the whole; that is, it sees the functions as expressions of the structure or system of relations. Both, therefore, are highly concordant with the structuralist method. The crucial consequence for Slater's Marxism is that he becomes concerned to show that myths are functions of three base relations, or three aspects of the determining social structure. These three relations are, as given by Slater (1970, p. 82):

1. Contradictions within praxis,
2. Contradictions between ideology and a changed praxis, and
3. Intellectual contradictions within ideology itself.

In true but complex structuralist style, Slater has posited an abstract universal structure as the source of the specific mythic discourse under observation. Typically, there is the central absence of the dialectic between these contradictions and their consequent ideology. Does the resultant ideology really resolve them? May it not act in conjunction with them and play a determining role in maintaining the contradiction? That is, might the contradictions be overdetermined? Where is the in-built explanation (the mechanism) of the changes in these contradictions? Might not the nature of the contradictions repress the emergence of an 'ideology-as-solution'? Are these relations or contradictions simultaneous historically with their ideology-as-solution? Might not the ideology-as-solution have been generated in an earlier social formation? What accounts for the form of these relations as contradictions? All these criticisms derive from my critique of the structuralist method and its lack of an adequate theory of the social nature of ideology.

Since those fundamental relations are concretely given in modern capitalism, according to Slater (1970), there must be a myth-producing agency. There is, and he contends that it is the mass media. He implies that the mass media are the *only* myth-producing agencies. The concept of the Absolute Source seems to have appeared again in the disguise of the mass media as the oracle of bourgeois mythology. He goes on, inevitably, to argue that the press is a function in a system of relations and expresses the relations that make it so in a direct, immediate fashion (Slater, 1970, pp. 95, 96). Its constituent relations are immanent within it. Thus every relation of signification within the system of press mythology is seen as a transparent function of the relations that give press mythology its function in the social totality.[6] As a natural consequence, Slater hopes that the use of the structuralist method will lead him through binary oppositions (relations) in the myth, through the contradictions for which the myths act as solutions and to "the contradictions in the *real* basis from which they are transformations" (1970, p. 96). My argument that structuralist thought was fundamentally idealist is evidenced in strength here. The concept of reading off social relations from ideological functions when put into Marxist terminology leads an avowed Marxist to try to discover the structures of society from their transformations in the realm of mythologies! To understand the real, Marxism starts from the real, not from spontaneous impressions of the mythical! Slater, like Levi-Strauss and all other idealists, reverses Marxist method and works backwards from the myth in order to get to the social structure, instead of beginning from the social structure in order to arrive at the myths and other ideologies of the day.

Without delving into the trivial minutiae of Slater's analytical practice, let us note that he proceeds to discern, from a "piece" of the press discourse of the period, a number of binary oppositions, e.g. the police get insufficient publicity/the demonstrators too much, the police are supported by the old/the demonstrators by the young. Each significant function of the myth ("pieces" of discourse) involves a binary opposition (a relation), and each function of that binary opposition involves another binary opposition. For example:

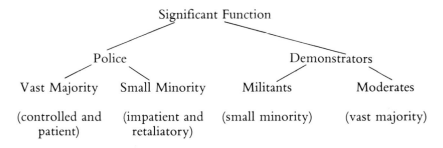

Some pieces of discourse are useless and ignored because they are found to be poor. They lack enough data. For a structuralist analysis to proceed "the text must provide contents and repetitions, at least" (Slater, 1970, p. 120). How similar this is to the method of content analysis which also requires contents and repetitions! The co-existence of content analysis and structuralism within the same wider empiricist epistemology forces both of them to look for the 'given' content and its repetition (which seems to provide more certainty of the 'givenness' of the content as data). Clearly, some pieces of the discourse are effectively denied social significance by Slater since they do not *appear* to be functions of the relations of signification he is looking for. At the same time, he argues that he knows the social significance of those rejected pieces since he is a "member of the potential public" (1970, p. 121)! This 'knowledge' of the code has no use for Slater because it must be "expressed explicitly for analysis", therefore he supposes that the news features, rather than the news stories, will contain the *full* ideological code at work in the press reporting of these demonstrations. So, he selects certain news features as "code sheets" for definitive analysis of the ideological formation at work, in addition to his analysis of the news stories. In brief, we can say that here we are observing a methodological manoeuvre, pragmatically entered into because the strict operation of the structuralist method on the news stories fails to deliver the goods, a fully illustrated ideological code which exhausts the content of the discourse. Structuralism fails in its own terms, and can only succeed on the basis of an implicit theory of the social meaning of the discourse. Without a developed theory of the social dissemination of news, and its production, structuralism fails to do the job Slater demands of it and he is forced to rely on implicit assumptions about the organization of newspaper discourse. Without social knowledge, structuralism is weak.

All the time during this investigation of the complex structure of ideological relations, the significant functions, which are allegedly constituted by these relations, are granted social significance. For example, the function "spy" is taken to summon up notions of "cracking international plots", saving the West from disasters, investigation of the enemy, etc. (Slater, 1970, p. 134). Slater is not supposed to know this without a knowledge of the constituent relations. He claims he does, as we have seen, because he is a "potential member of the public". This, of course, suggests that Slater, like several other structuralists, believes that there is in reality an area of public discourse which is shared by the overwhelming majority. This belief is forced on Slater if he is to justify his assumptions about the meanings of his data. Structuralism, like content analysis, needs to assert an ideological consensus on a vast range of matters in order to deduce the codes from the messages. Their similarity on this and other points is startling. My position here is that any consensus on the social meaning of terms is of a very limited nature indeed and is far less frequent than disagreement.

Having outlined a complex series of binary oppositions immediately underlying the selected pieces of discourse, Slater attempts to discover the contradictions for which these mythic relations are a solution. These contradictions are at the level of ideology (in his definition of the concept) which is said to mediate reality and myth. Ideology, unsurprisingly, seems to be equivalent to the "collective consciousness", a universal code of discourse. Earlier, Slater had commented on the repeated appearance of certain symbols or significant units:

> It suggests that at one and the same time the Press is using a pre-existent (ideological) language, and also transforming that language. It was a pre-existing language because in order to represent an event such as the demonstration in the first place it draws upon various codes already present in the "collective consciousness" of the public: Communists, trouble-makers, militants, foreign agitators, "Londoners", violence, revolution, extremists, etc. It transforms the ideological language to some extent, by changing the meanings associated with expressions formerly considered to have different, or otherwise quite common meanings . . . there is a real sense in which *nothing* happens . . . and what is "new" is not really news at all. (Slater, 1970, p. 142)

As the myth-producing agency, the mass media thus use the universal, "public" ideology as their instrument of production. Using Leach's concept of the creation and nature of the constitutive relations of ideology (Slater, 1970, p. 142; Leach, 1972), Slater then examines several examples of constitutive ideological relations (from his press reports) and seems to boil them down to one binary opposition: humanity/property. Are we to be surprised that this is the ultimate, deep structure of ideology when Hegelian Marxism, with its focus on the dialectical Logos, capital/labour, is combined with a structuralist method? The inability of structuralism and Hegelianism to conceive of unevenly and unequally related systems of social practice in a complex, historically determinate, social formation results in the attribution of major social myths to one Origin. Hegelian Marxism must posit that source to be the capital/labour structure, or, in its preferred terms, the opposition humanity/property. As regards the myth of the "student revolt", its origin, says Slater, is the ideological contradiction or structure: students-as-humans/students-as-investments (1970, pp. 169, 170). Students as humans are part of "Us" and have the normal characteristics of Everyman. Students as investments are the commodities of technological capitalism. When "rebel students" come along they "fuse the two roles" or, if you like, they exacerbate the contradiction for they are both humans and commodities. They can only be represented within the units of this structure and, therefore, three ideological solutions are possible (Slater, 1970, p. 171):

1. Rebellion is denied. If there are too many rebel students to make this possible the rebels are presented as the tiny minority, thus negating the rebellion.
2. The rebels are students-as-humans. That is, they are not really students at all. They do not work, or they are professional revolutionaries, or they cannot play student-as-investment roles properly.
3. The rebels are fulfilling their correct social function as intelligent, critical students. Perhaps the administration is authoritarian or old-fashioned.

Thus these three units of significance are said to be the three possible mythic functions of the same basic ideological relation or contradiction. Clearly, other mythic variations could be derived from the same basic ideological contradiction, yet Slater ignores them. For example, under his variant (1), a great quantity of rebel students could be dealt with ideologically as non-rebels simply making a sensible, 'human' protest. In practice, I have never seen the rebellion-denial interpretation take this form, but theoretically it could do. It seems to me that a whole range of forms are possible within the three frameworks outlined by Slater. But, if this is so, why are some manifested in press reports and not others? As a structuralist analysis, Slater's work fails to answer this question: he merely sketches out a logical structure or code which could generate many, variant messages. Moreover, it seems to be that other ideological formations were at work in those 1968 press reports; for example, ideologies of the nature of democracy and public order. How do these codes align with the code about students? Why do they align in a particular way during this period? The reduction of a complex admixture of ideologies, arising I would suggest from a variety of social structures and historically developed within a variety of social practices, to a monolithic epiphenomenon of the most general structure in a capitalist society, is a very crude operation indeed. But, of course, structuralism tends to reduce ideologies and societies equally to their most basic structures.

In conclusion, although Slater's work is an imaginative and advanced piece of research for its time, it really only describes an apparent ideological dilemma in the press reporting of student activism. It does not describe other features of the ideologies employed in the news reporting of the 1968 demonstations. It does not in any way adequately explain the historical, structural and practical sources of these ideologies and the conditions under which they entered the press discourse. Despite its apparent promise, in the last analysis, structuralism is very much like content analysis (of all kinds) in that the 'discovered' ideology is very much a presupposed product of the researcher's often very dubious sociological and political assumptions. This is not to say that the ideology discovered in the examined discursive materials is a fiction of the researcher's imagination, but that insufficient theoretical and historical groundings for the specificity of that ideology and its conditions of appearance are given by both content and structuralist analysts. They know the code before they start, but they do not tell us how, why and under what conditions they know. Their analyses, in short, do not satisfy the requirements of scientific work. I would say that to read an ideology in its discursive form of appearance necessitates a theory of its specificity based on sociological and historical evidence of its nature and origins—that is unavoidable. What can be avoided is the pretension that the method of reading derives its conclusions purely from an unselected set of data. This pretension must be replaced with detailed specifications of an ideology's nature, history and social conditions of existence; specifications which are open to the evidence and scrutiny of others.

Notes

1. For newcomers to this area, Lane (1970) provides an adequate introduction to structuralism.
2. It is interesting, in passing, to note the normative functionalism of Bauman's structuralism. Social life moves teleologically towards an ever greater order. This is not dissimilar to many statements in the work of Radcliffe-Brown and Parsons.
3. Such a production is the job of the philosopher and theorist—the weaver of complex ideological formations using preconstituted materials (signs).
4. From his ånalysis of Levi-Strauss's analysis, Slater concludes that Levi-Strauss actually has a social theory of myths up his sleeve, based on his use of "sequences" and "schemata" which represent the synchronic and diachronic "axes" of the myth. Levi-Strauss had stated that myth integrates synchronic and diachronic time referents (Levi-Strauss, 1968). This, however, is not an answer to my criticism since that theory of myth is unexplicated and very general, and, in any case, social significance is still granted to the functions prior to analytic categorization into "sequences" and "schemata". Slater senses this and weakly argues that "we do have to start somewhere" (1970, p. 52).
5. The struggle between Slater's orthodox Marxism and Levi-Strauss's idealism is explosive. Marxism loses (see Slater, 1970, pp. 73, 74). A more direct illustration is the whole of his Chapter 3 which revises Marxist theory by formulations which implicitly deny the feedback role and relative autonomy of ideology, in structuralist fashion, while in true Marxist fashion constructing, at a minimal level, a dialectic between relations and functions of signification.
6. To give Slater his due he is much more systematic than some other structuralists: he deftly places subsystems into wider systems and maintains his "cool". The fact that he has no solution for the problem of the inclusive nature of each totality does not seem to bother him.

5 The Semiology of Roland Barthes

Introduction

In this chapter, I aim to outline the essentials of the semiological method of Roland Barthes and to criticize that method briefly in the light of the critique of structuralism in the previous chapter. Structuralism and semiology are not necessarily identical but it is a fact that most modern semiological work, especially Barthes', is dependent on structuralist thought. Barthes' work is really the classic example of structuralist semiology. It is worth examining because it has influenced many modern analysts of culture, and because it is an applied, well developed approach to the reading of ideology. This examination is needed in order that structuralist thought can be adequately attacked. I have already indicated that I think that, whilst it appears to have much promise, structuralism is pretentious and insufficient. It does not deserve the following it has gathered; its substantial and mystifying influence therefore requires a substantial demystification. Consequently, it must be made clear that, although all of the chapters in this text are part of a cumulative development, this particular chapter is especially dependent upon the last. Again, I do not pretend to set out an exhaustive treatment of the author in question, merely to place his work within the perspective of this investigation into ideology and its reading.

The Concepts of Barthesian Semiology

For semiology, the apparent world is not merely an arena of people, matter and events, but a world of signs. Nothing exists purely in itself: everything stands for something else. As Barthes puts it:

> . . . as soon as there is a society, every usage is converted into a sign of itself . . . (Barthes, 1967, p. 41)

This is a useful insight into social life since it opposes the empiricist tendency to treat facts as things which speak for themselves. Semiology points out that things have meanings for people, a fact which forces the sociological observer to take into account the world of interpretations and its relation to the world of matter and structures. The danger is that the semiologist slides into a tendency to reduce social life to the life of signs and to neglect matter, history and social structure, as they determine not only physical behaviour but also the ideas which guide that behaviour (and transform it into social practice). As in other forms of structuralism, modern semiology is always in danger of reducing the historical event or actuality to a mere sign of a deeper, universal structure. A passage from Eco captures both the insight and the weakness of semiology:

> We only know a cultural unit communicated to us by means of words, drawing or other means. For the defence or destruction of these cultural units as for others such as /freedom/, /transubstantiation/ or /free world/ men are even ready to go out to meet death. Yet, death, once it has arrived, and only then, constitutes the one and only referent, or event, that cannot be semioticized (a dead semiologist no longer communicates semantic theories). *But right up to the moment before*, "Death" is mainly used as a cultural unit. (Eco, 1971, p. 23)

Freedom and oppression are, for Eco, merely signs of an ideological nature without any real basis.[1] They are "cultural units" without any economic or political substance. There is something of the modern phenomenological movement in this passage, too, in that, for the semiologist, all deaths other than his own are merely cultural units. Death is ideological until he dies.

Significance tends to be read into everything in such a way that, in semiology, the picture of social life becomes skewed. Julia Kristeva provides an illustration of this tendency:

> In his study of the capitalist system of exchange Marx showed that it is a semiotic system in which *money*, through a series of mutations, becomes the *general equivalent* or the *sign* of the work invested in the exchanged object. The economic system is thus a semiotic system: a chain of communication with a sender and a

receiver and an object of exchange—money—which is the *sign* of a piece of *work*. (Kristeva, 1973, p. 35)

She does insist, correctly, that work is not reducible to its outward signs, but, nevertheless, she has skewed Marx's arguments in attempting to illustrate the centrality of signs in social life. Money, after all, need not be the sign of work, it could signify a number of things. In its place in the mosaic of ideologies it carries many referents, such as status, or worth, or evil. What Marx "showed" was not that money was given its meaning by a semiotic system called the economy, but that the development of exchange relations (reaching its high point in capitalism) entailed the emergence of a general equivalent for use in trade. This general equivalent, eventually taking the form of money, is "that measure of value which is immanent in commodities, labour-time" (Marx, 1974, p. 97). Money, therefore, is an embodied form of value. Exchange relations give it the character of value itself. That is, its social character is not given by any semiotic system (economic or otherwise) but by a certain mode of economic activity. How that character is then signified ideologically by members of society is another matter, a matter for the study of semiologists. In short, Kristeva conflates the economic character of money with one of its cultural significations, the one which most closely reflects its economic character. In doing this, she converts the economy into a semiotic system or communication process. This act illustrates perfectly the dangers of semiological imperialism. Marx's own observations on the difference between an economic form and a symbol are instructive (emphases in italics by C.S.):

The fact that money can, in certain functions, be replaced by mere symbols of itself, gave rise to that other mistaken notion, that is in itself a mere symbol. Nevertheless under this error lurked a presentiment that the money-form of an object is not an inseparable part of that object, but is simply the form under which certain social relations manifest themselves. In this sense every commodity is a symbol, since, in so far as it is value, it is only the material envelope of the human labour spent upon it. *But if it be declared that the social characters assumed by objects, or the material forms assumed by the social qualities of labour under the regime of a definite mode of production, are mere symbols, it is in the same breath also declared that these characteristics are arbitrary functions sanctioned by the so-called universal consent of mankind.* This suited the mode of explanation in favour during the eighteenth century. Unable to account for the origin of the puzzling forms assumed by social relations between man and man, people sought to denude them of their strange appearance by ascribing them to a conventional origin. (Marx, 1974, pp. 93, 94)

In other words, it is too easy to see money as an ideological symbol when, first and foremost, it is an economic token: its symbolic, ideological forms only develop on the basis of its assured existence as an economic form.

Roland Barthes' commitment, as a semiologist, is to the discovery of the significance of social artefacts. He is not devoted to discovering the meaning of an item, but to extracting the structure of significations within the object which provides the parameter for any reading of it (see Genette, 1969). In other words, he tries to determine the code of significance within an artefact which, he asserts, sets the limits of variation of its possible readings. Thus, with a novel, he outlines the semantic code within it which acts to structure its possible meanings for a reader.

Various problems immediately arise. His research practice is not concerned with the social relations within which a phenomenon is set and acquires social character or form. He is not out to place a novel in its socio-historical context and specify the social meaning given to the novel by its historically loaded signifiers and its current situation. Returning to the question of money, it is as if Barthes sees money as a cultural unit whose basic meaning has public consent, but which is open to further interpretation; he wishes to identify that basic meaning. Such an asumption has not only got a long history, as Marx indicated, but it is at the centre of Barthes' work. His very purposes are thus unsoundly conceived. They are idealist in granting social forms merely an ideological character and source. They are dependent on the notion of consensus which is very dubious as a general theoretical premise. They have a static, functionalist character in positing a function based on a permanent consent, outside of its historical nature. In short, Barthes' semiological objective suffers from its structuralist constitution.

As I mentioned earlier, Barthes, like other structuralists, wishes to be a hermit and exclude all the social and historical features and sources of the cultural units under analysis. He wishes to extract a logical code of significance from each examined unit: as if one could do that without reference to the social and historical meaning of each significant unit. Thus, the terms or meanings (the significant elements) are seen as merely transient expressions of a deeper structure of signification:

> Semiology is the science of forms, since it studies significations apart from their content. (Barthes, 1973, p. 111)

But to deduce directly from a discourse (for example) the forms or structures of signification (the relations between terms and meanings in a discourse), it is necessary to grant the messages studied a definite meaning. On what premises does Barthes construct this meaning? Does he avoid the major defect of structuralist readings of ideology? How can one study meaning apart from its socio-historical context? Let us attend to his theoretical concepts to find the answer.

Barthes employs Saussure's distinction between *langue* (language or consensually sanctioned code) and *parole* (individual speech or use of the code). For Barthes, like Saussure, a langue is a social institution of a consensual nature:

> It is the social part of language, the individual cannot by himself either create or modify it; it is essentially a collective contract which one must accept in its entirety if one wishes to communicate. (Barthes, 1967, p. 14)

What Marx said, about those who separate form from content and then, in puzzlement at the problem they have created, ascribe the origin of the form to conventions, to the "so-called universal consent of mankind", seems to apply to Barthes' conception of langue or code. Language, in structuralist thought, becomes an "arbitrary function", to use Marx's phrase.

However, Barthes is no conservative 'social contract theorist' and hedges at his own conception of language structure as a consensual product of custom. He notes the "manifest affinity" between Saussure's concept of langue and Durkheim's concept of the *conscience collective*. Durkheim and Saussure worked in Paris at the same time and Saussure was aware of Durkheim's ideas. But Barthes does not investigate this historical connection any further. Instead, he argues that in most sign-systems the code is elaborated by a "deciding group" and not by the "speaking mass" (Barthes, 1967, pp. 23–27, 31, 32).[2] Like Slater, Barthes offers us a crude, functionalist, almost conspiratorial picture of a society's relations of signification as a function of ruling class power, a function dictated by the deep structure of society, the capital–labour relation. The main essay in Barthes' *Mythologies* is dominated by this picture of social ideology. The ruling class produce and disseminate the codes whilst the masses merely receive and use them.

Parole, for Barthes, is the individual, diachronic aspect of language: "an individual act of selection and actualization" (1967, p. 15). It is a combination of the ability of the "speaking-subject" to use the code to create discourse and the "psycho-physical mechanisms" which enable him to exteriorize the discourse. This concept reminds one sharply of the notion of *Homo significans* imported by other structuralists to solve the problem of the absent social theory of the emergence of significance. Man signifies—men interact—structures of signification are built up—language, or langue, becomes a social institution. Again, we can note the similarity between radical European structuralism and the conservative structural functionalism of Durkheim and Parsons.[3]

Langue and parole are said to exist in dialectical process—each of the two forms achieves its full definition only in dialectical unity with the other. It is within this dialectic that "linguistic praxis" exists:

> On the one hand the language is "the treasure deposited by the practice of speech, in the subjects belonging to the same community" and, since it is a collective summa of individual imprints, it must remain incomplete at the level of each isolated individual: a language does not exist perfectly except in the "speaking mass"; one cannot handle speech except by drawing on the language. (Barthes, 1967, p. 16)

This dialectical fusion of langue and parole is in practice the focus of Barthes' attention. He wants to extract the langue from the parole (the code from the message) and, thereby, to constitute "the problematic of the meaning" (Barthes' phrase, 1967, p. 17). References to dialectic are merely lip-service in Barthes' work, however. He sees the code or structure as determinant of the message or units of significance, but not vice versa. One *never* finds structuralist semiologists analysing the way the speaking mass change the code (against the wishes or interests of the deciding group) through their "linguistic praxis". Moreover, Barthes' dialectic is a purely formal one, it is in no way a materialist one: langue and parole are never actually placed causally within the boundaries of social practice (whether economic, political or cultural).

The second major distinction in Barthesian semiology is the distinction between connotation and denotation. Connotation is said to be that aspect or level of the discourse which contains the attitude, choice or intention of the communicating subject. Connotation is the realm where individual or private ideology intervenes in the collective or public language. Ideology for Barthes is thus an intentional layer of signification reflecting the social circumstances of the individual or group. It is a sectional appendage to the shared universe of denotative signs (Barthes, 1967, pp. 89, 90): a conception he shares with the American content analysts. This is, of course, the classic conception of ideology, pinpointed by Raymond Williams as the Napoleonic, political conception. *Homo significans* comes home to rest in Barthesian semiology as the vehicle and motivator of ideology.

Ideology, the stuff of connotation, is the product of a socially situated communicator, whereas denotation, the level containing the basic signs of any language, is seen as an arbitrary set of relations sanctioned by the "deciding group" and the practice of the "speaking mass". Barthes thus, in effect, distinguishes between language and ideology. Discourse is seen as a mixture of both expressed in linguistic form. Barthes tends to see denotation as the pure, social form and connotation as a sordid, motivated distortion. The latter is an ideological overlay which uses shared signs for its sectional interest:

> Entrusted with "glossing over" an intentional concept, myth encounters nothing but betrayal in language, for language can only obliterate the concept if it hides it, or unmask it if it formulates it. The elaboration of a second-order semiological system will enable myth to escape this dilemma: driven to having either to unveil or to liquidate the concept, it will *naturalize* it. (Barthes, 1973, p. 129)

Connotative systems of discourse using denotative signs are thus developed to "naturalize" the motivated ideology of the sectional, interested subject or group. Ideology is thus the unhealthy development of class society. It is thoroughly distasteful and muddies the water of denotative discourse:

> The fact that we cannot manage to achieve more than an

unstable grasp of reality doubtless gives the measure of our
present alienation . . . (Barthes, 1973, p. 159)

The task of the semiologist is to scrape away the layer of connotation, the site of the intentional concepts of ideology, and "liberate"
the significant (1973, p. 9). Connotative discourse is a parasitic
growth on the host, denotative discourse.

   Barthes' distinction and the way he develops it are both open to
question. Is the distinction, between a collectively shared quantity of
denotative signs and a quantity of connotative signs shared by
groups formed out of social divisions, a valid one? Barthes says that
the signified meanings of connotative signifiers are fragments of
ideology which have a "very close communication with culture,
knowledge, history, and it is through them, so to speak, that the
environmental world invades the system" (1967, pp. 91, 92). He
implies that denoted meanings have a very remote connection with
their contemporary social circumstances: as if, once settled a long
time ago by the deciding group, they have fallen into popular usage
and become collective institutions. It is certainly difficult to deny that
many signs have an established, collective meaning and that some
signs have acquired new, contemporary and sectional meanings. But
does that mean (1) that these denotative signs were not born out of
social practice and have never been connotative in nature, or (2) that a
distinction between language and ideology is justified? I think that
the answer must be negative in both cases. I would contend that what
are now taken as denotative signs were born in social practice: even
Barthes admits social influence in his assertion of the role of the
deciding group. Moreover, I think that the number of signs which
mean the same universally is not so great as he thinks. To use his
language, there is little left that is not infested with some ideology or
another. Furthermore, and this is the most fundamental point, does it
not depend on the social context of the usage as to whether a sign is
denotative or connotative? After all, even the definite article 'the',
which would seem to be as denotative a sign as one could get in
English, can be used in such a way as to carry a connoted meaning,
e.g. "He is *the* one", "This is *the* book on the subject", etc. I doubt if
it is valid to specify the existence of one general denotative code and a
separate series of ideological codes. Whether a sign is denotative or
connotative all depends on whose code we are talking about and the

context of the discourse. One cannot even point to a dictionary and say that there lies the denotative code of the English language. Every English dictionary I have seen contains highly sectional definitions of some words and highly eclectic definitions of most others. And I doubt whether this is just a sign of our contemporary alienation.

All signs are ideological in that they involve significations which reflect their social practices of origin and use. No discourse, or series of signs, exists which transcends either its social conditions of origin or its social conditions of current use. In every discourse, some signs are used denotatively and others carry wider connotations. The codes of signification which constitute these signs cannot be constructed abstractly and can only be determined in the light of their historical development and current social context. What the student of ideologies has to do when faced with a specific discourse is to determine which words carry the wider connotations and to establish that the others do not. The only way this is possible is through a thorough examination of the history or biography of the author, his social conditions of production, and the wider socio-historical setting of the discourse. One cannot decide which words, or sequences, carry the connotations without such a socio-historical knowledge: it is literally impossible. Those who pretend that they can do without this knowledge are fooling themselves and others if they claim that their work is scientific. Of course, for everyday spontaneous readings, readers automatically identify the connotative terms, but they only do this on the basis of their socio-historical knowledge of the reality in question, albeit a highly speculative, condensed, filtered, shorthand knowledge based more on spontaneous experience than careful research. Researchers generally have the facilities to investigate the validity of their superficial, first impressions: they should use them, instead of pontificating rampantly about the significance of a cultural form without looking further than its immediate appearance.

Barthes' distinction between denotation and connotation is thus inadequate. It bears the marks of a structuralist, static construction abstracted from history and society. My criticisms destroy it as it stands. However, as some readers may have noticed, to knock it down as a theoretical edifice is only to resurrect it as a methodological device. For, although a term may be denotative in one discourse and connotative in another, if we take any one discourse we need to establish some constants in order to detect variance. Unless we discover any historical or contextual evidence to the contrary, we would need in practice to assume that certain words carried their everyday meaning. This is not a satisfactory device, but it is all we have in this difficult area of research. We should certainly not elevate it into a theoretical distinction, for it is only a technique. Theoretically, we would bear in mind the principle that meanings of terms depend on their historical usage and current context. I do not think that transferring Barthes' theoretical distinction into a mere research technique is underhand practice: what is underhand, or at least deceptive, is to elevate a mere pragmatic technique into a theoretical distinction. The guiding principle in historical materialist readings of ideology is not an elevated technique but the theoretical principle that there is a genuine dialectical interpenetration between social relations and conditions, on the one hand, and forms of social significance on the other. This principle derives from, and specifies clearly, the Marxist concept of social practice as the subjective appropriation of the objective world under definite social relations; a concept which takes ideology as an integral feature and refuses to relegate it to an epiphenomenon of the economy or an outcome of the politically motivated, intentional consciousness.

The inaccuracy of Barthes' view that one can deduce the code embodied in a discourse purely from a reading of that discourse, without any socio-historical knowledge or assumptions, is rendered even more obvious when we look at the details of the semiological method, such as it is. In semiological terms, the structuralist concepts of 'relation' and 'function' are represented by the concepts of the *syntagmatic* and *paradigmatic* axes of discourse. If we take a written discourse, Barthes would say that the differences (or relations) which constitute the words (or functions) exist at the syntagmatic level and that the terms (or functions) available to a given system of differences (a langue) exist at the paradigmatic level. The syntagm is the fundamental operation of a discourse since the distinctions which constitute it divide up the continuum which is the "blur of reality". The creation of these distinctions or differences produces the "points of the structure" (the terms or the functions) (see Barthes, 1967, p. 64). Given a specific set of syntagms (or linguistic structure), only certain terms or functions are possible. Terms which are equal in that they serve as variants of expression of a particular structure in the system stand in paradigmatic relation to one another.

Given these structuralist concepts, when making a semiological reading of a discourse, the analyst uses what is called the *commutation test*. If it is supposed that a signification (X) is a function of relation of signification (A), then it is posited that there are other significant terms which could act equally as functions of relation A. So the analyst substitutes, in his/her imagination, the hypothetical terms for those in the text in order to confirm the suspicion that significant relation A is at work in this discourse. If the substituted terms do not alter the meaning of the discourse it is concluded that relation A (or syntagmatic form A) is in operation in the discourse (Barthes, 1967, p. 65).

The problem is that the semiologist does not specify the conditions under which it is supposed that X is a function of A. What assumptions are made in order to make this supposition and on what evidence are they based? Clearly, to make the commutation test work, one has to know the meaning of A in advance. One needs to know what A means in the discourse in question in order to investigate the logical distinction which it presupposes. But semiologists deny making use of socio-historical evidence in making their interpretations of the meaning: as we have seen, some, like Barthes, even suggest that the analyst should be cut off from socio-historical circumstance. Whose meaning, or what kind of meaning, is given to the terms then? One can only conclude that the meaning given is one which reflects the semiologist's own personal ideas and experience. In practice, of course, the semiologist, in making a personal reading of the meaning, must use socio-historical assumptions, theories and data. The net effect, therefore, is to base the reading on unevidenced or undeveloped socio-historical knowledge. This surely cannot meet the requirements of a science, which in my definition (and that of many others) demands either detailed evidence or developed arguments (or, preferably, both). Semiologists claim that their readings are scientific, but one can only conclude that they are statements of aesthetic or political preference.

A further problem with the commutation test can be briefly dealt with. By its nature, all it can produce is a description of the apparent relations of signification in the text and of the terms which appear to express those relations. This description can only be a static one of the apparent ideological formations at work in the discourse and contains only the mere hints of a theoretical explanation which specifies the sources, functions and direction of change of these ideological formations. Descriptions of phenomena which contain only a hint of the explanation behind them are not very helpful and often turn out to be misleading or inaccurate. One can best describe anything (and its effects) when one consciously and explicitly knows how it works. In connection with this general criticism of the semiological method, it is worth saying that it can easily lead to an overelaboration and extrapolation of an ideology. By furiously producing substitute terms, the semiologist can end up with a morass of interchangeable terms which of itself does not necessarily aid our comprehension. One could be left with an overcomplication of something fairly simple and an underexamination of the much less obvious (which could only be discovered using a socio-historically informed approach to the discourse).

Furthermore, Barthes argues that "it is impossible to guess in advance the syntagmatic units which analysis will discover for each system" (1967, p. 68). This may be true when we are examining the syntactic structures of a language, although I am not competent to say definitely. But it is certainly not true for the analysis of ideological structures, if we base our readings on socio-historical knowledge. Given that Barthes excludes, formally, such knowledge from his method, it would be impossible for him to be consistent and guess the structures in advance. But I do not think he *is* consistent because, despite what he says in theory, in practice he must make assumptions in advance about the operative relations of signification, based on his socio-historical knowledge, in order to intuit a meaning for the significant terms. On the basis of such a knowledge of a situation, one knows, for example, that a certain line of argument will be put forward by certain people in a meeting and one can test that knowledge by identifying the line of argument in its form of appearance in the ensuing discourse. Of course, such procedure does not always lead to accurate results, but using semiology one would never know whether the results were accurate or not. At least when one allows socio-historical knowledge to enter into the proceedings one can be proven wrong and can then begin to correct the error (thus refining and developing the theoretical knowledge guiding the method). In passing it is pertinent to mention here that socio-historical knowledge includes evidence about the previous ideologies expressed in the situation in question. I am not for one moment suggesting that one predicts certain ideologies as a consequence of social structures, historical events and material conditions alone: it is vital to take into account the past and present ideological structures, occurrences and conditions also.

Finally, by consciously studying ideologies on the basis of socio-historical knowledge, the researcher is less likely to mistake the apparent message of a discourse for the actual message. Semiology has no means of telling whether the apparent message is indeed *the* message. The historical materialist approach is more able to get beyond the apparent message to the actual social meaning of the discourse. Of course, semiologists may deny that they are searching for *the* meaning of a discourse, but what is "the code" if it is not *the* supposed meaning of the discourse? Phenomenologists may disagree, but Marxists hold the view that there is an objective, social meaning within a message, even though sometimes its purveyors and receivers may grant entirely different meanings to that message. Semiologists also hold this view, but they do not use a method which is ever likely to produce a satisfactory account of the social meaning of a message. Their method can only result in an apparent, asocial, logical code being presented as the objective, social core of the message. Moreover, one suspects that, despite their silence on their theoretical assumptions about the meaning of the message, semiologists are far more reliant on what they take to be the intention of the communicator than Marxists are. Marxist method would take into account authors' intentions of course, but because of its nature these intentions would be placed in their context and would rarely be the end of the matter. To paraphrase Marx, intentions are rarely the only causes of social praxis and phenomena.

Conclusion

In consciously attempting to separate ideological codes from their concrete contents, Barthes creates a world of abstracted, logical systems of signification. This world has lost its social and historical roots. Yet these very roots, as they are sedimented and filtered in the experience of the semiologist, must determine the meanings he gives to the message. Only by granting the messages under examination a definite meaning can their internal logic be abstracted. Thus, to supercede semiology as a research method must be to return forms of significance to the practical contexts in society and history which generate them and which enable us to read them. Discourses are in a sense like money: they are open to interpretation but nevertheless contain an inner character which is given to them by the social relations within which they function. Semiology is geared neither to the description of modes of interpreting signs nor to the discovery of the social character of those signs. Instead it interposes a mystical realm of abstract codes and avoids the key questions. Positivists in criminology (to take one example) have claimed ideological and political neutrality whilst establishing meaningless, abstract correlations between unexamined variables and neglecting detailed theories of the social nature of crime and its multiple modes of appearance. Similarly, semiologists like Barthes aim for hermetic neutrality and meaningless codes. Positivists of all kinds never face up to the task of providing theoretical accounts of the social nature of reality and the various modes of reading it. Barthesian semiology in this sense is the high mark of structuralist Positivism.

Notes

1. Not all signs are ideological from the point of view of modern semiology, as we shall see. In Chapter 2, of course, I defined ideologies as signs.
2. This argument is very reminiscent of Althusser's notion of the preparation of ideology within ruling class-dominated, ideological state apparatuses.
3. Compare Barthes on parole with Durkheim on the emergence of social institutions and Parsons on the emergence of shared value-orientations.

6 Neo-structuralism: The Marxist Avant-garde

Introduction

The search for a theory of reading ideology cannot end yet for, although we have distinguished two distinct, yet similar, modes of reading (formless empiricism and empiricist formalism), there remains a body of work which attempts to transcend these ideological modes and develop a dialectical materialist theory and practice of reading. This body of work can be entitled "neo-structuralism" because, as we shall see, it remains imprisoned with the web of structuralism and its associated weaknesses. I shall consider the effects of these deficiencies in selected writings from the work of Jacques Derrida, Julia Kristeva and Louis Althusser.

I shall not produce a comprehensive review of their texts since I am closely familiar with the whole writings of only one of the three, those of Althusser. All that I can achieve here are some indications of the inadequacy of their work, as far as I understand it. Hence my comments on Derrida and Kristeva are purely provisional—and await the translation of their major works into English. However, having said that, I must add that I am satisfied that one can grasp the general direction and substance of the work of Derrida and Kristeva, even from the small amount of their writing that exists in English translation. This degree of certainty arises not from a cavalier attitude to scholarship but from the fact that even small quantities of their writing can be readily comprehended if one has grasped the nature of previous theories of reading ideology and from the fact that their available works take the form of intellectual manifestoes, or pro-grammatic statements, which are fairly explicit. My discussion in the previous three chapters has described and criticized the existing methods of reading ideology against which the work of Derrida and Kristeva must be read. Like that of Althusser, their work warrants examination because it appears as the entire opposite of content analysis and offers us a Marxist approach.

Although all of Althusser's major works are in English translation (the most important for our purposes is *Reading Capital*), I would argue that, despite this plenitude, we cannot really grasp Althusser's theory of symptomatic reading (and its consequences for his reading of Marx) unless we set it in the context of other theories of reading. Set in its context of neo-structuralism and in its struggle with existing empiricist and structuralist tendencies, Althusser's mode of reading comes alive from the stylish ambiguity and convincing novelty of its formulation in *Reading Capital*. (It is vital to appreciate that Althusser is fighting empiricist and structuralist epistemologies: this appreciation is easily achieved since Althusser continually names his enemies. But, it is also vital to appreciate that Althusser's fight exists within the framework of neo-structuralism. The relations between the theoretical work of Althusser, Derrida and Kristeva should become clear as this chapter progresses.) For the moment, let us just note that, given Althusser's impact on world Marxism, it is obviously very important to understand the relation between neo-structuralism and structuralism, and, therefore, (again) this chapter must be read in the light of the previous three. I would say that, once digested, this chapter orders us to "decode" Althusser's interpreta-tion of Marxism on the basis of a more detailed knowledge of this neo-structuralist approach. This task is beyond the scope of this project, but it is of such obvious importance for the development of Marxism that I shall try in passing to give some indications on the key points at stake.

De-centring the Discourse

In our discussion of the analysis of form we gave air to the problems naturally flowing from the concept of structure. To reiterate only the main points, we examined the problem of movement or history, the problem of internal contradiction, the empiricism of the structuralist reading, the de-substantiation of the concrete elements of the structure, the logocentrism or teleogism resorted to in order to give the structure a context, the universal infinitude and asociality of the structure, and the problem of the combination of structures. All these problems arise from the static, formal, asocial, abstract concept of structure. Structuralism, in short, had taken the blood and fight out of history. Indeed, structuralism could be said to have taken the history out of history and left it with the rotting skeletons of form which act as signposts or monuments to an elusive, never-present reality. It is no wonder that structuralists talk of "archeology" (Foucault, 1974). They strip history of its flesh and bury the bones carefully in profoundly mysterious places; only to return with their semiological shovels to dig the whole thing up again and to leave joyful, proclaiming that they have "discovered" the signs of civilization. Structuralism has not just neglected the social context of the cultural message in its attempt to discover universals, as one reviewer has argued (Lovell, 1973); its basic concepts and consequent techniques logically exclude any concrete analysis of the social nature, movement and function of ideologies. Structuralism is totally antithetical to Marxism, to a *dialectical, materialist* analysis of phenomena. Structuralism fundamentally excludes movement and matter in its fetish for the static form. As such it stands radically opposed to Marxism.

The movement away from "pure" structuralism takes place (in the field we are considering) in France in the 1960s and 1970s, notably in the work of the *Tel Quel* group, a collection of Marxist cultural analysts and linguists whose work was produced in the journal *Tel Quel* and a series of texts on the theory and practice of reading ideology. Derrida and Kristeva belonged to this group. The movement clearly affected structuralism proper. Roland Barthes, in 1971, was arguing that there is no general semiological system and that each text had its own system. Agreeing with Derrida, Barthes now took the neo-structuralist view that each text must be seen in its "difference", as the accomplishment of many codes. Culler states Barthes' new position clearly:

> Reading must focus on the difference between texts, the relations of proximity and distance, of citation, negation, irony and

parody. Such relations are infinite and work to defer any final meaning. (Culler, 1975, p. 243)

The absolute meaning of the text had therefore disappeared. The text no longer had 'its structure'. Various readings of the text were now allowed. The stress had shifted from the Structuring Structure to the creativity of the reader in producing an "active reading".

Culler summarizes the *Tel Quel* position as a conscious rejection of structuralism (1975, pp. 241, 242). He says that the group would argue that the concepts of literary competence, the collective code, the semiological system, etc., are means whereby orthodox culture is frozen and preserved. The concepts of structuralism are denounced because they are said to deny the value and existence of creative violations of cultural conventions. The *Tel Quel* group, states Culler, would emphasize the possibility of several different readings of the text, or cultural artefact, and would reject anything which would grant one reading a privileged status. Derrida has expressed this emphasis well:

> . . . the absence of an ultimate meaning opens an unbounded space for the play of signification.

> . . . the joyful Nietzchean affirmation of the play of the world and the innocence of becoming, the affirmation of a world of signs which has no truth, no origin, no nostalgic guilt, and is proferred for active interpretation. (Both passages from Derrida, 1967, quoted in Culler, 1975, p. 247)

Reading ideology now becomes the creative practice of signification where past, present and future significance all enter play as active features. The analyst must "let his hair down" and enjoy the human capacity to create sense and meaning. Any critical reading will do, since no-one is privileged in this socialist Utopia of classless readings. Such is the position of *Tel Quel* at its most general level. Structuralism would appear to have given way to an avant-garde humanism pleasuring itself in the aesthetics of creative reading. Let us examine this apparently remarkable shift in more detail and see how it relates to Althusser, Kristeva and Derrida.

Jacques Derrida rejects the classic Saussurean structuralism embraced by Barthes' work as "logocentric" in that it grants an Absolute Meaning or Source to the text. For Derrida and Kristeva, the view that the empirical words or sounds are simple expressions or representations of the structure is characteristic of all previous Western philosophy of the sign. Like Althusser, they see Leibniz and Hegel as the best exponents of this "representativism" (Derrida) or "expressivism" (Althusser). Giving a discourse a "centre" is to give it "a definite origin" and to make each visible part of the system an expression of the invisible structure. "Centring" the discourse, therefore, argues Derrida, closes the play of the elements which that discourse inaugurates. "The concept of the centred structure is in fact that of limited or founded play" (Derrida, 1967) and it thus testifies to the presence of an ideology, since, like Althusser, Derrida sees ideology as a closed discourse, one that prevents further development. Derrida, therefore, rejects the very basis of structuralism when he renounces the notion of discourse with a fixed structure or centre. In place of the all-powerful structure, which dictates the meaning of the empirically visible elements of a discourse, Derrida develops the concept of the *system decentré*, the decentred structure. In this concept, each reading displaces the centre of the discourse. For Derrida, every discourse has a surplus of meaning and this surplus creates "a play" in the process of signification. Each term in the discourse may have "normal" usages, but it refers us to other possible meanings. These possible meanings may involve reference to past connotations, or present connotations, or, indeed, they may involve the creation of new references. Derrida argues that meaning is a function of differences between terms, *à la* pure structuralism but for him the relations between the terms are infinite and all have potential for producing meaning. Hence every reading is an active process of signification which decentres the orthodox, customary meaning of the discourse by its invocation of other, less orthodox, private meanings and references.

This general outline of Derrida's analytic position shows that the concept of the denotative structure of language survives but now it exists alongside the concept of the continual displacement of that structure by every new act of reading. The structure, in other words, is always being connotatively displaced. It is no longer the limit to the possible meanings of the text, as pure Barthesian semiology would have it. In fact, the structure must give way to the active reader, rejoicing in his "Nietzchean affirmation of the play of the world and the innocence of becoming".

We can now examine more precisely how Derrida constitutes his theory of the decentred structure.[1] Firstly, he urges us to see all signification as a "formal play of differences", or as a formal play of "traces". This concept of the play of differences can be grasped more easily if we remember that pure structuralism (found in Saussure, linguistics and Barthesian semiology) saw the structure as a system of differences which specifies the units of the structure and thus constitutes their significance. Derrida argues that the fact of a system of differences means that no element ever exists in a discourse purely in itself, reflecting nothing but itself. As an element in an infinite system of differences, an element of discourse is merely a "trace". It is a mere "notation" or transient flash of significance in an infinite sky of meaning. Such an element, therefore, contains traces of the rest of the system. It does not exist in itself in the discourse but as an element in a chain. It thus reflects other elements in the chain, some being visible in the discourse, others invisible, others absent altogether. Every element in a discourse therefore carries traces of related elements from the system of differences. It is in this sense that Derrida goes on to argue that no element of the system is ever simply absent or present in the discourse, "there are only differences of differences and traces of traces". The whole system of infinite significance is, therefore, *forever potentially* present in any discourse. It is *ever, already-given in its presence* and is thus the most general concept of Derrida's semiology.[2] Derrida gives the ever–pre-given structure of significant differences the term "the gramme". Semiology, for Derrida, must therefore become grammatology—the study of the infinite plane of the significant traces.

The gramme is a structure and it exists in movement. It is the systematic play of traces or differences called into movement in the praxis of signification. It is a structure but not a static, synchronic one: "Differences are the effect of transformations" (Derrida, 1967). These shifts in the structure of significance which effect differences lead us to the centrality of signifying practice, of "semiotic activity", for Derrida's neo-structuralism. The gramme, or ever–pre-given structure of significance, only exists in and through its activation in signifying activity. The play of traces is no mere slogan, it is Derrida's concept of the active employment of the potential structure of significance in practice. Every text or discourse is thus a production, which can only be read against another text or discourse—that text or discourse which was unconsciously transformed or reflected in the production. Derrida points out that the notion of "epis-temological break" (an obvious reference to Althusser) is misleading since every new discourse is always reinscribed in an old fabric which must be continually, and interminably, undone. Discourses only exist as transformations of other discourses, as grammatologically situated productions, and can never escape the formal play of the structure of differences. They are always constituted by the traces in them of the other elements of the system.

It is interesting that Derrida comments, in puzzlement, that "grammatics" is introduced by him at the moment when he appears to have "neutralized all substance". He is reflecting on the fact that material substances such as speech, books, etc., all appeared to have collapsed under the weight of his concepts of gramme and semiotic praxis, and the critique of Saussurean expressivism (which saw the empirical world as the mirror reflection of the structure carried and mediated by the motivated subject). It is interesting because always Derrida puts the structure, the system of differences or gramme, before all else. "There is no presence outside of and preceding the semiological differance [the gramme—C.S.]" (Derrida, 1967). He goes on to argue that we must begin with the systematic production of a system of differences before we can talk about code/message and langue/parole distinctions. In other words, semiologists can only begin to construct abstract, metaphysical codes or structures out of the units of a message on the basis of their (own) systematic production of a set of differences. To put it bluntly, Derrida's position is that significance is always actively produced in semiotic practice and the semiologists' work is no exception. Every discourse is a creative reading of the world, acting upon and constructing a chain of differences, and there is no discourse outside this practice, yet, at the same time, there is no significant practice without the system of traces which is ever-already-pre-given. Nothing precedes the gramme or system of traces. Derrida should not therefore be surprised when grammatics appears a substance vanishes; for Der-rida's grammatics are yet another celebration of the Structure or Form at the expense of its content, which is relegated to an "effect". Thus, for Derrida, the structure of the discourse is for ever being decentred by its active receivers or "readers" but *only* because the field of the significant is such an infinite structure, an endless chain of systematic relations. The infinitude of the system of significance provides *the surplus meaning* which all readers can actively exploit in their semiotic practice. The ever-already-givenness of the gramme is thus the basis for the always-creative practice of signification.

Derrida has attempted to rid us of the notion of the Logos, the Absolute Source Structure, by conceptualizing signification as creative work. Both the text and its reading are productions. Every discourse has its difference as a creation of a possibility already present in an infinite range of linked possibilities.

Julia Kristeva also rejects the ideological aspects of semiology and spends much time criticizing them, arguing that she wants to combine semiology and Marxism to create a science of ideology (Kristeva, 1969, 1971, 1973). For Kristeva, semiology, to become a science, must continually analyse its own postulates:

> Semiotics cannot develop except as a critique of semiotics . . . Research in semiotics remains an investigation which discovers nothing at the end of its quest but its own ideological moves, so as to take cognizance of them, and to start out anew. (Kristeva, quoted in Culler, 1975, p. 245).

Semiology must continually decentre its own structure. This may seem to leave semiology in a state of *avant-garde*, cultural masturbation, based on the pleasure of producing new meanings. This would, of course, be acceptable if it renounced its claims to scientificity and its links with Marxism: semiology as an artistic or propagandist practice would be an honest and valid proposition. However, Kristeva wants a semiotic science and founds her claims on a position identical to Derrida's. For Kristeva, the "infinite memory of significance", represented in Derrida's concept of the gramme, is termed the "geno-text". This structure serves as the "substratum" (Culler's term) to any actual text:

> . . . the geno-text can be thought of as a device containing the whole historical evolution of language and the various signifying practices it can bear. The possibilities of all language of the past, present and future are given there, before being masked or repressed in the pheno-text. (Kristeva, quoted in Culler, 1975, pp. 246, 247).

Like Derrida, she holds that the only concept that can serve as the centre for her analysis is a concept of the infinitude of significance. She also rejects Saussure's emphasis on the signifier as the combination of material letters on the page of the text. This is empiricist—the letters or words are really only "supports" (Althusser's term) for the structure of differences which is always present; just as human agents are only the supports of the structure of the social totality in Althusser's Marxism.

Kristeva, like Derrida, wishes to produce readings unrestrained by a particular cultural theory. She, too, wishes to live in the permanent revolution of a continually decentred, ideological structure. Culler points out that her own readings, in practice, actually operate "Quite restrictive conventions of reading" (Culler, 1975, p. 250). Kristeva would probably be satisfied with the defence that her "reading conventions" were in a state of permanent de-centredness:

> At every moment in its development semiotics must theorize its object, its own method and the relationship between them; it therefore theorizes itself and becomes, by thus turning back on itself, the theory of its own scientific practice . . . (Kristeva, quoted in Culler, 1975, p. 251)

This is a self-justification of the most obvious kind. Any reading is permissible because its validity is guaranteed by its existence as an expression of the geno-text. It may not be scientific at first, but if the reader looks at the assumptions of the reading, and theorizes them as an activation of an ever-present geno-text, he can then say that his reading is fully theorized and scientific. We may note that no recourse to any outside consideration is necessary—the scientificity of the practice is guaranteed internally. This point was worth mentioning at this stage because we shall see later that Althusser guarantees his own scientificity in the same way (without any reference to anything outside the sphere of difference brought into play by the theorist himself). The plane of systematic references activated by the practice of the analyst (or the theorist) defines its own objects, concepts and methods; scientificity is thus internally constituted, as a mere point within the system of differences.

Again like Derrida, Kristeva believes that semiotic gestures should be seen as semiotic practices with the same status as other social practices (Kristeva, 1971, p. 37). Their social value lies in the "global model" of the world suggested in their practice; bearing in mind that one should always relate the global model to the specific phase of the country's social development and not lapse into teleology and projectivism.[3] This is the nearest Kristeva gets to relating semiology to the world outside her busy hive of semiotic reproduction. Her main project is *semanalysis*. This would be a form of analytical semiotics that attempted a typology of signifying systems, it would attempt:

> . . . to dissolve the constitutive centre of the semiotic enterprise such as it was posited by the Stoics, and this would mean the interrogation of the fundamental matrix of our civilization grasped in its ideological, neuralgic locus. (Kristeva, 1973, p. 34).

In other words (and as usual with the neo-structuralists, we do need other words), the project of Kristeva's semanalysis would be to call into question the whole theory of knowledge in Western thought. This project would be of the utmost importance for "contemporary thinking" since the sign is "the foundation of our culture" (Kristeva, 1973, p. 35).

Ideology may well be crucial to capitalism's future, but Kristeva's approach will not carry us very far. Her main concern seems to be to "think the constants of [our] culture" in order to pose, "once more", "the problems of the signifying act" and to reformulate them. Kristeva is concerned only with the infinite grammatological possibilities of reformulating the problem of formulation (or signification); she seems to care little about the relation of her formulations to the real world, the world of social relations which present immediate appearances. The process of formulation and signification seems as important to her as the process of money-making to the capitalist. As Marx notes, it is not money but money-making that entrances the capitalist: in neo-structuralism it is not knowledge but the process of knowledge-producing that interests its proponents. This would appear to be true of Derrida and Althusser as much as of Kristeva. As Althusser puts it:

> Unlike the "theory of knowledge" of ideological philosophy, I am not trying to pronounce some *de jure* (or *de facto*) *guarantee* which will assure us that we really do know what we know, and that we can relate this harmony to a certain connexion between Subject and Object, Consciousness and the World. I am trying to elucidate the *mechanism* which explains to us how a *de facto* result, produced by the history of a knowledge, i.e., a given determinate knowledge, functions *as a knowledge*, and not as some other result (a hammer, a symphony, a sermon, a political slogan etc.). I am therefore trying to define its specific effect: the

knowledge effect, by an understanding of its mechanism. If this question has been properly put, protected from all the ideologies that still weigh us down, i.e., outside the field of the ideological concepts by which the "problem of knowledge" is usually posed, it will lead us to the question of the mechanism by which forms of order determined by the system of the existing object of knowledge, produce, by the action of their relation to that system, the knowledge effect considered. This last question confronts us definitively with the *differential* nature of *scientific discourse*, i.e., with the specific nature of a discourse which cannot be maintained as a discourse except by reference to what is present as absence in each moment of its order: the constitutive system of its object, which in order to exist as a system, requires the absent presence of the scientific discourse that "develops" it. (Althusser and Balibar, 1970, pp. 68, 69).

Like Kristeva and Derrida, Althusser's object is the mechanism of the production of significant systems, i.e. their mode of production. Like his fellow writers, he is concerned to protect his work from the field of ideology and to understand scientifically the mechanism of signification. And, like them, he seems to cut off his theoretical work from the project of making sense of the world as it appears in practice. We will return to Althusser; however, I would suggest that, although he poses knowledge production as a question, he does in fact build the answer into his construction of the question. The mechanism that produces the knowledge is presupposed: it is the system of differences at work for the theorist. The "systematicity of the system" of theoretical concepts makes the "knowledge effect" possible (Althusser and Balibar, 1970, p. 68). Like Derrida and Kristeva, Althusser posits scientificity as a trace within a system of traces. Scientificity for the neo-structuralists is constituted internally by every semiotic system, and every science is a semiotic system.

Returning to Kristeva, her "semanalysis" would base itself on two main concepts: Marx's concept of work and Freud's concept of the unconscious. Signification as an act of unconscious production is thus the centre of Kristeva's field of differences. The process of signification as work involving a formal play of differences becomes her base-point. And, having defined her object as semiotic practices (in my terms, the sphere of cultural practice), it is not surprising that she focuses the would-be semanalysis on literary and poetic texts. After all, as Kristeva says, these texts, more than any other type, carry a "surplus of significance" which provides the material for an approach which orients itself to "the pre-signifying and pre-conscious work" that the text exposes. This surplus of significance will undoubtedly give her much scope for creative readings and re-readings of the unconscious work "exposed" in the text.

As with Derrida, we find that Kristeva focuses on the active production of significance in the field of 'literary or artistic creativity'. Both of them seem to be attending to the question of the mode of production of creative art, of how an artist can operate a field of differences to creative effect. This involves both of them in a recovery of Freudian psychoanalysis since the active creativity must necessarily be unconscious (since neo-structuralism rejects the authorship of human subjects). It is thus a fit ending to this brief exposition to note that Kristeva and Derrida displace the God of Structure and replace it with the artistic practice of decentring the Structure. As much as they bring social practice in to play, their neo-structuralism is an advance. But, inasmuch as social practice only means the creative artistic praxis of literary and poetic work, this advance is limited. Furthermore, inasmuch as they see the semiotic practice of art as simply the creative decentring of the Orthodox Structure of Conventional Normative Discourse through the operation of an already-pre-given, infinite *Structure* of Significance, Derrida and Kristeva have not left the bounds of structuralism.

A Critique of Derrida and Kristeva

It seems to me that these writers have simply replaced the deep structure of consensual denotation with the even deeper, infinite structure of possible meaning. Or, perhaps more accurately, they have added to the structure of orthodox meaning an opposite which is presupposed by it. By locating ideologies as the expression in semiotic praxis of a structure of ideological significance, however infinite and complex in its differentiation, they have not moved one step away from Hegelian expressivism, despite their statements to the contrary. Ideology is still its own source and master. We are still left with an abstract, universal structure which lies in wait for the beginning of any significant practice. The emphasis on practice is a very important advance but it is retarded by its location within the remnants of a structuralist approach. Derrida and Kristeva have only talked about practice activating and developing a pre-given structure: they have failed to specify even at a general level, the *social* origins and locations of ideological structures as elements within specific social practices. Consequently, they fail to develop the notion that there are only specific ideologies reflecting the various social divisions of labour. The concepts of gramme and geno-text are simply metaphysical since they posit an abstract structure with no social location whatsoever. Kristeva and Derrida have destroyed the concept of the structure of the visible text, but only to replace it with the concept of the structure of every text, the gramme. Thus they have not destroyed the structuralist concept of structure but merely displaced it to a more abstract level. Consequently, all my previous criticisms of structuralism (mentioned at the beginning of this chapter) are applicable to their work.

Creative but unconscious praxis in the works of Kristeva and Derrida is a conceptual tool for the comprehension of *avant-garde* art. The concept of social practice in the context of their thought is not only crippled by its function as an agency for a mysteriously pre-given structure of meaning, but also by its restriction (in effect) to creative work in the field of art. Science demands that we sweep away the tautologous notion of ideology (ideology as an expression of itself) and move towards the analysis of the social conditions and relationships necessary for the emergence and development of particular ideological forms. In the work of Kristeva and Derrida, material conditions and the social relations of practice seem to be unimportant, yet, as I have argued, one can only understand ideological forms as material elements within social practices composed of other material elements and social relations. Without this historical materialist concept of the labour-process, their work simply reproduces the metaphysical concept of 'creation' as the human expression and development of a prior presence. Such a concept has only a fragmentary grasp of any actual social practice: it seems to be merely an idealistic representation of artistic practice.

Relegating creativity to the unconscious does not solve the problem either—it simply helps to conceal their concept of the production as the work of a human agent activating an ever-already-present, monolithic structure. Rendering Jesus unconscious would not make him any less the agent of the Deity. Nor does the de-centred structure solve the problem. It still posits the existence of an unconceptualized, dominant ideology (the structure to be de-centred) and, moroever, perpetrates the notion that even the liberative act of de-centring is only the expression of a collectively shared, cosmic structure of significance.

The concept of the pheno-text or gramme, the infinite structure of significance, seems to be yet another structuralist universal. It is slightly different from Levi-Strauss's 'structure of the human mind' but it still retains the character of a vague, ahistorical presence. If it was clear that they were arguing that, since the time when man ceased to be an animal and developed ideology, each particular historical social structure begets a particular macrostructure of significance which limits all forms of ideological expression, then that would be an interesting proposition. However, their emphasis on the infinitude of significance in any historical period, and on the ability of creative de-centring work to conjure up any past, present or future meaning, clearly forces us to criticize them for setting up another cultural universal. Just like Leach, they appear to be operating a concept of the primeval continuum of significance, out of which creative men carve interesting chunks. In a typically structuralist vein, they have expropriated the history from history and left us with the skeletons of the universal structure. I, for one, am less interested in skeletons than in the bodies they inhabited and the part these bodies played in the development of social life. Reducing history to forms is not an activity that is begotten by Marxism, in my view, but rather one begotten by structuralism. Marx never sanctioned the reduction of history to the expression of cultural universals or the consent of mankind.

Derrida and Kristeva do not in any way take the study of the significant out of the ideological sphere of Cultural Studies. Significance and signifying practice remain in the domain of 'culture' as though culture was some element of society separate from social practice. In Marxism, ideologies are an integral element in social life. In Cultural Studies, culture is usually something produced by the upper and middle classes in their leisure time; a conception that conceals the fully social nature of ideology. For all his faults, Barthes had at least tried to demonstrate the *diffusion* of "myth" throughout the social formation. Unfortunately he also suffered from the conception of myth (a form of culture) as the production of the ruling classes: dominant ideology thus remained the privileged product of the bourgeoisie. Derrida and Kristeva have failed to challenge this pervasive notion and to place ideology in its general location in social practice. They *have* universalized ideology inasmuch as they posit a pheno-text of significance, but this concept fails to grasp the general concept of the place of ideology in social practice which enables us to develop a knowledge of the historical origins, specificity and development of any particular ideological formation. Their conception of a generalized ideological structure is too metaphysical to lead us to any such theoretical development. Derrida talked of the movement of the gramme when he argued that significant differences were the "effect of transformations". However, he did not provide us with the concepts with which to think the nature of these transformations. The transformations of the gramme appear as a general assertion, an article of faith. Derrida fails to develop the concepts adequate to the socially situated movement of ideological forms. Had he and Kristeva begun to think of ideologies as necessary elements of specific social practices, then the concepts to explain the movement of ideologies could have been constructed. But, without connecting ideologies to the elements and relations within specific social practices, it is impossible to do anything but posit a Mysterious Movement of an Absolute Structuring Structure.

These remarks close our critique of Derrida and Kristeva. I have not put to them the three questions on their reading of ideology (the questions outlined in Chapter 3) because these questions can be best answered by dealing with neo-structuralism as a whole. We must examine Althusser's "lecture symptomale" before the questions can be addressed to the whole approach. Before Althusser, however, let us briefly look at Jonathan Culler's response to the work of Derrida and Kristeva.

Culler's Critique

Culler begins his critique by arguing that the *Tel Quel* group's position is subject to its own arguments. For him, the fact that a text can be read in a number of different ways does not demonstrate the lack of structure in the text so much as the complexity of the reading process:

> If each text had a single meaning, then it might be possible to argue that this meaning was inherent to it and depended upon no general system but the fact that there is an open set of possible meanings indicates that we are dealing with interpretive processes of considerable power which require study. (Culler, 1975, p. 243).

Thus, for Culler, the principle of the de-centred structure, adopted by the *Tel Quel* group, is just another principle of interpretation that centres the discourse under study and consequently it is just as ideological as any other principle of interpretation or reading. Moreover, the ideological reading of *Tel Quel* is particularly weak because it specifies that any reading of the text is possible. Culler finds this apparent anarchy unsatisfactory since it forgets that there are conventional ways of reading. It is one thing to try to change the rules for reading but it is equally valid, says Culler, to study the conventions that actually do commonly operate in the current social situation. Despite this criticism, however, Culler clearly shares with Derrida and Kristeva the view that meaning can only be constituted by semiotic systems, a view that denies the ability of social relations to constitute the form of things-to-be-signified, and to necessitate particular relations of signification.

The perpetual self-transcendence, advocated particularly by Kristeva, does not secure invulnerability from current ideological influences in Culler's view. Firstly, he points out that, in order to transcend orthodox readings, one has to study existing established semiotic conventions—it is a step that cannot be avoided. I think that this criticism is misguided since *Tel Quel* do not deny that conventional readings must be examined before any progress can be made. Kristeva's whole position is based on a process of critique of orthodox conventions, clarification of the concepts of the critique, application of the new concepts in a reading, reclarification of the mode of reading and self-criticism, a new application, and so on. Culler's second point is that there is no such thing as a freedom to create meaning since every creation implies a rejection or destruction of other possible meanings. Each reading has its own limits and constraints. Therefore to search for the totally creative reading is Utopian in the extreme since there will always be limits and constraints to any mode of reading. From this correct observation (which I do not think the neo-structuralists would disagree with anyway), Culler then jumps several steps in the argument to the position that no reading can escape from the existing conventions of meaning:

> Whatever type of freedom the members of the Tel Quel group secure for themselves will be based on convention and will consist of a set of interpretive procedures . . . What I should like to argue, then, is that while structuralism cannot escape from ideology and provide its own foundations, this is of little importance because the critiques of structuralism, and particularly of structuralist poetics, cannot do so either and through their strategies of evasion lead to untenable positions. Or perhaps one should say, more modestly, that any attack on structuralist poetics based on the claim that it cannot grasp the varied modes of signification of literature will itself fail to provide a coherent alternative. (Culler, 1975, pp. 252, 253).

He goes on to direct us:

> Rather than try to get outside ideology we must remain resolutely within it, for both the conventions to be analyzed and the notions of understanding lie within. If circle there be, it is the circle of culture itself. (Culler, 1975, p. 254).

In other words, all readers are trapped within the circles of their personal ideologies and there is therefore no point in trying to break out. All the literary critic can try to do when reading is "participate in the play of the text" and to isolate the "series of forms" in the text "which comply with and resist the production of meaning" (Culler's phrases, 1975, p. 259). Criticism should focus on "the adventures of meaning" and make the text "interesting" (p. 262). Culler thus abandons structuralism as a method and redesigns it as a "kind of attention" paid to the various ideological codes articulated by a text. But his return to structuralism is not a return to a structuralism for pleasure (the pleasure of making pretty and "interesting" patterns out of the text in order to combat "boredom"). Pleasure, he argues, is not the only value of a structuralist reading: "Literature offers the best of occasions for exploring the complexities of order and meaning" (Culler, 1975, p. 264). We are thus to return to an 'open' structuralism, according to Culler, in order to understand how "man" makes sense of the world. And, predictably, he finally reasserts structuralism's concept of *Homo significans* and assumes that by understanding "man's" ways of reading we will understand the world we live in:

> Man is not just homo sapiens but homo significans: a creature
> who gives sense to things . . . To know oneself is to study the
> intersubjective process of articulation and interpretation by
> which we emerge as part of the world. (Culler, 1975, p. 264).

Culler thus ultimately resides in the same *avant-garde* home as the
neo-structuralists: a place of pleasure, continuous introspection and
contemplation of the order of things. It seems that the modern
middle classes share much the same ideology as their ancestors,
although today it takes some remarkable forms. Culler may differ on
the question of Marx, but, like Derrida and Kristeva, he adopts a
mode of reading which prides itself in its infinite regression. And,
like them, he is not content to see his practice as merely aesthetic, he
wants to claim some scientific status. But how can transcendental
meditation be a science?

Derrida and Kristeva may have failed to establish the materialist
concepts for the reading of ideology, but at least they rejected the
logocentrism of the human subject as Absolute Creator of meaning.
Culler's relapse into a kind of phenomenological subjectivism takes
us no further in our quest for an adequate theory of reading ideology.
He never left the realm of spontaneous readings of discourse and thus
became enmeshed in its circle of insecurity based on the question:
how do we know? Because the answer to the question is not available
at the level of spontaneous analysis he could not find it, and resorted
to idealistic contemplation. However, the solution is not to give up
and assert the fact that, at the level of ideology, all is subjective.
Rather the task is to develop a knowledge of the social conditions
under which specific ideologies arise and develop and thus to move
from superficial, spontaneous readings to more certain, more evidenced, more theorized and more careful understandings of the
contexts of our different experiences of the world. All is indeed
subjective at the level of ideology: what theory must achieve is a
knowledge of the objective, social and historical conditions which
produce and maintain the phenomenal forms and modes of seeing
that structure the vision of the human subject. Rather than a
phenomenology, we need a knowledge of the complex fusions of
objective phenomena and subjective perceptions in the formation of
a social ideology. Only when we understand the socio-historical
contexts of these fusions can we begin to decipher our own
experience and that of others.

Althusser's "Lecture Symptomale"

Re-reading Althusser's theory of theoretical discourse in *Reading Capital* in the light of the work of Derrida and Kristeva is quite startling. What becomes obvious very quickly is the similarity between his concepts and those of Derrida. I hope that in what follows I can indicate the basis of this obviousness.

Just as Derrida rejoiced in his anti-Positivist "world of signs which has no truth, no origin, no nostalgic guilt" where the "innocence of becoming" is regularly affirmed, so Althusser submits there is "no such thing as an innocent reading" and enjoins us to share in his "adventure" of reading Marx's *Capital* (see Althusser and Balibar, 1970, p. 14). To be more accurate it is Althusser *and friends* who read *Capital*:

> The studies that emerged from this project are no more than the various individual protocols of this reading: each having cut the peculiar oblique path that suited him through the immense forest of this book. (Althusser and Balibar, 1970, p. 14)

Is this to say that each reading of *Capital* was seen as purely subjective? Since Althusser goes on to confess that he and his colleagues are all philosophers and that they had engaged in "philosophical readings", it seems clear that he locates the guilt of the reading not so much in its subjectivity as in its application of a philosophical approach to the text:

> To read *Capital* as philosophers is precisely to question the specific object of a specific discourse, and the specific relationship between this discourse and its object; it is therefore to put to the *discourse-object* unity the question of the epistemological status which distinguishes this particular unity from other forms of discourse-object unity. (Althusser and Balibar, 1970, p. 15)

The philosopher's problem of knowledge, therefore, guides their paths through "the immense forest" of *Capital*. A grid, composed of a system of philosophical differences, is thus placed over *Capital* and a reading is made of "Marx's philosophy".

Althusser feels no shame about the reading: "It is a guilty reading, but one that absolves its crime on confessing it" (Althusser and Balibar, p. 15). His position here is practically identical to that of Kristeva and Derrida. Neo-structuralism is continually making active readings, criticizing their assumptions and developing new ones; for example, Kristeva seemed to accept a state of permanent de-centration of the structure as the normal state for neo-structuralism. This continual self-examination ensured that semiotics always "theorized itself" and always existed as "the theory of its own scientific practice". Semiotics, therefore, practised in a permanent state of scientificity: a state justified for itself from within. Althusser's philosophy appears to be very similar to Kristeva's semiotics and Derrida's grammatology in that the practice of all three is self-justifying. All three programmes represent attempts to specify a relation between a proposed field of significant differences, operating unseen within any given text or discourse, and the explicit concepts and objects of that text or discourse.[4] All three modes of exploration operate by concepts which provide a safety net, i.e. they all use the notion that any reading is permissible provided its constituting system of significance or "grid" (Althusser's term) is systematic enough to prove itself necessary. The systematicity of the reading thus ensures its own validity and necessity.

Althusser rejects Hegelian models of reading which provide an "immediate reading of essence in existence" as "fetishist", and claims that Marx inaugurated a scientific reading in *Capital*:

> *Capital*, on the contrary, exactly measures a distance and an internal dislocation (décalage) in the real, inscribed in its *structure*, a distance and dislocation such as to make their own effects themselves illegible, and the illusion of an immediate reading of them the ultimate apex of their effects: fetishism. (Althusser and Balibar, 1970, p. 17)

The text of history "cannot be read in its manifest discourse" and is the "inaudible and illegible notation of the effects of a structure of structures", Althusser argues. Similarly, a theoretical discourse cannot be read from its immediately visible text as though that text was the direct expression of its author's vision. Althusser thus inaugurates the important concept of the dislocation of the significant functions of a discourse from their relations (or structure) of signification. Derrida and Kristeva did not make this point explicitly, but, clearly, since they rejected expressivism and posited the pheno-text as an expression and repression of elements of the geno-text or gramme, they implied a definite concept of the dislocation between the pheno-text and geno-text. The visible elements of significance in the pheno-text were not just related to each other but also to invisible but present elements and to elements of significance absent altogether from that text. The neo-structuralist structure is always de-centred. Ben Brewster's Glossary definition of Althusser's concept of "dislocation" is interesting:

> Althusser argues . . . that the relations between ideology and the other practices, between the different practices in general, between the elements in each practice, and between ideology and science, are, in principle, relations of *dislocation*, staggered with respect to one another: each has its own time and rhythm of development. (Althusser and Balibar 1970, p. 312)

The principle of the de-centred structure has thus been applied to the social structure: each element of social life has its own "relative autonomy" or internal specificity, subject to the determinations of other elements, the whole being arranged in a structure of unevenly weighted parts. Relative autonomy and the weighting of elements are also features of dialectical materialism. Consequently Althusser, correctly, notes that Marxism thinks of the social formation as a "structure-in-dominance", a structure of dependent but independent, elements dominated by one heavy element, the sphere of the economy.

Examining Marx's reading of the texts of Adam Smith, Althusser finds that Marx provides two methods of reading:

1. A "grid" reading. Marx reads Smith spontaneously through the grid of his own thoughts and finds him lacking, ridden with "oversights", etc. This reading concerns itself with the observation or identification of the weaknesses in the object-discourse and does not trouble to reflect on the reasons for these inadequacies.
2. A "symptomatic" reading. This reading identifies the connections between the visible and invisible in a discourse. Any "oversights", inadequacies or concepts invisible to the theoretical discourse in question are seen to be built into its vision or problematic as part of its whole field of operation. Althusser argues that Marx does this kind of reading but never consciously talks about it. It is unconscious to Marx but nevertheless, it is argued, it is an integral part of his theoretical discourse. Like his first reading, Marx's second reading measures one text (his own) against another (e.g. Smith's). But what marks off the second (symptomatic) reading

from the first is that *Marx's text is "articulated with the lapses" in Smith's text.* I shall attempt to explain what Althusser means by this.

It is this attribution of a method of symptomatic reading to Marx that marks the operation of the concept of the de-centred structure in Althusser's theory of theoretical discourse. Therefore we must examine this symptomatic reading in detail.

To understand *lecture symptomale*, we must realize straight away that Althusser sees knowledge as a production:

> What political economy does not see is not a pre-existing object which it could have seen but did not see—but an object which it produced itself in its operation of knowledge and which did not pre-exist it: precisely the production itself, which is identical with the object. (Althusser and Balibar, 1970, p. 24)

Shades of Derrida here as Althusser introduces the notion of the "theoretical problematic" as a semiotic field! Althusser seems to share Derrida's notion of the play of differences created by semiotic production because he has introduced the neo-structuralist concept of a semiotic field created by discursive practice. In Derrida's terms, semiotic practice produces a field of signs linked to and drawn from the gramme; for Althusser, a theoretical problematic is the articulating instrument of theoretical practice—it is a field of concepts drawn from and linked to the web of existing theory and ideology.

For Althusser, all scientific knowledges contain a theoretical problematic:

> This introduces us to a fact peculiar to science: it can only pose problems on the terrain and within the horizon of a definite theoretical structure, its problematic, which constitutes its absolute and definite condition of possibility, and hence the absolute determination of *the forms in which all problems must be posed*, at any given moment in the science. (Althusser and Balibar, 1970, p. 25)

A theoretical problematic is a product of theoretical practice [defined by Althusser as the transformation of ideology into knowledge by means of theory (1970, p. 316)]. But where does the operative theory come from? Theoretical practice? But surely that would be tautologous! Theory would simply derive from theory. Althusser's reading of Marx has ignored the many asides in *Capital* (and elsewhere) to the economic and political interests of the political economists. These asides may be *ad hoc* and untheorized but they cannot be ignored. By focusing on Marx's supercession of Political Economy in theory, Althusser renders the process of theoretical transformation totally autonomous. This problem reappears many times in Althusser's works in the forms of 'the relation between Marxism and political practice' and 'the general relation between theory and practice'. A similar problem exists for Derrida and Kristeva in that they fail to transcend the notion of the ideological source of ideology. This problem (which has become known as the problem of theoreticism) is very important for Althusser's position and one that remained unsolved in his prior text, *For Marx* (1969). In the text he had specified the notion of scientific knowledge as the product of work done on ideological formations by scientific theory (pp. 182–193). That notion opened up the problem which he creates again in *Reading Capital* (1970). In *For Marx* the problem was indexed with a footnote declaring that the concept of theory "obviously deserves a much more serious examination" (1969, p. 184n). In the passage quoted above from *Reading Capital,* Althusser again posits the theoretical problematic as the "absolute and definite condition of possibility" of a science. In my view this begs the question: what connection does the production of science or theory have with the ongoing production of social life (in its various forms)? After all, there are other necessary conditions for science; notably, the scientist must eat and obtain shelter—this simple point means that we must ask about his position in the structure of social life and in what ways this position influences his science. Like Derrida and Kristeva, Althusser seems to propose that a theoretical discourse is a dislocated expression of a theoretical structure and that this structure exists purely in theory, i.e. abstractly and asocially. In this strict sense, Althusser has not left the terrain of a structuralist problematic. The forms which theoretical problems take are governed by the theoretical problematic. Is this not the same as Derrida's view that forms of significance (past, present and possible) are governed by the gramme or Kristeva's view that the forms of the pheno-text are governed by the geno-text? Althusser seems to be operating the same neo-structuralist concept of the mysteriously appearing, grand structure which determines all forms of the content of a discourse. The theoretical problematic seems to stand in relation to theoretical discourse as does the gramme to the "formal play of differences" in an actual statement.

Althusser goes on to argue that this concept of the theoretical problematic removes the subjectivity of theorizing and reading:

> Any object or problem situated on the terrain and within the horizon, i.e., in the definite structured field of the theoretical problematic of a given theoretical discipline, is visible. We must take these words literally. The sighting is thus no longer the act of an individual subject, endowed with the faculty of "vision" which he exercises either attentively or distractedly; the sighting is the act of its structural conditions, it is the relation of immanent reflection between the field of the problematic and *its* objects and *its* problems. (Althusser and Balibar, 1970, p. 25)

Thus the reader or theorist is unwittingly the unconscious agent of his theoretical structure or problematic. Althusser footnotes the fact that, as his own work is *consciously* (note the paradox) anti-structuralist, the concept of immanent reflection used in this passage presents problems. It certainly does, since it is a classic structuralist concept! How similar this is to the other neo-structuralist works which by-pass 'the human subject' through their conception of the text as the dislocated expression/repression of the geno-text or Structure! Althusser's footnote refers us to a later section of *Reading Capital* but this section fails to solve his difficulties.[5] The section concerned simply argues that the organization and order of succession of concepts in a theoretical work are underpinned by the "systematicity" of the system of concepts in the theoretical problematic and that a concept's meaning is given by its place and function in the totality of concepts (Althusser and Balibar, 1970, p. 68). These are classically structuralist notions. The problem is indexed by Althusser's uneasy use of two favourite structuralist terms "synchrony" and "diachrony" (he argues that the synchrony and diachrony of the concepts are given by their place and function in the theoretical structure).

The reason why Althusser designates this mode of reading the structure of a theory in its absences and presences at the level of the text's theoretical concepts as a method of "symptomatic reading" is as follows: under "certain very special critical circumstances" (unspecified by Althusser), the theoretical problematic produces "the fleeting presence of an aspect of its invisible" within its visible field of discourse (1970, p. 27). To the spontaneous grid reading, this fleeting presence of the invisible appears as a theoretical lapse, weakness or oversight. To a symptomatic reading, the presence of the problematic's invisible field (its "repressed" concepts) at the level of the visible is a *symptom* of the "unconsciousness of the text" (1970, p. 317), its theoretical problematic; just as some of the patient's utterances are for Freudian psychoanalysts a symptom of the structure of the psychic unconscious. It is interesting to consider that the term 'symptom' can mean 'sign' and that 'semiology' is the science of signs or symptoms. Althusser's 'discovered' mode of reading in Marx, therefore, seems to be no more than an imposition on Marx of a neo-structuralist or radical semiological approach to phenomena. The similarity of terminology between Althusser and the structuralists simply indexes the fact. However, it would be wrong to say that the neo-structuralists are simply structuralists. They definitely remove the concept of the immediate expression of the structure in its effects and definitely construct the valuable concept of semiotic modes of production, two important moves away from structuralism. However, on the other hand, we should not exaggerate the differences; neo-structuralism is just a new, developed form of structuralism. What conceptual developments neo-structuralism has made simply displace the concept of the Absolute Structure to another, more abstact, level; they do not remove it altogether.

A symptom is defined (in the 1971 Oxford English Dictionary) as "a perceptible change in the body or its functions, which indicates disease, or the kind of disease". Symptomatic reading is thus a very accurate term for the neo-structuralist mode of reading since it expresses the fact that this group of theorists see the Structure as a thing in movement. In this sense, their conception of the Structure is a *dialectical* one—a distinct advance on structuralism. And, because the Structure (the problematic, gramme or geno-text) is in continual transformation, movement or "dialectical mutation" (Althusser's term), it is constituted two-sidedly by its presences and absences. Thus the symptomatic reading observes the dis-ease within the theoretical problematic as it moves; the dis-ease being constituted by the antagonism between the two poles of the problematic, its recognized concepts and its unrecognized or repressed concepts. As such, symptomatic reading is an advance on ordinary structuralist readings, which only observe the recognized or 'visible' concepts of a static problematic or ideology and fail to discern the totality-in-movement of the structure composed of visible and invisible concepts in connection. Unfortunately on the other hand, being a form of structuralism, neo-structuralism fails to locate its discovered forms, or structures, within the *social* totality and fails to define the concept of the importance of the contents or material substance of a form. Neo-structuralism has been very important in introducing the concepts of Structure-in-movement and contradictions-within-the-Structure, but it has failed to put the Structuring Structure into the social totality, to give the elements of the Structure any real materiality and historicity, and to solve the problem of how to conceive of structures in combination.[6]

These failures can be illustrated by pursuing Althusser a little further. Althusser's concept of the theoretical problematic and its effects is remarkably similar to Derrida's concept of the gramme with its appearance in traces. Althusser also talks of the production of theory using a spatial metaphor like Derrida. These two similarities can be indicated by the following passage:

> Hence, if we wish to preserve the spatial metaphor, the paradox of the theoretical field is that it is an *infinite* because *definite* space, i.e. it has no limits, no external frontiers separating it from nothing, precisely because it is *defined* and limited within itself, carrying in itself the finitude of its definition, which, by excluding what it is not, makes it what it is. (Althusser and Balibar, 1970, p. 27)

This may appear to be sheer gobbledegook or dialectical metaphysics, but, in my view, Althusser is attempting to specify the concept of a created, discursive space in movement. He is trying to steer clear from static concepts of structure and to embody movement in his definition of the problematic. Thus he sees it as a disengaged theoretical space, "limited within itself" and "marked inside itself", created by a productive mechanism—the knowledge's mode of production. This concept is practically identical to Derrida's concept of the infinite sea of differences in which semiotic practice introduces a particular play. And, as regards the form of appearance of the field of differences, Althusser talks of "illegible notation" and "the fleeting presence of an aspect" while Derrida talks of "traces" and "traces of traces". Not only do they both use the same stars-in-the-night-sky image to indicate the profound degree of mediation between the structure and its effects, but also they share the view that the absences of the text are as indicative as its presences.

Althusser argued that the distinguishing character of a Marxian symptomatic reading lies in the fact that the reader's text is articulated in the lapses of the real text because (he says) Marx occupied the terrain of the unconscious text of his victims. Only on the condition that the reader through his theoretical work has occupied both the conscious and unconscious terrain of the theoretical problematic under examination, can he achieve a symptomatic reading of that problematic's written, theoretical texts. The theorist or reader must, literally, conquer the territory of his predecessors before he can make the advance of opening up new theoretical space for the creation of knowledge. He must grasp in full the thought structures in existence before he can locate and resolve their inadequacies: for only by understanding the mechanism (the structure) of their production of knowledge can he eradicate it, or improve upon it, and so create new knowledge. It may be observed that this is rather obvious to anyone who has engaged in any kind of sustained enquiry and that it does not take all this complicated language to express the fact that "one has to master the field of knowledge before one can advance it". I may be doing Althusser an injustice but, at this point in time—after this long and arduous deciphering of his discourse, this observation seems to be fully justified. To say that a theoretical text is always inscribed in and against the field of significance of another text is surely to state the obvious. Moreover, the fact that is so obvious is suspicious, to say the least. My suspicions lead me to suggest that ironically the obvious substance (yet magical appearance) of Althusser's symptomatic reading corresponds to an absent concept of the social origins of theoretical revolutions (and stagnations). Althusser's discourse focuses solely on the movement of theory, as if it went on in a vacuum; none of his concepts reflect upon the relations between theoretical products and their social conditions of existence. Althusser's view of theoretical revolutions is idealistic and descriptive in merely referring to the apparent differences between knowledges, and the apparent, purely theoretical, structures which produce them. "Theory evolves from theory" is as bourgeois-ideological as "ideology evolves from ideology"—it is equally tautological and equally descriptive. Symptomatic reading, therefore, is simply a thorough way of describing theoretical differences. *That is all* Marx does in the passage given so much attention by Althusser (1970, pp. 20, 21). Consequently, symptomatic reading is not so markedly different from grid reading—it is simply the reading theorist's reflection on the differences between his grid and that of the object-text which he has comprehended and superceded.

Just as Kristeva produced a concept of semiotics as a continual reflection on its own field of differences, so too has Althusser produced a mode of reading which continually reflects on its own differences. Symptomatic reading simply produces a list of differences between two theoretical grids and explains those differences in terms of the different structures of the two grids. In an era of increasing surplus labour, it is interesting to note that *lecture symptomale* is very much a surplus reading; the basic form of reading is grid reading. Normally, theoretical advances should be possible on the basis of grid readings. However, the symptomatic reading, by its very nature, will clearly give the theorist a greater degree of certainty over the novel nature of his concepts and an apparent explanation of the inability of other problematics to produce his discoveries. Perhaps, then, a symptomatic reading of Marx (to produce the specificity of his differences) has been produced at a time when there is a felt need for a development and/or a redefinition of basic Marxian concepts in the light of threatening tendencies such as Stalinism, anarchic humanism, adventurism, reformism, etc. Does the uncertain Marxist retrace his steps of theoretical origin at times of crisis in the socialist movement? Perhaps. But should he then generalize his retreat as a new, "Marxist" theory of reading? No. It seems to me that Althusser's symptomatic reading is, in one way or another, itself merely a symptom—a symptom of a type of Marxism (in a specific political-historical setting) in retreat, retracing its steps, in order that it can go forward on a more correct and sure footing. But, on the other hand, the practice of symptomatic reading is not thereby an incorrect procedure in itself: at times, theory must be reworked and retraced in order to advance. However, symptomatic reading is only a rigorous, double-checking reading most suitable to periods of (or Parties in) theoretical stagnation or turmoil; it should not be generalized to the level of an absolute, scientific mode of reading. Any such generalization would mean condemning theory to a perpetual reflection on its own premises; a fate that would send Marxism round in circles. Certainly, critique, re-examination and theoretical reflection are, in certain historical conjunctures, vitally necessary but only inasmuch as they enable the further production of adequate theories of social developments. Like Kristeva's reflexive semiotics and Derrida's grammatology,[7] Althusser's symptomatic readings of philosophical analyses threaten to be an infinite regression into insecure introspection and an obstacle to the development of adequate knowledge of social developments.

Theoretical reflection is valuable when it produces more fruitful general concepts than presently exist. General concepts are necessary if one is to develop any concepts of the particular. However, it should never be forgotten that the object of theoretical introspection and review is to provide general concepts that can be developed in the particular. The production of general concepts in itself is not the ultimate end of theoretical review; such a motive could only succeed in providing massive and intricate webs of generalities with no grasp on the particular. Such general theory would be abstract and one-sided with no concrete character as a reflection of the movements of the real world. In short, the object of Marxism should not simply be to reach "the threshold of Marx's philosophy".

Althusser's reading is indeed "guilty" in that its object is to recognize "the infinite extent contained within its minute space: the extent of Marx's philosophy" (Althusser and Balibar, 1970, p. 30). In his view, "we are all seeking this philosophy". Having found it, other readings of Marx and Marxism will be possible. At this point, says Althusser, "before it is too late", we will be able to understand correctly "the reasons for this unreason" (1970, p. 34). By unreason, Althusser refers to the ideological deformities of Marxism such as the "cult of the personality". Althusser seems to assume that all the problems of global socialism stem from a crisis in Marxist theory and that continual philosophical re-readings will resolve that crisis. My position on this should be clear from what I have said already, but let me reiterate some basic positions:

(1) Any such crisis in general theory does not of itself explain the current problems of practice. No doubt, the problems of theory are connected to the problems of practice: theoretical problems have been generated by certain movements of revolutionary practice and problems in practice have been generated by certain movements (or lack thereof) in theory. But one cannot be a Marxist and see theory as an Absolute Structure generating all the practical problems of the

surface text of history. Rather, one needs to examine the social conditions which have produced theoretical deviations: theory only exists in social practice. Rediscovering the truth of Marxist theory cannot be done by purely philosophical investigation, it also requires a knowledge of the social changes that produced the changes in the theory.

(2) Continual philosophical re-reading of Marx and Marxism will not provide anything but a developed super-abstract philosophy. What is needed is the development of appropriate general concepts and their particular counterparts in order that Marxism can provide adequate theoretical analysis of social developments presenting problems for revolutionary socialist practice. A developed philosophy, in itself, does not provide even general concepts because it is a *backward step* into the abstract analysis of the basis of conceptualization as a whole. Philosophy simply generalizes the actual methods of sciences—that is, it works on sciences—it does not actually produce a science. Socialism certainly has its own epistemology but that epistemology renounces idealist philosophy (as bourgeois ideology) and places the principles of knowledge within their social context. Hence, its key principle is that of the materialist dialectic, the recognition of contradictory development in concrete situations. Now, it is certainly true that many Marxist works are undialectical and the restoration of the dialectic to Marxist theory is today an urgent theoretical task. But that restoration can only be realized in a materialist way through the theoretical analysis of particular social developments, not in the practice of concocting endless streams of general permutations made possible by the dialectical approach. Marxism is not just dialectical in orientation, it is also materialist. Certainly dialectical philosophy is potentially "infinite", only waiting for philosophers to produce its extended "space". But strings of potential abstractions are irrelevant! They would simply be empty speculations on what could be. Rather more immediate is the employment of the dialectical principle in the development of the necessary concepts which enable us to grasp faithfully the particular developments in the global social structure. Dialectical materialism is an approach which grasps social phenomena in their movements and which was built on a rejection of metaphysical philosophies pointed upwards towards the heavens rather than downwards towards earth. Althusser's philosophical readings, aimed at putting the dialectic

back into dialectical materialism, threaten to take the materialism out, just as other forms of structuralism have taken the history out of history. After all, if one has grasped Marx's critique of philosophy in his early works and the nature of materialist dialectics practised in the later works, one should put this comprehension into a theoretical practice of explaining the latest social developments rather than a practice of propounding an idealistic theory of theory. The lost dialectic is a result of a number of social changes; it will best be restored through the dialectical materialist analysis of these changes and their implications for general Marxist theory.

I would not like to leave this critical discussion of Althusser's *lecture symptomale* without registering the fact that, in my view, Althusser's reading of Marx is very valuable. It has produced, or at least encouraged, a re-awakened interest in the question of ideologies. He and his colleagues, through their actual readings, have observed, albeit descriptively, the intervention of bourgeois ideologies in Marxist theory. The central object of Althusser's work seems to be the role of ideology and it seems to me that, at the present stage of historical development, as in the past, the role of ideologies is a very important one. The development of the Marxist theory of ideology in general, and of particular ideologies and their mode of intervention in the social formation in particular historical conjunctures, is therefore a vital task. Concepts of philosophy, semiotics and significance which (1) do not specify in themselves the specific connections between ideology and the social structure, and (2) remain at the level of generality, will be of little value in practice. It is interesting that Althusser's post-*Reading Capital* writings show some awareness of this point. In the Foreword to the Italian edition of *Reading Capital*, he talks of his conception of philosophy as theoretical and likely to "induce 'speculative' effects". In an interview in 1968, Althusser still maintains a concept of dialectical materialism as the philosophy of Marxism and as a necessary weapon of proletarian revolution, since it enables "the defence and development of theory" (Althusser, 1971, pp. 15–25). He seems to have moved to a position identical to the one expressed here: that theoretical development is the important thing and that 'reading adventures' represent a tendency to speculative and retreatist thinking. Moreover, in this interview there seems to be more of a sense of the historically specific nature of the need to defend and develop theory: there is less sense of the permanent necessity and scientificity of symptomatic reading. In short, Althusser himself now seems to be looking forward to the relation between theory and practice rather than backward to the philosophical practice of producing systems of super-abstract generalities. In his later self-criticism (Althusser, 1976), he reaffirms his belief in philosophy as "class struggle in theory" (in the last instance) and thus anchors the break with his work in his famous texts (1969, 1970). Gone is the notion of some asocial, ahistorical philosophy of philosophy. Even epistemology is now seen as socially rooted in history. Marxism is now not seen to be validated by or dependent upon its dialectical materialist epistemology; instead it must be seen as proletarian science which arose amongst the working class and its allies in the course of the struggle against capitalist exploitation and repression. It is no longer epistemology but politics which secures the theoretical unity of Marxism. There is no time to discuss the matter here, but Althusser does seem to have gone from one extreme to another. Marxism is surely not validated by either its view of knowledge formation or by its current political line, but by the ability of its theories to appropriate the movement of social reality in cogent analyses and thus to win people over to the cause of socialism. Althusser's latest position begs all the questions and suggests that the truth of an argument will be settled by its author's class alignment in politics.

Ideology Detection in Neo-structuralism

The neo-structuralist problematic sees ideology as a closed discourse: one which makes unself-conscious assumptions and therefore lacks systematicity. Science is predicated by the systematicity of a discourse. Scientific discourse is not closed at any point since it constitutes an infinite system of elements. Hence the neo-structuralist analyst claims to read ideology scientifically (or detect it) by reading a discourse through the concepts of his or her own field of signification and identifying the closures and silences in the field of logical signification of the object-discourse. Consequently the neo-structuralist is looking for the logical breaks in the chain of significance in the discourse, its blind spots and its gaps.

In other words, the analyst's discourse is juxtaposed against the discourse of the object-text, and the discourse that has weaknesses is deemed to be the ideological one. The object-discourse is said to be read against the reading-discourse, or, as Derrida would have it, one text is inscribed within the lapses of another, and the text with lapses is the one with the ideology. For Kristeva, of course, the next thing to do would be to check back on the winning discourse to see if its infinite systematicity is real. With this mode of reading, of course, the field of discourse reading the text can be found to be ideological just as much as the text's discourse itself. In this sense there are no guarantees in this method that the discourse of the text is the one that is the object of reading; for if the "reading field" or grid is found lacking in comparison with the text's discourse, then it is the one with the ideological lapses and the one that is the object of the reading practice. In such an instance, we could say that it was the reading-discourse that had been read! Frequently, it will happen, of course, that lapses are found both in the reading-discourse and in the read-discourse. In that case both discourses are ideological and there is a frantic search for systematicity: this is reflected on the surface in the mind of the reader as a "crisis in theory", or, perhaps, as "an intriguing problem".

This mode of reading ideology is an advance in two important ways. Firstly, there is the concept of the object-discourse as actively signifying in relation to the active field of signification of the reader. Secondly, there is the concept of the active nature of the reading-discourse in relation to the actively signifying object-discourse. In other words, both the ideologies of "the reading" and "the read" are considered *active*. They are seen as active because the practice of the reading activates them. The reader operates his own field of significance in reading and by that act he also activates a field of reading in the text. In short this concept of the reading process is a *dialectical* one: it posits a movement between the reading- and read-discourses. The reading-discourse is only constituted in the practice of reading the read-discourse and the read-discourse is only realized in the activity of the reading-discourse. The concept of the given, static structure of a text is abandoned and in its place is substituted the concept of the de-centred structure created by an active reading. It is important to note that, in this dialectical conception of reading, the ideology of the read-discourse is not given to all-comers—it is *produced*, in the reading practice, by the work of a more systematic reading-discourse on the less systematic read-discourse.

Thus it is that ideology is detected by the production of closures, breaks and lapses in the read-discourse. These closures, breaks and lapses exist at both the visible level of explicit significance and the invisible level of implicit or absent significance. There are no guarantees that they exist in the text and can only be produced by a reading practice employing a more systematic, more scientific field of significance. This is the neo-structuralist theory and practice of reading ideology. Clearly it is a self-conscious or reflexive mode of reading; it not only reads (with its grid) but it also notes the differences in mechanism between itself and its object-discourse. This mode of reading thus involves both grid and symptomatic reading. It reads and then talks about its reading. This is peculiar to all three protagonists of neo-structuralism discussed here. It was clearly expressed by Althusser in his explicit enunciation of the two modes of reading (grid and symptomatic) in Marx, but it is equally clear in Kristeva. The following passage illustrates her view of neo-structuralist reading (in the form of semiotics) as a grid reading which constantly questions its own structure:

> For . . . if the *raison d'etre* of the semiotic enterprise from the time of the Stoics to the present day has always been to found scientific abstraction in posing the *sign* and in so doing allowing the constitution of science (including linguistic science) as systematisation and formalisation, semiotics is now called upon to question these foundations, the foundations of science (and of linguistics) and to work towards the constitution of a *theory of knowledge* in which the project of linguistics, duly questioned, will itself be integrated. In other words, having provided the positive foundations of metaphysics and/or science, semiotics now offers itself as the area of the interrogation, analysis and criticism of metaphysics and/or science that they may be refounded in a new theoretical gesture (of which all that may be said is that it is practised as a critique of metaphysics). (Kristeva, 1973, p. 25)

This text can be seen as a perfect example of the philosophical nature of the neo-structuralist reading. This reading does not discover the pre-given structure of a pre-given text in classic empiricist style; rather, it claims to construct a critique of the text, out of the relation between itself and the discourse of the text, and then examines the conditions of difference (the breaks) between the two discourses which enabled that critique to take place.

But does not this make the neo-structuralist reading simply a kind of reflexive or dialectical structuralism? After all, as in ordinary structuralism, the reader still reads the problematic of the text, its discourse, from the *empirical* absences or presences from the words of a book. It is interesting when listening to Althusserians talking about symptomatic reading that they often talk as if the book itself was empirically absent.[8] Williams has noted this problem also in his brief discussion of Althusser's *lecture symptomale*:

> But, in Althusserian theory, what "lecture symptomale" is required to do is to locate the discrete subject and object in each problematic. The indexical reading of questions and answers does not allow this, at least *without inaugurating a mystery about the connection between what is absent and what is present,* that is the questions and answers which are a kind of incomplete present image of the absent problematic. (Williams, 1974, p. 49)

Indeed, there is a "mystery" in Althusser's thinking over this question of the empirical text, and, to my knowledge, the usual tactic in the Althusserian method is to gloss over this problem of its status (and existence) by an implicit assumption that the symptomatic reader does not see the words etc. of the actual book in front of him. It appears almost as if the object-discourse is whisked in from nowhere by the activation of the reading-discourse. This impression is reinforced by another one—the impression that Althusser ignores statements (actually empirically present) in *Capital* which do not suit his purposes. Now, should that be surprising to us after our analysis of structuralism? For, after all, do not structuralists see the actual words and sentences as mere manifestations of the "deep structure"? From what we have seen already, "pure" structuralism or semiology does not see the elements of the structure as anything but the playthings of the relations of the system. As we have seen, for pure structuralism, the elements of a structure have no internal specificity, relative autonomy nor history. Consequently, in a dialectical form of structuralism which emphasizes reading as a practice and specifies a dialectic between the unconscious discourse of the reader and the unconscious discourse of the object, we should expect to find that the object-discourse is defined entirely by the existence of the reading-discourse, as its dialectical counterpart, its geno-text, or "necessary condition of existence", and that the mediating material, the empirical book, is rendered almost totally immaterial.

Not only does neo-structuralism tend to ignore the elements of the structure (especially the signifiers) like structuralism proper, but it commits a second structuralist crime in assuming (1) that the object-discourse is directly readable through the text without any other recourse, and (2) that there is a centre to be de-centred. The first assumption specifies, even if implicitly, that the analyst can read the words in their "real" or "true" meaning. Thus, in reality, neo-structuralism engages in the structuralist practice of reading the Structure in its effects. Somehow, despite all the talk of dislocation and mediation, the neo-structuralists must assume they know the meaning of the words in their normal use in order to discern the Structure of the text. The second assumption connects to the first. The neo-structuralists assume the normal meaning of the discourse in order that they can de-centre it as the structure of the text. One clearly cannot de-centre a structure unless one can read its presence. This assumption has implications—primarily, that there is a Dominant Ideology, ever-already-present in the discourse of a text. This implication may sound fine to the radical ear, but the problem is that we are back to the universal Absolute Source notion. Neo-structuralism does not question the assumption of a Dominant Ideology, which exists *ever-present in the text* like the "Universal Structure of the Human Mind" (Levi-Strauss); rather, it conceals it by the procedure of an "active reading" which de-centres the Structure. In effect, the neo-structuralist method contains within itself a structuralist denial of the movement, transience and social nature of ideologies; rather, these ideologies form a Structure with no specific origin (or condition of existence). Like structuralism proper, neo-structuralism whisks in its Absolute Source—only the difference is that this time the "whisking in" is consciously done under the aegis of a dialectical 'active reading', performed by a systematic field of significance. In neo-structuralism, ironically, the Structure of Orthodoxy is set up by the concept of de-centring the Structure and, on their own admission, neo-structuralists create their opposition whilst creating their own discursive system. The Dominant Ideology, thus, is as much a product of their fertile imaginations as is the Structure of the Human Mind; it remains a Metaphysical concept with no concrete, social or historical reference.

In conclusion, ideology detection, in this problematic, is the effect of the difference in systematicity between two theoretical discourses brought into contact by the practice of reading. The systematic discourse can detect the closures and breaks of the ideological discourse by juxtaposing itself with the other in the practice of reading. Naturally enough, this problematic also produces a "science". The science is constituted by the systematic discourse. In simple terms, then, science for neo-structuralism is not a body of theory which explains the mediations between the real structure of things and their immediate forms of appearance in social practice, but rather that field of significance which most systematically connects itself, or, if you like, that body of concepts which explains itself the best. Although questions of science must remain largely outside the scope of this discussion, one comment can be made.

It seems to me that, although, neo-structuralism carries a useful definition of science, the problem of the data remains. It is fair to say that theoretical problematics in a sense produce their own "data" and, consequently, that if they can make sense out of that data they are "knowledges" or "sciences". But, this is to solve the question of science one-sidedly. If science involves some form of 'cognitive appropriation of the real' (paraphrasing Marx), then scientificity must lie in the connection between cognition and reality, and not in the field of cognition. Empiricism errs in locating the site of the problem of scientificity in the field of the real, but neo-structuralism (like phenomenology) seems to go to the other extreme by locating the problem in the sphere of cognition. Neo-structuralism seems to have resolved the question of science at the level of theory rather than at the level of the connection between theory and reality. Systematicity provides no guarantees, in my view, that the theory is an accurate and explanatory 'cognitive appropriation of the real'. Scientific theory may be systematic; however, its condition of existence is not systematicity but rather that it explains the nature, mediation and movement of practical appearances and thus acts as the theoretical expression of concrete social relations (see Marx, 1955, p. 95). As Marx said (emphases by C.S.):

> Of course the method of presentation must differ in form from that of inquiry. The latter has to *appropriate the material* in detail, to analyse its different forms of development, to trace out their inner connexion. Only after this work is done, can *the actual movement be adequately described*. If this is done successfully, if the

life of the *subject-matter is ideally reflected as in a mirror*, then it may appear as if we had before us ₐa mere a priori construction. (Marx, 1974, p. 28)

Just because a theory is systematic does not imply that it has explained, or reflected in the abstract, the mechanism and movement of appearances. For example, a systematic theory could occur which explains the internal structure of a social phenomenon at one point in time, yet, because of quantitative changes in that phenomenon over the next period of time, it may change its quality or structure.[9] In consequence, our systematic theory would no longer explain or faithfully reflect the internal structure of the phenomenon. Furthermore, this theory may not even have noticed the changes in the phenomenon because its authors were so busy checking their epistemological assumptions. As a result, it would be unaware that it had ceased to be the theory of the data, and a theory which is not the theory of some thing or condition is only a *general* theory with no immediate relevance to social practice. The new data would be available to the theorist with his systematic theory—*yet, because he was so anxious to be systematic and non-ideological, he would not have made the ideological observations (of the surface changes) necessary to enable and stimulate the development of the old theory.* In short, a scientific theory of social life must not only always check its own assumptions, it must also constantly keep abreast of changes in the phenomenon as they reflect themselves (albeit in complex, mediated fashion) in people's ideological impressions (either in the practices of everyday life or in research practice). Any science that concentrates on systematicity, reflexivity or self-consciousness alone is likely to become theoreticist, speculative, metaphysical, abstract, idealist, old-fashioned, useless and impractical. In the same way, any science that only concentrates on recording new, apparent developments in the world is, on the other hand, likely to become empiricist, pragmatic, 'trendy', unsystematic, illogical, practical but partial, lacking in perspective and fragmented.

My final point on neo-structuralism concerns the fact that Althusser's version restricts itself to complex and systematic or theoretical discourse, whilst Kristeva and Derrida restrict their work to literary products rich in surplus meaning. It would seem that the concepts of neo-structuralism specify the need for it to provide discourses of substantial depth. Without this depth of meaning or width of space created by the theoretical or artistic discouse, neo-structuralism simply cannot work in practice. We should not be surprised that it restricts itself to advanced theoretical disciplines (Althusser), or literature (Kristeva and Derrida), film (Metz) or medical science (Foucault). Neo-structuralism, although its practitioners never admit it, needs *data*. How ironic! The theory that dispensed with the concrete in favour of the Structure finds that it cannot work without forms rich in substance! The real world has come back to haunt the formal skeletons of our structuralist metaphysicians! Just as Slater found that he had to use newspaper editorials thick with ideology in order to make the Structure of Bourgeois Ideology produce the connotations of news reports, so, too, the neo-structuralists require code-sheets rich with repeated connotation to enable them to read off the Structure. One can only conclude that structuralism in all its forms is heavily reliant on its data, even though its practitioners deal with data simply as an effect of the Form. Structuralism grants the elements or substance of a structure no inner determinations and, paradoxically, this is ultimately reflected in its practitioners' search for rich discourses to analyse. Structuralism needs texts rich in ideological substance so that it can proceed with its abstract analysis of their forms without the social nature of this substance becoming problematic.

A mode of reading ideology which wishes to attain scientificity needs to theorize (1) the social nature of ideology-in-general, and (2) the social nature of a particular ideology, before the reading takes place. The scientific identification of ideology, in other words, can only proceed on the basis of an elaborated social theory of ideology-in-general and of the social nature of any particular ideology. Neo-structuralist readings proceed on an inadequate concept of ideology-in-general. They presuppose that the weaknesses in the read-discourse, which they produce, are indicative of the presence of ideology-in-general: hence ideology-in-general is implicitly defined as an unsystematic or closed discourse. Such a definition fails to specify the social conditions for ideology and remains at the level of a description of ideology's effects. Furthermore, neo-structuralist readings proceed without a concept of the social and historical specificity/materiality/objectivity of the particular ideology under examination. Hence they do not, within themselves, provide a theorized identification of an ideology within a definite social and historical conjuncture. All they can provide is an identification of the effects of ideology-in-general within the specific form of appearance of a specific ideology. Their claims to specific "sightings" must as a result remain, in effect, spontaneous, lacking in evidence and polemical. As such they may have great political value, but cannot claim scientific status. The in-built weakness of all forms of structuralism is their refusal to attend to the historicity, materiality and specificity of the substance of a discourse. Viewing content as a mere manifestation or effect of a deep, general semiotic structure, they are unable in practice to identify the precise objectivity of that structure. All that is possible in their practice is the identification of the general effects of ideology on a substantive discourse; and, even then, as I have argued, such an identification remains questionable because of the problems with the definition of ideology implicit in the reading practice.

A Note on the Relation between Althusser's Neo-structuralism and his Reading of Marx

It is not possible here to develop a full analysis of the effects of Althusser's neo-structuralism in his reading of Marx owing to the magnitude of the task. However, given its importance for the socialist movement and given its relevance to the comprehension of the Marxism in this project, I think a note should be made on the question.

The main effect of Althusser's neo-structuralism lies in the question of the elements of the structure. So far I have only analysed this question at a very general level. However, when we look at Althusser's reading of Marx, the critiques in the previous chapters begin to bite with sharp teeth. Neo-structuralism, as we have seen, writes the elements out of significant existence. Althusser's work shows the effects of that in two important ways. Firstly, in his *lecture symptomale*, as we have already noted, there is no discussion of the objective meaning of the words, i.e. of the connection of signs with their constitutive social relations (that is assumed), and their structure is constituted immediately and subjectively from them. Secondly, and more importantly, the *Structure* of the social formation is said to constitute the individual human subject:

... the real protagonists of history are the social relations of production, political struggle and ideology, which are constituted by the place assigned to these protagonists in the complex structure of the social formation . . . The biological men are only the supports or bearers of the guises (Charaktermasken) assigned to them by the structure of relations in the social formation. (Althusser and Balibar, 1970, p. 320)

Here we see a classic example of structuralist idealism and metaphysics: ideas or concepts make history whilst people only act out the role that is set for them by the concepts. Althusser makes the categories fight the battles of history in *Reading Capital*. We know what Marx would have said (emphases in italics by C.S.):

Economic categories are only the theoretical expressions, the abstractions of the social relations of production. (Marx, 1955, p. 95)

The same *men who establish* their social relations in conformity with their material productivity, produce also principles, ideas and categories, in conformity with their social relations. (Marx, 1955, p. 95)

If we abstract thus from every subject all the alleged accidents, animate or inanimate, men or things, we are right in saying that in the final abstraction, the only substance left is the logical categories. Thus the metaphysicians who, in making these abstractions, think they are making analyses and who, the more they detach themselves from things, imagine themselves to be getting all the nearer to the point of penetrating to their core—these metaphysicians in turn are right in saying that things here below are embroideries of which the logical categories constitute the canvas. (Marx, 1955, pp. 92, 93)

... the moment you present men as the *actors* and *authors* of their own history, you arrive . . . at the real starting point, because you have abandoned those eternal principles of which you spoke at the outset. (Marx, 1955, p. 100)

M. Althusser, like M. Proudhon, has made ideas produce history, whilst, for Marx, people make history under the conditios in which they live. Althusser has failed to grasp the interpenetration of the opposites, subjective and objective, because of his structuralism. The forms of subjectivity (consciousness) are determined by the social relations within which they act, yet the existence of these modes of consciousness is purely formal or abstract until they are realized in definite social practices, and in that process of realization they recreate, or revolutionize, the social relations of production. Althusser can only see the Structure, social relations (whether they be economic, political or ideological); human practice is erased in favour of abstract categories which use people as agents. Marx sees people as authors as well as agents. He holds a dialectical comprehension of the two aspects of human existence in social formations. The humanist Marxists are one-sided in allowing people an authorship outside their role as agents of social relations, Althuserian Marxism, on the other hand, is equally one-sided in refusing to see the authorship involved in social life. Both humanism and anti-humanism are non-dialectical positions. For Marx, social life involves the located dialectical combination of the objectivity of matter with the subjectivity of people. Ideology is not simply a "level" of the social formation but an aspect of structured, human practice.

Althusser's neo-structuralism has thus led him to write people out of history in *Reading Capital* (1970). Like all forms of structuralism, Althusserian Marxism only leaves us with the skeletons of the Structure. It is true that capitalism predicates people as "creatures" (Marx) of the system, but some people did create, and most people daily recreate, that system themselves, not in the abstract but under the conditions of specific social practices. Without the work of people the capitalist system would collapse. Althusser's "supports" are vital to all social systems known to history as are the supports of a building (he talks of supports as agents, implying the absence of subjective determination). But forms of consciousness do determine the forms taken by material things and that includes the social relations of practice. Social relations of practice indeed determine forms of subjectivity, but only inasmuch as the subjects continue to reproduce those social relations. Althusser has reduced this highly material and complex dialectic to the historical interplay of abstract forms, or (in Derrida's terms) to a play of differences in a structure, and the historical materiality of the consciousness of the subject is denied the specific degree of effectivity which it has at every level of social practice in every epoch of human history.

Conclusions on the Extant Methods of Reading Ideology

If my analyses in this section of the book have been correct, then it is clear that the existing methods of reading ideology are unsatisfactory. Taking them as a whole, their general defect is that they assume more about the meaning of the words of a text (or, the meaning of the significant units) than they explicitly discover. That is to say, the relations of signification (constituting various ideologies) which these methods allegedly discover are largely assumed *a priori* on the basis of unexplicated premises. This general criticism can be broken down into its component parts in order to clarify the way forward:

The dangers of empiricism

It was one thing for Saint-Simon and Proudhon to observe spontaneously that poverty and misery appeared to be endemic to modern Western economies. But it was another thing altogether when Marx explained that the inner logic of the capitalist mode of production necessitated the existence of poverty and misery on a national and on, eventually, a global scale. Correspondingly, the political remedies of Saint-Simon and Proudhon,[10] far from undermining the capitalist system, would in fact perpetuate it, because they were not founded on principles alien to its logic.

Similarly, it is one thing for content analysts and structuralists (of all kinds) to observe spontaneously that a text contains some sort of ideology, but it is wholly another thing to explain and identify, in one and the same moment, the exact specificity of the ideology in that text. Just as the scientific comprehension and identification of poverty and misery is dependent upon a theory of their conditions of existence and appearance, so, too, the scientific identification of an ideology must be based upon a theory of its conditions of existence and appearance. This is not to imply that we need science before we know what poverty and misery feel like. However, it is to imply that, without science, poverty and misery can be attributed by their recipients to the Will of God, the Laws of Nature or the National Interest and hence become transformed into something other than what they really are (e.g. eternal 'facts of life', 'acceptable living conditions' or 'just rewards'). Without its scientific identification, an ideology can be attributed to individual bias or the social functions of an institution, and so become converted into something else, such as the expression of human uniqueness or institutional corruption.

The problem is the age-old one in social science of the danger of empiricism. What seems to happen is that when a phenomenon is observed spontaneously, the observer associates it etiologically with the circumstances in which it appears. For example, in orthodox criminology, research of an empiricist kind has observed the co-existence of poverty, criminal behaviour, broken family ties and delinquent juvenile gangs within working-class neighbourhoods. From this sighting, criminological researchers have gone on to correlate crime with poverty, broken homes, working class values etc. Rather than seeing all these circumstances (including crime) as normal exigencies of life for a class with a specific position within a particular social structure (and, thus, comprehending the connections between social structure and class conditions), the theory-less researchers took the appearances and attempted to make them explain each other. Similarly, in political economy, observers such as Malthus noted the conjoint appearance of poverty and 'surplus' population, and proceeded to explain poverty by the fact of surplus population.[11] What the political economists cannot grasp is the fact that poverty and a relative surplus population of labourers are *necessary* conjoint effects of the accelerated accumulation of capital, the essential inner mechanism of capitalist societies. Like orthodox criminology, political economy lacks explicit, systematic theory and continues by confounding appearances with their causative mechanism.

Until a social science learns that the outward appearances or impressions gained in social practice are not identical with the inner essences of social structure, it remains trapped within a vicious circle. The trap is set when appearances (*A* and *B*) are statistically correlated on the basis of the idea that their regular co-existence proves that *A* causes *B*. In such a research practice, what inevitably emerges is the problem of "the other variables". A correlation may be statistically established but the researcher in practice can never actually prove that the variables are causally and exclusively connected. Consequently, there are increasing cries for improved statistical technique and a tendency to link increasing numbers of variables together. Eventually a situation is reached where all the conjoint appearances of an apparent social setting are statistically correlated in a multifactorial analysis and the researchers are presented with the problem of weighting their causal efficacy. At this point, if theory is not brought in from the cold, the discipline must go on to study weighting and scaling methods and the cry for better techniques takes on a new form. After that, the original problem of explanation is a mere Holy Grail—never to be captured, but always sanctioning the adventure of the quest. Research projects become valued in terms of the technical excellence of their methods and the researcher is judged by his ability to provide an imaginative discussion of the results of his applied technology. Good statistical techniques and a butterfly imagination become more important than systematic theorization which describes and explains the emergence of the social mechanism producing the phenomenal appearances. In this process, what gets lost is the point that statistically significant correlations of appearances merely indicate that their conjoint existence is no coincidence and that the explanation of one of them will probably be at least a partial explanation of the other (see Willer and Willer, 1973).

The practice of empiricist epistemology tends to push etiological social science into a cul-de-sac. It seems to divert attention from the specificity of a thing and direct research towards its forms of appearance. The peculiarity of empiricism is its insistence on the transparency of the real. It thus effectively limits the development of theory; the precise reality of the real becomes overshadowed by the technology for linking appearances. Implicit assumptions and ideas direct this technology, but are rarely confessed in public. In the reading of ideologies, we observed these same effects. Content analysis, speculative criticism, semiology and lecture symptomale are all practices which fetishize an unexplicated technique. They are all characterized by the woolliness of their application and the implicit nature of their founding principles.

Spontaneous reading of ideologies from their forms of appearance is a practice likely to locate the source of an ideology in the immediate circumstances of its appearance in any particular social setting. On the one hand, the humanistic readings of content analysis and speculative criticism tend to see an ideology as the expression of a human author's "world-view", inculcated perhaps by "professional socialization" or "political indoctrination". On the other hand, the anti-humanist readings of the structuralists and neo-structuralists tend to produce a view of an ideology as the consequence of the social function of the practice in which it is expressed. Thus, in readings of press reports, spontaneous readings of a humanist variety result in the ideology being blamed on the journalists, whereas those of an anti-humanist variety result in the ideology being attributed to the social function of the press. Both these tendencies have a similar weakness: they conflate the nature and origin of an ideology with the circumstances of its specific historical form of appearance. Reading practices which attempt to read off the essence of an ideology from a specific form of its social existence (in a discourse or practice) are likely to lead to the regular confusion of the conditions of existence of a specific ideology with those of its appearance in a specific historical instance.

Dialectical materialism, the method of Marxian analysis (and perhaps all sciences), demands that things be grasped not only as they appear in a particular manner and context in a given social practice, but also, and most importantly for the purposes of explanation, in their conditions of existence and forms of development. Because of this, and because Marxian theory holds that each ideology is generated within a specific social practice, it is not possible to read with certainty the presence of a determinate ideology in a particular phenomenal context without (1) a theory of the specificity of that ideology as it is given by its generative social conditions of existence, and (2) a theory of the structure of the phenomenal context itself. What happens to an ideology after its birth must not lead us into thinking that its essential nature is identical to any of its specific, historical forms of appearance. We can only begin to trace the different forms adopted by an ideology when we have specified its inner and unique character. The existing methods of reading ideology carry no such specifications and, therefore, cannot justify their sightings to any satisfactory degree; at least, not without adducing evidence which is prohibited by their explicit methodological canons. Ideologies only ever exist in situated movement and to determine their presence and role in each situation it is vital to distinguish between their conditions of existence and their forms of appearance: existing reading methods neglect this distinction to their cost. Without a conception of the specificity of the ideology in question, the analyst cannot identify the range of signifying units capable of relating to a range of signified meanings. These two related sets embody the historical forms of variation of an ideology and a knowledge of them is necessary (logically and historically) to the reading of an ideology's presence in a specific significant form. Relations of signification are never just whisked out of the imagination, they are always pre-constituted by history. Empiricism may think that it can do without a theory of history, but its neglect does not prevent history from creeping in through the back door of the reading imagination. How then can empiricist reading practice sort out the contingent from the essential and cause from effect? Without analytic categories to capture the origin, nature and mediated development of the ideological form, empiricists cannot specify precisely the determinations which congeal in the concrete significant entity.

The mystification of commonsense

No one needs the mystifying language of structuralism or the magical use of statistics by content analysis in order to carry out a spontaneous reading of ideology in its forms of appearance. Anyone alive can engage in such a reading. Only speculative criticism avoids the charge that its procedures and terminology glorify and conceal what are essentially commonsense reading practices: at least, that particular method is honest. All the other methods must lead to the uninitiated believing that their own spontaneous readings are inadequate.

The everyday practice of reading other people's discourse can be usefully contrasted with the empiricism of the practices of the scholars dealt with here. This contrast will expose that empiricism even more starkly than the theoretical criticisms made so far. In ordinary, practical social existence, we are continually "reading" other people's discourse. It must happen a thousand times a day. What methods do we routinely use to establish, for all practical purposes, the meaning the communicator is conveying? How do we discern ideology (or, as it would be known in workaday parlance, bias, prejudice, slant, interest, intention) on a routine, practical basis? It is obviously outside the scope of my analysis to answer this question in any depth; however, I would suggest that there are certain common techniques:

1. The perception of repetitions of statements, words or phrases.
2. The perception of assumptions contained in certain statements and accompanying gestures.

3. The observation of inconsistencies within an argument or between the argument of one day and that of the next.
4. The observation that certain topics are never dealt with in the discourse.
5. The grasp of the general drift of a systematic discourse or series of discourses.

Repetition, assumption, inconsistency, neglect and substance are all read routinely as significant discursive phenomena. The perception of their existence leads us to make interpretations or readings of that significance; interpretations which are purely speculative and are often recognized as such. These readings take on a more certain, dogmatic character when we can link them to other facts relating to the speaker or writer, e.g. his job, his domestic relations, his reputed character, his explicit statements of his attitude to life, and so on.

The fact is that all these techniques for the attribution of significance are used by the academic readers criticized in this text. Content analysis in its pure form uses method (1) and in its less pure form it includes methods (2) and (5). Information theory, if it was operationalized in this field, would concentrate on method (2). Speculative criticism tends to focus on methods (1), (2) and (5), although in its well-developed forms, such as literary criticism, all the methods would be used. Structuralism uses method (1) implicitly and methods (2) and (5) explicitly. Neo-structuralism again uses (1) implicitly but explicitly employs the other four methods. In passing, we can note that this comparison of use of everyday reading techniques indicates the validity of the neo-structuralist claim to engage in a highly "rigorous" reading practice.

The empiricism of all the reading practices dealt with in this work is illustrated by this analysis. Practical, everyday, spontaneous reading techniques are the very foundation of the academic reading practices. My conclusion that, essentially, the allegedly scientific modes of reading ideology promulgated hitherto are spontaneous and thoroughly empiricist seems well-founded. Like everyday practices of reading ideology, they have remained content with the view that ideology is transparent in its effects. The underdevelopment of their theories of ideology prevents them from rising above spontaneous reading to something more scientific. In fact, I may be doing an injustice to non-academic readers of ideology; everyday readings arguably take more account of the history and context of a discourse than do academic readings.

It seems to me that to improve on commonsense and to establish a reading practice which could make some claim to scientific status, it is necessary to investigate in detail the conditions of existence and appearance of an ideology. With knowledge of its nature, history and context, an ideology's appearance can be established and described with more certainty and precision than that of the methods of commonsense. Having said that, however, it would be wrong to urge the renunciation of spontaneous reading. Let it be clear that I am not suggesting that spontaneous reading can or should be abandoned. It must always be with us (and will often be the first kind of reading practised by the researcher). Indeed a spontaneous reading may offer new insights and generate new ideas for further systematic investigation. Science develops out of commonsense, not apart from it. However, what should also be stressed is that scientific investigations can enlighten and sensitize commonsense. More knowledge of the history, nature, forms and functions of bourgeois ideologies should assist proletarian organizations in their political struggles. Subjectivity needs no apology; nor does it need to be dressed up in scientific garments. The proletariat has no need of the bourgeois scientist's self-justifications. However, using the available facilities, the social scientist in bourgeois society can improve upon spontaneous readings to heighten the spontaneous consciousness of the exploited classes through the production and dissemination of detailed knowledge about important ideologies and their social nature. The methods of reading ideology criticized in this book do not offer much to those deprived of research facilities which they could not have discovered for themselves.

The politics of science

The practices of reading ideology discussed here are, ultimately, no more than spontaneous efforts in the political struggle for the ideological hegemony of the working classes. It is true that by allowing evidence strictly prohibited by their methods, or by operating on implicit knowledge about society and history, the products of some researches have gone beyond that which could have been observed spontaneously. But that is incidental for my purposes. More important is the fact that these methods are essentially political with a subsidiary scientific pay-off, rather than essentially scientific with a subsidiary political pay-off.

It is worthwhile recalling that quantitative content analysis emerged in the service of the U.S. government during a period of war (both military and ideological), that the speculative critics have often got clear political purposes (e.g. Young was concerned to demystify stereotypes of deviance and link them to the power structure), that Barthes, the leading semiologist, desired the liberation of true signification from the stifling myths of bourgeois ideology, and that Althusser wanted to restore Marx to himself in order to rejuvenate Marxism-Leninism. Basically, the practice of ideology detection hitherto has involved one side claiming that the other side purveys ideology and legitimating that claim by legislating (overtly or covertly) for the scientificity of its own reading. Content analysts back their claims to scientificity with statistics, structuralists back theirs with talk of magical, universal structures, and the neo-structuralists point to the super-systematicity of their general concepts. To be fair to the speculative critics, many of them would not lay claim to scientificity. However, many of them would lay claim to an extra sensitivity or political correctness which adds a different kind of legitimacy to their readings. On the whole, the practice of reading ideology in discursive materials has merely involved the blanket specification of an opposed viewpoint as ideological. The practice so far, therefore, has been the site of an ideological struggle over the real. There has been little debate over the precise nature of the ideological: ideology has simply been identified in its difference, as the version of 'the truth' which differs from that of the reader. It has been the proclaimed outcome of a clash between two different forms of spontaneous, political consciousness.

I have no desire to cite my proposed scientific programme for the study of ideologies outside political conflicts. I merely conceive of the relationship between reading ideology and politics in a different manner to other writers. Firstly, political purposes and values are best aided by soundly conceived research. Put bluntly, science serves radical politics better than speculative commonsense: that seems to be true whatever context one applies it to. The 20 odd years which Marx spent bookworming in his den to produce *Capital* have served socialism better than a million rapidly produced, ill-conceived polemics. Secondly, political values must be uppermost when deciding which ideologies to investigate systematically. To call for scientific research is not to call for pointless burrowing in libraries. Thirdly, the produce of science can be used by the radical polemicists who prefer, or are forced into, the production of popular literature.

What I want to develop and encourage is a reading of ideologies which is fully informed by a theory and knowledge of history: a reading which knows what it is looking for and can support its identifications strongly. The reading of ideologies cannot remain bogged down in empiricism and polemic because it is politically urgent to be able to trace the history and source of specific, politically effective ideologies. Spontaneous identification and public berating of such ideologies are not enough: they are likely to have only minimum plausibility, except to the converted. Ideologies need to be placed in their historical origins, contextual variations and social functions for their public exposure to be fully effective. Scientific investigation serves these ends. Scientific enquiry is distinguished from spontaneous observation by the fact that it employs developed theories which improve on simpler or previous notions, refined methods which are sharper than cruder instruments, and carefully established data (or appearances) which its theories explain. The reading of ideologies has been almost entirely lacking in an explicit, developed theoretical base and its implicit assumptions operated without check on appearances of a limited and unquestioned nature. Without a theory of the precise materiality or historical specificity of an ideology, the work has barely risen beyond the level of a slanging match.

The question of circularity or hermeneutics

> . . . it seems necessary to understand the social context in which this play [*Hamlet*—C.S.] was written in order to interpret it, whilst at the same time we have to interpret *Hamlet* in order to understand that context. (Keat and Urry, 1975, p. 173)

Is it the case that thus far I am assuming something which contradicts the argument inherent in my critique? If we investigate, as I am saying we should, an ideology's historical sources and previous forms of appearance, do we not at some point have to assert the meaning of significant units of a discourse without any other resort?

Given an historical period chosen for research, how do we read the first relevant signification within that period without recourse to prior historical evidence? Do we select and read it spontaneously? If not, do we regress into the past—a course which leads us into a regress to the Original Signification? To avoid this absurd regress, what assumptions do we make? This colossal question in its present form and in other forms has necessitated much thought by myself and by others. I venture an answer with some trepidation.

To begin with, I could argue that I am insisting that the historical materialist reading of ideologies starts with social relations and determines the ideologies which they necessitate in their practical operation. It does not start with discourses and induce from them their generative social relations. But, to say this is not in any way to forget that to establish a knowledge of social relations, the historical materialist can only work from the initial evidence, the appearances of social life. But this evidence is composed of people, institutions, events, social practices and apparent beliefs. In other words, the initial evidence has embodied within it the effects of social ideologies (the very objects of the ultimate analysis) as well as the effects of social relations. To establish the existence of certain social relations, therefore, would we not have to read the ideologies-to-be-studied spontaneously? We could not justify our reading by an as yet undiscovered knowledge of social relations. Nor could we ignore the existence of the relevant social ideologies since they are inherent in the initial evidence: to determine the social relations underpinning the appearances of social life we would need to understand the ideologies which corresponded with, or at least were co-ordinated with, those social relations in the human production of specific social forms. If this is a correct analysis, historical materialism is caught up in the hermeneutic circle, just like other approaches (albeit in a way peculiar to itself): to read the social ideologies we need to know the social relations at work, but to comprehend social relations we need to know the social ideologies at work. So to dismiss the hermeneutic problem as a problem of bourgeois philosophy is false: it is also a problem for Marxian analysis.

How then is the problem resolved? Keat and Urry suggest that mediating the gap between a discourse and its social context are a series of shared rules of communication which enable communicators to understand each other (Keat and Urry, 1975, pp. 173,

174). Consequently praising the project of ethnomethodology, they argue that the discovery of these rules enables us to bridge the gap between discourse and context on the grounds that the rules of communication inhere within both discourse and context. Whilst allowing that Keat and Urry did not set out to resolve the hermeneutics problem systematically, it is nevertheless true that they beg the obvious question: how do we determine these rules of communication without assuming an *a priori* knowledge of them? Using either the discourse or the context as a justification is inadmissible since that use itself raises the question of circularity.

Martin Hollis takes the debate much further (see Hollis, 1967a, b, 1977). Simplifying his sophisticated discussion (not entirely out of recognition), we can say that Hollis also argues that we need to know the rules in operation before we can understand either a discourse or an action. Both "social action" and discourse can only be understood as "the rational expression of intention within rules" (1977, p. 186). Rules, for Hollis, are the social context of either discourse or action. Once we understand the rules we understand the discourse or action. To understand the rules, Hollis correctly argues, it is not enough to employ a bilingual or an "insider" for that merely displaces the question (or passes the buck) without answering it. What is necessary is to assume that the discourse or action is rational:

> To grasp the rules, I must grasp the thoughts; to grasp the thoughts, I must grasp the rules; I can break the circle only by imputing rationality. (Hollis, 1977, p. 153)

This assumption gave the researcher a "bridgehead" into the problem and enabled him to link thought with thought and thought with real referent: thus enabling him to induce the operative rules of communication and/or conduct and to understand the meaning of the discourse or action. Once we understand the rules we can go on to identify irrational actions and inconsistent statements: the bridgehead assumption is only of an *a priori* kind, it is not intended to be an empirical one.

Clearly, Hollis's notion of the bridgehead is crucial. Let us examine it more closely:

> To establish a bridgehead, by which I mean a set of utterances definitive of the standard meanings of words, he [the anthropologist—C.S.] has to assume at least that he and the native

> share the same perceptions and make the same empirical judge-
> ments in simple situations. This involves assumptions about
> empirical truth and reference, which in turn involve crediting
> the natives with his own skeletal notion of logical reasoning.
> (Hollis, 1970b, p. 238)

In essence, it seems to me, that this proposal is analogous to the
semiologists' assumption of a denotative code and the structuralists'
assumption that newspaper editorials are code-sheets for the
ideologies at work in the condensed discourse of the news reports.
But how can we make this assumption without presupposing that
we understand the social context of the discourse? Here, of course, I
give social context a much wider meaning than do Hollis (1977) and
Winch (1973), who limit it to the realm of subjective norms or
ideological rules. Without assumptions or knowledge about the
economic and political realities of a situation, our assumptions about
denotative codes, ideological stocks or symbolic rules are literally
impossible to justify. I do not disagree with Hollis that we need to
assume the predominance of rationality: to disagree would be
irrational since it is plain that to understand an exception it is
necessary to know the rule. But what I would contend is that to
assume rationality *a priori* is vacuous unless it has empirical viability.
Now, to discover the rationality of a statement in a particular social
context one would need to know the details of the social context,
broadly defined. If capitalist X announces publicly that worker Y,
standing motionless outside the factory holding a placard, is a
"wrecker" and "a threat to industrial peace", it would be impossible
to understand the rationality of X's statement without a knowledge
of the economic structure within which they exist. Merely to impute
rationality of itself would not enable us to say anything. In short,
Hollis's solution is no solution at all and we appear to be back
where we started.

This apparent conclusion is shored up by the fact that Hollis
admits at the end of his book, *Models of Man* (1977), that his main
thesis (that rational action is its own explanation) is best suited to
individual actions and fails to account for the construction of social
contexts (in the broad sense) and social revolutions. He, himself, is
forced to conclude that reason-explanations are only "the alpha" and
structural accounts "the omega" for plausible (his term) socio-
historical accounts. He thus implies that the imputation of rationality

is only a minute methodological device in the analysis of societal phenomena, which are constructed by much more than individual negotiations. However, our conclusion is a deceptive appearance. To take it as valid and to berate Hollis for his analytic individualism would lead us up a blind alley. In his diatribe against structural accounts, Hollis has in fact posited something which we can share: that, normally, social practices contain an inner rationality which is a part cause of the eventual social product. In my view, that rationality should not be located solely within the practitioner's mind; it is a contingent rather than necessary possibility that the practitioner correctly understands the links between his movement, his purpose, his material context and his social relations. Rather, the inner rationality of social practices necessarily lies within the connections between their constituent elements. It is in the light of the connections between movement, purpose, material context and social relations that we can say that a practice is rational. The internal logic of a social practice constitutes its rationality.

It seems to me that when historical materialism attempts to specify the social structures which account for the appearances of social life (the given, available evidence—carefully scrutinized, of course), it is in fact implicitly positing that social structures are *necessarily* linked with those appearances. Events, institutions, statements, geographical contexts, demographic trends etc.—the palpable appearances of practice—what are these things but merely the discernible elements of practice? All the historical materialist does is to specify the social relations which necessitate the discernible appearances selected for study and all that is done is based upon the (usually implicit) assumption that the links are not contingent but necessary. Thus, Hollis is right. It *is* necessary to make an *a priori* assumption in order to begin to unpick the complex interpenetration of structure, context and signification. All that the researcher sees at first is the condensed unity of diverse determinations: concrete appearances. These fleeting moments do not leave signposts to their inner structure: they are very reticent creatures. So we need a bridgehead, but Hollis's *a priori* assumption is inadequate for the analysis of social phenomena, as he himself concludes. It is not enough to assume that the actor is rational, acting intentionally according to normative or ideological codes. Nor is it sufficient to add the assumption that we all see the same physical entities. For the assumption to be sufficient we also need to assume (1) that the discourse or action is carried out within the parameters of certain social relations, and (2) that the social relations, the subjective state and the physical context are linked to each other in a causal matrix. In short, the bridgehead assumption of historical materialism has four constituent elements: subjective rationality, physical reality, social structure and the internal logic of a practice.

It is my contention that historical materialist analyses make this bridgehead assumption all the time, yet rarely elucidate it. Hollis is correct to say that the elucidation of such an assumption is necessary and that one cannot argue that the hermeneutic must simply be resolved empirically. Empirical research is theoretically based and theories must be made plain. If any Marxist objects to my submission on the grounds that assumptions about rationality are things done by bourgeois philosophers, my reply would be that these assumptions are made for a reason: try doing an analysis of a discourse without any bridging assumption. As I have said, we do not need to accept just any bridging assumption. The one I have put forward seems to contain all the elements necessary to begin to decode the ideological components of social artefacts or discourses in a situation where one has no further resort (such as a developed socio-historical knowledge).

The bridging assumption appropriate to historical materialism clearly centres on its key concept of social praxis as a societally located, historical action carried out by actors, purposively in the light of their ideologies, within specific structural and material contexts. Like any other *a priori* bridging notion, it stands to be disproved in some particular instances, e.g. where a discourse bears no necessary relation to its context or the actor's purposes. But, like other bridging assumptions, it is necessary in order to be able to establish the 'irrationality' of such phenomena. Similarly, it has a practical function—to enable the researcher to begin building up a knowledge of the ideologies of the people studied. Our assumption is necessary in two key situations:

1. Where the research starts from scratch and the researcher is trying to establish the social relations which explain a number of carefully established, empirical, historical regularities. The discovery of the social relations is dependent upon a knowledge, however provisional, of the ideologies contained in the practices which produced the historical regularities.

2. Where the researcher, as posited at the beginning of this section, has selected an historical period on the basis of a knowledge of social relations and wishes to read the first relevant discourse within that period.

It could be said that the second situation is easier for the researcher than the first because he has at least got a knowledge of the relevant social relations and can therefore posit certain necessary ideologies. In the first situation, he has to make commonsensical guesses about the social relations at work. It could also be said that, on (say) a 48th analysis of an ideology at a later historical juncture, the researcher does not need the bridging assumption at all because he has detailed socio-historical knowledge, built up from the previous 47 analyses, about the nature of the actors' ideology, the situations in which it is operative, the forms it takes, the social relations it presupposes, and its relation with the other elements of a particular social practice.

Both these things could be said fairly but it should be clear that what successive analyses achieve is the filling out and refinement of the initial assumption. That is, the frequency of analysis does not do away with the assumption but merely gives it empirical substance and a more advanced theoretical form. The bridging assumption is always operative, it merely becomes easier to employ as the analysis is repeated. In other words, successive analyses produce increasingly precise (theoretically and empirically) approximations to an understanding of the relation of necessity between an ideology and its social context. In the end, there would probably be such an ideal, mirror-reflection between ideology and context that "it may appear as if we had before us a mere *a priori* construction" (Marx, 1974). In general, our initial *a priori* construction would probably have acquired a number of qualifying conditions, but such improvements could only benefit subsequent researches. In particular, the initially assumed connections between certain ideologies and specific contexts would probably have long been superceded by a much more explanatory notion of those connections. If we were only looking at the connections within one culture, the first few analyses would probably establish the basic structure of the final conception. For that final conception to be developed further, a cross-cultural study would be needed.

One further misunderstanding must be corrected before we conclude this section. It is not necessary, in my argument, to abandon the use of bilinguals, translations, insider's accounts or actors' own accounts of their beliefs. All I am saying is that, like Hollis, I do not believe that these devices can be used outside a bridging assumption. The information which they provide is itself subject to the requirements of that assumption and can be judged accordingly. That is, translations must make sense in the light of the physical situation, the subject's purposiveness, the social structure pertaining, and the historico-logical relations between these three elements of practice in a given societal context.

In conclusion, the problem of hermeneutics is a vicious one and cannot be ignored. All hitherto resolutions depend on some bridging assumption which enables the researcher to begin decoding the discourse or ideologies under study. In my view such assumptions are necessary, otherwise mindless empiricism ensues. Existing assumptions usually involve the positing of a social consensus over norms, denotative codes, or modes of reasoning. All these are inadequate in my view. I have replaced them with an assumption that requires no consensus but which supposes that most social signification is connected necessarily to a social context, composed of purposive action, ideologies, material circumstances and social relations. Thus, to begin decoding, the researcher needs a little information and plenty of guesswork about the social context. Ideology is an integral part of social practice. That has been my thesis all along. It thus acts appropriately as my bridging assumption into the problem of reading ideology. In a sense, the history of knowledge is the history of bridging assumptions and my own is merely the product of the perceived inadequacy of previous assumptions and also, of course, of the social contexts which lead me to elaborate on this truth rather than on any other. Rational action is not its own explanation: even good approximations only ensue from a socially contextualized focus on specific aspects of reality. The study of ideology is not merely limited to the study of false consciousness, as Hollis would have it; good reasons may explain our beliefs to a degree, but they are only one element of our social practice—there are others which are also determinant.

Existing modes of reading ideology are thus insufficient. A more explicit method is required based on the understanding of social relations: a method which therefore requires the general concepts and specific theories to comprehend history. Fundamentally, the emphasis has now been shifted from the internal relations of the discourse to the contexts in which such relations are generated, operated and maintained. Since internal discursive relations are still important we need not throw away our old commonsensical methods of identifying them; rather they continue, but under the aegis of an explicitly theorized method of reading ideologies. Method is not abandoned but developed. Barthes' desire to consign reading to the pleasure of the humanities makes no sense since any reading involves socio-historical knowledge (Barthes, 1977). Commonsense methods, however reflexive or however spontaneous, now operate within the application of the "bridging assumption", which turns out to be our initial thesis. Once the bridgehead into the historical material is established, repeated analysis provides successively greater approximations of the relations between ideology and social context, approximations which give us a knowledge of the specificity of social ideologies and enable us to identify their operation in contemporary culture with some certainty.

Notes

1. This section draws mainly from Derrida's programmatic statements of 1970 and 1972.
2. We can note how Derrida's concept of the structure-in-movement of significance is extremely similar to Althusser's concept of the social structure:

> Instead of the ideological myth of the philosophy of origins and its organic concepts, Marxism establishes in principle the recognition of the givenness of the complex structure of any concrete "object", a structure which governs both the development of the object and the development of the theoretical practice which produces the knowledge of it. There is no longer any original essence, only an ever-pre-givenness, however far knowledge delves into its past . . . There is no longer any original simple unity (in any form whatsoever), but instead, *the ever-pre-givenness of a structured complex unity.* (Althusser, 1969, pp. 198, 199).

3. By "projectivism", Kristeva (1971) seems to mean guesswork or speculation. Structuralism always masks simple materialities with the convoluted terminology of their essences or forms. The very incomprehensibility of the structuralist discourse is built into its thinking: it *is* hard to express essences in simple terms.

4. Foucault's "archaeology" seems to represent the same operation.
5. The very fact of the footnote at this juncture (Althusser and Balibar, 1970, p. 25) indexes again the problem of structuralism in Althusser's discourse.
6. Althusser's concept of the social totality as a structure-in-dominance is not the advance it seems. It simply operates the neo-structuralist view of the dislocated, non-expressivist relation between the base structure and its effects. Thus the economy is seen as the basic structure of a social formation and politics and ideology are its organic, although relatively autonomous, products. However, Althusser's conception does move a step away from the notion that each element in a system is equally weighted; he is able to conceive of unequal weighting of elements and of the uneven development of different elements.
7. And, for that matter, Alvin Gouldner's "reflexive sociology": see Gouldner (1971).
8. See, for example, Taylor (1972, esp. pp. 342 and 349). See also Hindess and Hirst: "These concepts [of modes of production–C.S.] are abstract, their value is not limited by the analysis of the concrete. As concepts they can have a theoretical function even if concrete conditions to which they are pertinent do not exist, have not existed and will not exist" (1975, p. 321). As the authors note, because they do not analyse "concrete conditions" they cannot be accused automatically of speculation. However, they do seem to ignore the issue of the relationship of concrete conditions to the construction of their concepts. Do these concepts "work" in the analysis of concrete conditions? How important were historical analyses of concrete conditions for the construction of the concepts?
9. See, for example, Marx on the quantitative changes that led to qualitative changes in the very nature of the English mode of production (1974, p. 192).
10. The reorganization of society by a scientific and Christian elite and the enforced exchange of products at their value, respectively.
11. ". . . by the absolute over-growth of the labouring population." (Marx, 1974, p. 594).

Part Three

Reading Ideologies in the Law: An Historical Materialist Method

7   An Historical Materialist Method of Reading Ideologies

It is, in reality, much easier to discover by analysis the earthly core of the misty creations of religion, than, conversely, it is to develop from the actual relations of life the corresponding celestialised forms of those relations. The latter method is the only materialistic, and therefore the only scientific one. (Marx, 1974, p. 352, n.2.)

Introduction

The critique in Part Two has indicated the weaknesses of existing reading methodologies and the basis of a new approach (the threads of which I shall pull together at the end of this chapter). However, it has also made it clear that Marxism has not yet extended its basic concepts very far. This feeling is promoted by the fact that my conclusion on reading method throws all the weight onto the following theoretical categories: social practice, social relation or structure, necessity and appearance. These general categories need to be explicated further in order to make my proposed historical materialist reading method a viable tool for empirical analysis. It is true that to do empirical analysis one would need to rely on the more specific categories of capital, feudalism, the earlier modes of production, bourgeoisie, petit bourgeoisie, proletariat, etc. But it seems to me that these concepts are in a different group to those centred on the general concept of social practice. Thus I feel justified in limiting myself in this chapter to those theoretical specifications which are immediately necessary for the formulation of a general method of reading ideologies.

The implications of this procedure are interesting. Firstly, it is clear that the formulations in the texts of Marx are insufficiently elaborated to enable the immediate description of a general reading method. Secondly, knowing that ideologies are simple or complex significations generated in specific social relations and practical contexts is not of itself enough to enable us to do improved empirical analysis. Thirdly, the latter requires us to focus on the conception of social practice and that means that, like voluntarist or bourgeois sociologies of meaning, Marxism needs to explicate a conception of the micro level of social life. Fourthly, one is reminded of the centrality of praxis in Marxian thought. This concept has got lost over the last few years in the process of explicating Marx's theory of international capital and its necessary implications. As outlined here, the conception of social practice plays the same role in Marxian analysis as do various models of man in other intellectual traditions: it is a fundamental conception that underpins all the more specific concepts. We are reminded that, although the post-1845 writing of Marx explicates the dynamics of specific economic practices in a way which contradicts his earlier works in many respects, it is still true that Marx juxtaposed his concept of social practice and the bourgeois concept of individual action in the manuscripts of 1844:

> Not only is the material of my activity given to me as a social product (as is even the language in which the thinker is active): my *own* existence *is* social activity, and therefore that which I make of myself, I make of myself for society and with the consciousness of myself as a social being. (Marx and Engels, 1975, p. 298)

> Above all we must avoid postulating 'society' again as an abstraction vis-a-vis the individual. The individual *is the social being*. His manifestations of life—even if they may not appear in the direct form of *communal* manifestations of life carried out in association with others—*are* therefore an expression and confirmation of social life. . . . Thinking and being are thus certainly *distinct*, but at the same time they are in *unity* with each other. (Marx and Engels, 1975, p. 299)

Despite the Feuerbachian character of the 1844 manuscripts, a distinct conception of social practice takes shape. There is a break in

Marx's work in 1845 but one can only understand it as a break because of the very continuities which sustained his theoretical development.

Social Practice in General

All ideologies originate within social practices and, once formed, are integral to their operation and development. Ideologies can also be operative within social practices other than their necessitating practices. They may act in the structuring of new practices. Some practices may tolerate or use ideologies developed elsewhere. Origination, tolerance, use, maintenance and structuring capacity are all possibilities which must be distinguished and examined for their function in a social formation. A social formation is a totality of social practices interconnected in a variety of ways and fundamentally circumscribed, ranked and influenced by the structure of economic (social) practice.

It is necessary to explicate the common elements, or general internal determinations, of social practice because there is always a danger that social practice will be reduced to an originating human subject. Social practice is not just the chosen action of its human agents, although it may appear as such to people in practice.

Every social practice is relatively autonomous. That is, it has its own dynamic and context, whilst remaining related to other social practices. Its internal nature and its relation to other practices are mutually interpenetrating opposites within a given social formation; a situated interpenetration which is the theoretical key to the empirical, historical analysis of the state of any one practice.

The internal composition of any social practice is as follows:

A. The elements
   1. Raw material or matter worked upon.
   2. Human beings in conscious activity.
   3. Means or instruments of the action.
   4. The social and geographical context of the action.
   5. The immediate, material product of the action.
B. The class and technical relations between these elements, i.e. the social relations.

This definition represents a development of Althusser's and Balibar's conception (see 1970, pp. 165–181 and 209–225) in the light of my observations on their work in Chapter 2. Ideologies, in my conception, are active features of elements 2 and 4. It is through human action and interaction that they are integral and active elements of all social practice.

I have included social and geographical contexts within this definition simply because they are not external to social practice. There is an interpenetration between a practice and its containing social formation. This relation is effected not only in the forms of elements 1–3 but also in the social and geographical context in which a practice is located. Practices do take place in typical socio-geographical contexts and, at a minimum, we can say that not all such contexts permit their operation. Moreover, practices necessitate certain socio-geographical conditions. Consequently, such conditions must be seen as integral components of social practice. For example, "the city" is not an external thing separate from advanced capitalist economic practice, but an integral element of its functioning.

All social practices have these components. How then do we distinguish one social practice from another? By their raw materials, their purpose, their produce, their socio-geographical context or their instruments of production? One thing is clear: it is theoretically possible to distinguish practices by any of the five elements of their operation, and different classifications have been tried, but it should not be forgotten that the elements of a practice are only constituted as such under the aegis of specific social relations. That is, one has to remember that social practices only exist as integrated totalities. Thus, to distinguish between them at the level of the particular, one must compare them as wholes. Similarities or differences in one element will not be decisive. No one criterion is decisive: although it would not be out of order to compare historical practices according to their instruments of production (for example), providing one did not use this element as the only distinguishing criterion. The decision, I think, rests on the balance of total similarities and differences. Of course, this is only to consider distinctions between individual practices *in themselves*. One can distinguish between them in terms of their social function, for example, in terms of their effects on ruling class domination. It must, however, always be remembered, when doing this type of comparison, that essentially different practices could have the same social function. One can distinguish between substantially similar practices according to the differences in the social relations under which they are carried out, but this would only be justifiable as a study in the effects of different social structures. One could go on, but the point is clear: comparisons on various criteria can be made providing that their purposes are made clear and that their limitations (in the light of the theoretical model) are recognized.

Ideologies are important features of social practice since (1) they define the purpose of the practice, (2) they define the actor's reasons for engaging in the practice and his mode of engagement (and disengagement), (3) they form part of the social context of the practice, (4) they will effect the shape of the product, (5) they will be generated within the practice, and (6) they will be embodied (as past forms) in the material conditions (the raw material, the tools, the geography, etc.). Some practices will involve ideologies more centrally than others: compare brick-laying with news production. Note, however, that I make that point whilst at the same time maintaining that brick-laying is not a purely economic, ideology-free practice. Clearly, where ideologies themselves are the tools and raw materials of the practice they have an exceptional importance in relation to the other elements. Thus the role of ideology in some practices is more complex than in others.

One final point on social practice in general is that it could be said that my model seems to generalize outwards from economic production. Am I working on an economic analogy? The answer is no. If a practice can be thought of which fails to conform to this model then the model is wrong and needs development. Even thinking itself conforms to the model, given that I hold significations to be real entities. The fact that economic practice conforms to the model is only to be expected if the model is correct. It should be realized that I choose this conception rather than any other (e.g. the concepts of behaviour, action and conduct) not because Marx seemed to hold to it but because it seems to be a better conception for analysing the patterns of social existence. It seems to offer more insights, generate more questions and lead to less confusion than any other conception. Behaviour and social action are too narrow to grasp the full social nature of human movement. 'Behaviour' ignores the integral and connected relevance of matter, structure, context and ideas. 'Action' mitigates the relevance of matter, structure and context. Patterns of human movement seem to me to be differentiated according to the connections between conscious people, matter, structure and contexts. One cannot understand a physical movement by a human being outside of its context (material, structural and ideological) and the ideologically constituted reasons for its commission and procedure. The concept of social practice, as outlined here, forms the matrix of historical materialist knowledge.

For the purposes of general analysis, it is useful to simplify matters. To this end, a typology of social practices is often employed. I would wish to continue this device provided that the types have some value in their own right. Social practices can be, and often are, usefully dealt with in three different types: economic, political and cultural. The criterion of the classification is rarely made clear. I would like to continue this trichotomy on the basis of the criterion of the produce of the practices. Thus, economic practices are distinguished from others by the fact that they result in use-values (whether for personal use or exchange); political practices are distinguished by the fact that they result in forms of institutionalized social power; and cultural practices are distinguished by the fact that they result in the expression of forms of signification (or ideologies). I suspect that this classification criterion is often used unconsciously by many writers. It certainly seems useful for any general discussion of social practices which does not want to be limited to a specific social formation.

Political practice in most societies will primarily refer to legislation, armed repression, the administration of social power, propaganda by politicians and the organization of parties.[1] Social ideologies have an important role to play in such practices in that the production, administration and maintenance of social control (or, the control of social power) often depends on the ideologies of the controllers as much as on their fire-power. Not only do political principles on which control is justified require enunciation, but also the application of the principles and the winning of consent for the principles require practices which operate with a heavy ideological component. I want to introduce here the following corollaries of my arguments so far:

1. Specific ideologies will emerge within specific forms of political practice, reflecting the structure of these forms as they exist in a

specific social formation. Such ideologies may penetrate other types of social practice and take economic or cultural forms.

2. Ideologies produced outside political practice may enter into it and take on a political character, thus acting to determine the shape of political practice.

3. All ideologies, simple or complex, must be considered for their potential or actual bearing on the decisions and balance of power within society.

Corollary (2) is usually recognized, corollary (3) increasingly today, but corollary (1) is much neglected. The relation between ideology and politics is clearly not a simple relation between externals, nor is ideology merely the vehicle of political expression; nor, we might add, can politics be reduced to the conflict of ideologies.

In most societies, cultural practice means art, music, science, the dissemination of news, ritual, the dissemination of beliefs, literature, drama, dance and other forms not covered by this list. Significations play the fundamental role within cultural practice because not only are they the end result but also they usually form the raw material of the practice and heavily structure the means of production. As in economic and political practice, people in cultural practice draw heavily upon the properties of nature. This conception of cultural practice is much wider than Althusser's concept of ideological practice, defined as "the transformation of one relation to the lived world into a new relation by ideological struggle" (Althusser and Balibar, 1970, p. 316). This concept is too restrictive for general analysis. Althusser distinguishes scientific practice as a qualitatively different type: this seems to resolve (for him) the problem of where to put science when one employs a narrow concept such as ideological practice. Althusser would not want to say that Marxism is ideology. It seems to me that scientific work is one form of cultural practice because the accuracy of significations is not a distinguishing feature within cultural practice. Why formalized significations of the world and its dynamics should be seen as qualitatively different from musical or literary significations when both may signify in an accurate and enlightening way is not clear in Althusser's work. I would suggest that scientific practice has all the general features of cultural practice but that it is distinct within its field because of its methods, its formalized statements, its use of evidence and its public nature. Althusser elevates scientific work in a way that mystifies it. His notion of the dialectic of scientific practice as one internal to theoretical thinking forgets (1) that scientists' reliance on 'practical intelligence' and 'outside' ideologies is often great, (2) that scientific work is carried out within social relations and contexts which determine the procedure and produce, and (3) that what counts socially as "science" is often a matter where wealth, power and ideology play a greater part than logic, even in the 'natural' sciences.

Several important conclusions can be drawn from my conceptualization of this form of social practice:

1. Specific ideologies are generated in cultural practice, reflecting the social structure (relations) of such practice.
2. Ideologies generated in economic and political practice may operate in cultural practice and adopt cultural forms.
3. Ideologies generated in cultural practice may become operative in economic and political practice and take on appropriate new forms.

These conclusions should be contrasted with some of the twentieth century Marxist analyses which reduce ideology to an epiphenomenon of the economy or a specific class. Not only do I find my own conception of the place of ideology in social practice preferable to those analyses, but the notion of the social relations of cultural practice seems a particularly fruitful one. It maps an area of territory which has been relatively unexplored: the relations of exploitation, oppression, control and co-operation, which structure various modes of cultural practice. The notion of ideological social relations has had much currency in the last few years, but, in my view, it fails to capture the practical relations which are so important in cultural life. It tends to be used to refer only to relations within ideology, or between significations, and thus escapes the crucial realm of practice. Contrasts between ideologies are important but they must be rooted in the lives of people, in practice, and this includes the relations of cultural practice.

Finally, it must be remembered that this classification of social practices is only one possible classification, one which is particularly useful for general analysis. It may get into difficulties when one is trying to do a political analysis of "the current situation"; here, the classification may hinder rather than help. But, even in political analysis, clear definitions of concepts is important and obscure general categories are frequently obstructive to a good understanding. In empirical analysis, this classification is a helpful background, although it is necessary to be aware that in modern capitalist societies, particular institutions may involve complex combinations of the economic, the political and the cultural. For example, as capital spreads its greasy palms, most forms of practice become 'economized' and their original character is complcated and subjugated to the demands of capital.

Social Relations and the "Necessity" Thesis

But on no account do men begin by "standing in that theoretical relation to the things of the external world". They begin, like every animal, by eating, drinking, etc., hence not by "standing" in a relation but by *relating themselves actively*, taking hold of certain things in the external world through action, and thus satisfying their need(s). (Therefore they begin with production.) Through the repetition of this process, the property of those things, their property "to satisfy needs" is impressed upon their brains; men, like animals, also learn to distinguish "theoretically" from all other things the external things which serve for the satisfaction of their needs. At a certain stage of evolution, after their needs, and the activities by which they are satisfied, have, in the meantime, increased and developed further, they will christen these things linguistically as a whole class, distinguished empirically from the rest of the external world . . . But this linguistic designation only expresses as an idea what repeated corroboration in experience has already accomplished, namely that certain external things serve men already living in a certain social connection (this is a necessary presupposition on account of language) for the satisfaction of their needs. (Marx, 1975, p. 190)

. . . since for an individual, the need for a professional title, or the title of a privy councillor, or for a decoration, not to speak of such things as rice, maize or corn, or not to mention meat (which does not confront the Hindus as the means of nourishment), is only possible in some quite definite "social organization". (Marx, 1975, p. 205)

Like many other passages quoted in the present work, these observations from some of Marx's last writings indicate the most fundamental thesis in the historical materialist study of ideologies and forms of social consciousness. This thesis can be expressed as follows: the emergence of an ideology or signification (or "designation") has *as a necessary condition of its existence* a particular social relation. Now, it is certainly true that there are other necessary conditions for the existence of an ideology (e.g. being alive, having a brain and at least some of the senses, effective means of production of basic means of subsistence), but these conditions are necessary for the existence of any social phenomenon. Means of designation are also necessary for the existence of ideologies, but again, these are presuppositions of *any* ideology, But a specific relation between a signifier and a signified requires a specific condition—the existence of particular practical social relation:

> Language is as old as consciousness, language *is* practical, real consciousness that exists for other men as well, and only therefore does it also exist for me; language, like consciousness, only arises from the need, the necessity, of intercourse with other men . . . Consciousness is, therefore, from the very beginning a social product, and remains so as long as men exist at all. (Marx and Engels, 1976a, p. 44)

Since it is that very relation between signifier and signified that is the crux of an ideology, it must be emphatically stated that ideologies originate within social relationships. Put another way, specific forms of human co-operation are necessary conditions of existence of specific relations of signification. It is to be noted that my interpretation of Marx (and the quoted passages from Marx themselves) in no way supports an economistic or class reductionist view of ideologies. Social relations take more than an economic form.

Of themselves, the elements of social practice are incapable of generating specific ideologies, and that includes the human element. That is not to say, of course, that individuals cannot manipulate signifiers, signifieds and relations of signification in such a way as to create potentially new ideologies; nor, for that matter, is it to deny that a computer could concoct potentially new designations. What must be understood is that significations are social affairs otherwise they are meaningless: they must refer back to the structure of social existence, otherwise they are annulled as signifying forms. Signification only exists if it exists in a social form. It does not need a universal usage or a consensus, but it does require (referential) significance within some socially constituted grouping. It exists for me and, therefore, for others; however, it only exists for me because it exists socially, and therefore (actually or potentially) for others. Language, like consciousness, only arises out of the necessity of social relations.

I have implicitly attacked the individualistic approach to this question, but it requires a final nail in its coffin. Returning to our 'inventor' of ideologies and the computer, is it not the case that computers are limited by their programs and that the most idiosyncratic recluse of an inventor is limited by his experience (past *and* present)? As Marx himself realized, some people can raise themselves subjectively well above their social context, but, and this is the killer blow for individualism, *they only do so on the basis of that context.* Don't recluses require a regular income from capital? Don't individualists tend to have middle-class jobs? Don't 'free-thinkers' benefit from their wide experience within different classes, cultures and societies? Don't 'drop-outs' contain within their ideas the reflections of experienced social contradictions? Doesn't the most novel ideology signify only on the basis of its reference to social life? Significance is only constituted socially, by origin, by terminology, and by reference. Durkheim captured the point well in *Suicide*:

> . . . at the very moment that, with excessive zeal, he frees himself from the social environment, he still submits to its influence. (Durkheim, 1970, p. 214)

As Marx put it, men are forever the creatures of their social relations. Both potential and actual ideologies are necessarily outcomes of social relations; significance forever lies within the circles of social practice.

Now, to some readers, this may seem a commonplace. So why emphasize it? Because often the thesis has been carelessly used. It has usually been reduced to one of the following incorrect propositions:

1. Social context influences people's thinking. (This implies that the context is entirely external to the thought and does not penetrate within it, that thought is non-social and can freely think its way round the entirely separate obstacles of context.)
2. Society tells us what to think. (This reifies social formations and

makes them external to social practices. It implies a notion of ideological consensus.)

3. Everything an individual says and thinks in a given situation is entirely an outcome of that situation itself. (This confuses necessary and sufficient conditions of existence. It forgets history and/or biography. It fails to distinguish origin from expression.)

4. Ideologies are only operative within the social relations which generate them. (Thus forgetting that ideologies are carried and authorized by people who engage in a variety of social relations and who are able to 'spread the word.)

5. Social relations are activated and maintained separately from the ideologies of the activators and, therefore, can only change through internal dissolution. (Ignoring the fact that social structural contradictions breed contradictory ideologies and the fact that people bring ideologies to social relations: thus underestimating the role of ideology in social change.)

6. Particular ideas suit particular situations. (This is a version of 1 and 3 favoured by cynics. It is usually founded upon an ahistorical notion of human nature as self-interested or manipulative.)

If one adds to this list the tendencies of economism ("ideologies only result from economic social relations") and class reductionism ("ideologies only result from classes and class contexts supplied by economic social relations") which also represent gross distortions of the Marxian conception, then one has a catalogue of theoretical disasters and blunders, a catalogue which has opened Marxism up to charges of determinism, an overemphasis on class, economism, cynicism, negativism, structuralism and sociologism. A lot of "isms" which hit the right targets very often. No wonder Marx denied being a Marxist!

The necessity thesis is a theory of the logical and historical necessity of the emergence of a particular ideology out of a particular social relation. It is not a theory of situations, of social influence, of suitability, of likelihoods or tendencies, or of man in general. The thesis holds that for a particular social relation to be carried out on a regular basis, certain ideas are required to be present as a *sine qua non*. Without these ideas the practice is impossible socially and thus ceases to be a social practice. Now, since social practices entail the purposive living out of certain social relations in a specific socio-geographical context, it must be the case that these ideas are the reflections of those relations (the assumptions or beliefs which make them socially operable), and that the ideas adopt their historical imagery, terminology and elaborated substance from the material circumstances, existing ideologies and socio-geographical contexts which constitute the environment in which they are brought to life. That is to say that the phenomenal character of these ideologies will vary with the context but that their essential structure only ceases to be activated when the generative social relations entirely disappear. This is not to say that people with opposed ideologies entering the social relations in question cannot modify, negotiate, privately reject or ignore the structurally generated ideologies; but it is to say that the latter ideologies are still generated by their necessitating social relations.

By now it should be clear that the Marxian thesis is not particularly geared to the explanation of individual beliefs or of such complex individual creations as the novel. In principle, these individual uses of ideology are explicable in Marxian terms but by the nature of the Marxian premises such things are the most difficult to explain. It is much easier to explain and read social patterns than it is to explain and read the discourse of an individual. Yet it is not true when commentators say that a complex act of individual creativity, such as a novel, defies Marxian reading and account. No decent Marxist would ever argue that the individual is the same as the social. It is totally predictable that the individual act never seems to fit the social analysis perfectly. Each individual surely embodies a unique configuration of social experiences, structures and ideologies. Yet that of itself in no way suggests that social matters are not afoot! The brilliantly unique novel does not negate Marxian analysis at all: new configurations of ideology in a text are themselves a reflection of the social relations experienced by its author. Marxian readings do not just identify single ideologies in accordance with their origins, but also identify combinations of ideologies according to *their* origins. If one adds to this an investigation of the ideologies of the reader and of the reader's social relation to the text, one even has the basis for Marxian aesthetics. The only thing that I am prepared to concede to the critics is that the strict operation of a Marxian method would *in practice* be unable to exhaust the full significance of something like a novel, since it would simply take too long. But there is no method in existence which can, in practice, do that anyway: every method selects. Marxian analyses would tend to focus on the main social ideologies in a text in relation to their current significance in a particular historical context and would tend not to explore in great depth the significance of the text for its author and his/her biography.

To illustrate the Marxian thesis one is forced back to *Capital*. Since the thesis depends on a knowledge of social relations, its practical application is limited by the lack of knowledge of social relations outside the sphere of the economic. I could make speculative analyses but they would lack certainty and detail. For example, it seems to me that the authoritarian social relationship between a university lecturer and a university student in the workplace is one which produces ideologies of deference. The technical relation between teacher and taught, however, only needs respect and co-operation, not deference. Less traditional social relations of university teaching, in my experience, definitely reduce the existence and effects of deference ideologies. Similarly, the social relations in which the modern domestic labourer operates seem to necessitate ideologies of personal worthlessness, subservience, conservatism and pragmatism. However, given the lack of adequate empirical research based on a developed theoretical knowledge, permit me to use *Capital*.

In *Capital*, Marx demonstrates that the regular production of capital depends in part upon the generalized exchange of commodities between private owners. Where exchange is a dominant social relation, the ideologies necessitated by it become dominant social ideologies. The dominance of the exchange relation in a capitalist social formation at a particular level of development, of course, means that these ideologies take a specific form which corresponds to the nature of the particular form of capitalism and to the exact conditions involved. Moreover, since exchange relations are not peculiar to capitalist economies, there is the further complication that the ideologies in question did not originate in a capitalist context. However, despite these complications, the basic thesis is still applicable. The following ideologies are necessitated by a generalized, exchange relation:

1. The ideology of ownership. To exchange goods, a legal personality must physically control or possess those goods and that possession must be recognized by the other party to the exchange.

That is, the crucial thing is that possession is socially recognized or validated. Exchange cannot take place on a regular, orderly basis without the parties' recognition of each other's valid possession. Ownership is the ideology of valid possession. It necessarily goes hand in hand with ideologies of "right" and "property", and, on the negative side, with an ideology of illegal possession or "theft". Regular, orderly exchange requires that possession is not taken without consent. Ownership and theft are simply two ideological sides of the same structural coin. Clearly, the ideologies of ownership, right, property and theft did not originate within capitalist societies and have taken various forms, both simple and complex, in the different societies inhabited by regular exchange. Where exchange is central, as in capitalism, not only are these ideologies very developed and complex, but they are also dominant ideologies in the wider society and play key roles in law, philosophy, religion, political doctrine, mass communications and everyday discourse. This applies also to the rest of the ideologies necessitated by exchange relations.

2. The ideology of the legal personality. Surplus and scarcity, in conjunction with the historical needs of people, force the exchange of goods. People are thus brought together, to the exchange, as representatives of the produce which must change places. People thus act as personifications of their produce. Regular exchange demands that the parties recognize each other as the valid representatives of their produce, as legal persons. Legal personality is vital to valid exchange.

3. The ideology of the contract. Exchange demands that the parties recognize that each other's will resides within the goods. The necessity for the goods to change places must be imputed to the minds of their representatives. Without this, the exchange would not be validated and the situation would be one of mutual theft: a patently ridiculous notion on which to base an economic practice. The exchange of goods must therefore be seen as a *consensus ad idem* or a meeting of minds and wills. What is ultimately a relation between differentially located economic practices of production thus becomes seen as an ideological consensus between intentional, free agents. This notion of the contract, needless to say, is fundamental and extensive within a capitalist society.

These three ideologies are inseparable from the regular practice of exchange. They are integral to its constitution. It cannot exist without them. Just to emphasize the nature of the thesis, it must be said that this is also true in a socialist society. Even if the concept of ownership is that of communal or social ownership, even if the concept of legal personality is that of a publicly elected dealer, and even if the concept of contract is that of a socially approved planning agreement, nevertheless, the existence of the exchange relation is working its necessary ideological effects. Indeed one could forcibly argue that the very concept of the socialist mode of production is dependent upon the full extension of the concepts of ownership, personality and contract which are born but crippled in capitalist societies.

My illustration of the necessity thesis also brings out the nature of legal rules as ideologies necessitated by general social relations and sanctioned by the institutions for the execution of 'social power'.[2] The particular ideologies discussed above form the backbone of those legal systems which exist in societies where exchange is a dominant social relation. It was thus not simply a case of contingent historical borrowing when Roman legal codes were drawn upon heavily by Western legislators and jurists. In this connection it is worth noting that once an ideology has been adopted within another practice, its development has a twofold aspect: (1) as an element of its originating practice, and (2) as an element of its appropriating practice. Thus the law of contract is not always in touch with the ideology of contract current in the economic practice of the producers, distributors and consumers; this is the basis of the *fictio juris*. Indeed, producers, distributors and consumers may have different versions of the contract ideology based on their differing positions within economic practice, and it is then a question of political power, not economics, as to which version becomes legalized. There is no good reason to assume, in general, that legal ideology is identical to the equivalent ideology in everyday practice. Nor is there any reason to be surprised when we find that a modern ideology was first pronounced a thousand years ago, in essence if not in phenomenal form. History is not the abstract, logical movement of categories but the structured movement of people in practice.

To say that social relations necessitate a particular ideology is not to argue that ideology is produced by abstract forms. An ideology is only produced when its necessitating social relations are realized in practice. Conflict and crisis can shatter this production. Ideologies only emerge when their constituent social structures are generalized in the practice of a group of society; they have no ephemeral existence outside the life-blood of social practice. Moreover, once an ideology has emerged, its generative social relations can only be practically realized under the guidance of that ideology. Thus, withdrawal of assent to the ideology can result in a standstill in practice, just as much as the cessation of the practice can lead to a shattering of the ideology. Social practices involve the conjunction of forms of co-operation and ideology in definite social and material settings. Forms of co-operation are mere abstractions without ideologies, people and matter to activate them. Antagonisms within a social structure are only perceived by people within the forms of ideology available to them: a structure never presents itself directly to the eye. Structures are blind, and conscious men are their guide-dogs. Sometimes it is a case of the blind leading the blind, and not just in capitalism; it takes guide-dogs, conscious people, to lead structures to their logical conclusion—guide-dogs who are themselves often blind to the historical logic of that ending.

Ideal-typically there would be a vicious hermeneutic between social structures and their necessary ideologies. That is rarely the case in practice, however, because of contradictions, mobility and context. Always the relation of necessity is mediated by people with different ideas, the effects of other practices and considerations of material circumstance. But mediation and counter-tendency do not negate the thesis, they merely point to the locatedness of any dialectic between structure and ideology.

The Mechanism of Spontaneous Observation

Given the conceptions elucidated above, I can now outline the mechanism of spontaneous observation. This model ("model" in the Realist sense, see Keat and Urry, 1975) may not seem vitally necessary to the development of a theory of ideology, but, nevertheless, its elucidation should help the reader to see (1) the way in which I conceive the operation of ideology in practical observation, and (2) the way in which bodies of simple ideology can be built up into extensive ideological formations. After all, the conditions of emergence of an ideology are one thing and the consequential movement of that ideology in practice is another. I am particularly concerned with the role of ideology in observation for three reasons:

1. To counteract phenomenological versions of the process of observation.
2. To counteract tendencies in Marxism to simplify the whole process by reducing vision to the effect of the structure and thus to make appearances the rulers of consciousness.
3. Observations, or what are taken to be facts or evidence, underpin the products of philosophical consciousness, such as laws. Thus the elucidation of spontaneous observation helps us to tie together what may otherwise come to be seen as disparate phenomena.

Spontaneous observation is a human function within social practice. It occurs within all types of social practice, although some social practices are specifically geared to the production of spontaneous observations (e.g. news reporting, government research units). In my conception, spontaneous observation in itself involves a human being in a particular practice viewing, through the grid or spectacles of particular ideologies, material forms with specific modes of appearance shaped by their presence within a social structure. This vision is itself conducted within the operation of specific social relations in specific material and social contexts. Condensed into this formulation are several theses.

Firstly, the observer never sees the thing in itself in some pure visionary vacuum. Whether it be a rock, a person, or a movement, the thing is only ever seen within the context of the practices in which both it and the vision figure. Thus, it is presented for vision in a particular way by the fact of its location in the structured setting of a practice. The practical structure itself determines the appearance of the material form. But also, the physical context of appearance and the conscious manipulations of the practitioners will determine that appearance. These determinations are themselves interconnected and so the presentation of the matter is usually overdetermined. However, this is not a necessity. Structure may co-exist with the elements of practice in a disjointed and/or contradictory relation, leaving an ambiguous appearance.

Marxists will be familiar with the observations of Marx on the fact that the place of a thing within a social relation often results in its appearance concealing its true nature. However, there is no need to forget that people can actively present things in specific ways which conceal their structurally determined appearance. Deliberate presentation itself, of course, is an act carried out with its own social imperatives. Nor should it be forgotten that Marx's analysis is applicable well beyond the economic sphere. Finally, when social relations are not working normally (for example, because of a conflict between the parties which results in non-cooperation), the way things appear is different and the normal veil of appearance can be seen for what it is, merely a socially contextualized appearance. In such times of crisis and conflict, social structures, individual characters and material objects are often seen for what they really are (in themselves). The normal practical interpenetration which gives their social appearances a natural character is shattered and both substance and social form become available to view.

Secondly, no social being is ever *tabula rasa*. Biography and the multiplicity of current experiences mean that the individual's vision can be fruitfully (if not elegantly) described as an ideologically structured grid. It is this grid which is placed over the practical appearances in the process of observation. Some appearances are seen as they are, some are seen in part, and some are not seen at all. But always the appearances available are mapped according to the ideological grid of the observer, which means that even if the totality of the material core of the appearance is observed, it is only observed in the tone, context and light of the ideologies in the observer's head. One man's street procession may be another man's political struggle. The multiple features of the meaning of the appearance for the observer requires a knowledge of his/her ideologies. Of course, vision is not often a split-second affair. There is often time to check and look again: ambiguous appearances come into focus. But this makes no odds: even the circumspect scrutiny requires ideological guidance.

Over the last thirty years, many writers have demonstrated time and time again that vision is coloured by concepts, values, assumptions and rules. This devastating critique of empiricism, which has offered us great insights into the ambiguity of reality and the importance of selective perception, has also frequently been overstated. One is often given the impression that what is visible is that which is in the mind of the observer already. In more sophisticated versions of this, it is argued that the social character of the visible thing is attributed to it by the observer's ideology and that the observer only sees a physical entity. Both these phenomenological theses are at odds with the conception developed here, which insists that matter is seen spontaneously as it presents itself socially. Observers' ideologies are indeed determinant but so also are the structures and contexts of the visible. The subject–object relation is real in practice, but the object only appears in practical process and no subject has innocent vision. Observations are thus ideologically filtered appearances: literally, impressions.

Thirdly, no subject–object relation exists outside the practice in which the observation is made. Observation is thus heavily structured by (1) the social relations of the practice, (2) the limits to vision set within that practice, and (3) the specific ideology necessitated by that practice. For example, the news reporter sees events in terms of a conception of news. The patterns of social life are selected into events and non-events, stories of human interest and non-stories etc. This selection is done at high speed to meet daily production targets in a competitive industry and some aspects of a story are more accessible than others. Social structure, practical parameters and practical ideologies are extremely important conditions under which the observer views the appearances of reality. It is an extremely unfortunate thing that much sociological analysis has neglected the practical context (in the widest sense) of observation and thus neglected its practical determinations. The conception outlined here, on the basis of Marxian principles, offers an extremely fruitful model for the analysis of spontaneous observation. No longer can we rest content with merely pointing to the deceptiveness of reality or the selective perceptions of the observer. Marxists have emphasized the former and phenomenologists the latter, but neither have systematically placed observation in its proper place, in social praxis.

This conception of observation has an implication of great importance for the reading of ideologies. What research must bear in mind always is that an observation is partly determined by the appearances observed, partly by the observing ideologies and partly by the social relations under which the observation took place.[3] Too often in the past, analyses of the ideological content of discourse have completely ignored the observed appearances underpinning that discourse, and then proceeded to assert that the discourse could only have been made on the basis of the ideologies indicated within it. In thus declaring the discourse to be ideological, such studies have implied that it had no basis in social reality. Perhaps this is one reason why the Marxian conception of ideology is equated with the notion of false consciousness. This is not to say that an observation statement is non-ideological and justifiable (in terms of accuracy) *because* it has an apparent basis, but it is to say that social appearances make some statements very justifiable. In other words, the analyst must be careful not to assume the mono-causal operation of an ideology when the observed appearances may also act to produce the observation. Of course, the analyst has to check in each case whether the justifying appearances have in fact been observed. Also, in practice, even if an observation is justified by apparent reality, usually what the observer does is to locate the observation in his/her ideological map of the world. The observation thus becomes woven into the complex ideological fabric which serves the observer as a philosophy. In reading ideologies we must always distinguish between (1) the observing ideologies, (2) the observed appearances, and (3) the relation between the two in an elaborated discourse. Only by studying this latter relation can the analyst begin to see the effects of the ideologies under study. Thus, not only do ideology readers have to study social relations in order to form precise notions of an ideological form, not only do they have to study history to see which vocabularies are used by an ideology and in what contexts, but they also have to study the social reality which the ideological form is supposed to refer to.

My conception of spontaneous observation does need further elaboration but there is no space here. Suffice it to say that within this conception one can see how new appearances are mapped in terms of old significations (ideologies), how the old term develops new referents, how the new referent sometimes requires a development in old significations and how a basic relation of signification comes to acquire, on the one hand, a whole range of meanings, and on the other, a whole range of signifiers. Of course, with use, old meanings and signifiers fall away and the relation of signification appears in a current form with its history concealed to the spontaneous imagination. The constancy of the relation of signification itself, despite shifts in its meaning and changes of personnel amongst its signifiers, is a testimony to its continuing necessity in a particular social practice, and thus to the continued operation of specific social relations. Signifiers may change radically and meaning may shift and develop but as long as the generative social relations still persist then the significant relation will also persist. Thus, exchange relations will always demand an ideology of contract, however it is signified and however the meaning of contract varies. Of course, a meaning can only vary so far before it becomes a different meaning altogether and not all signifiers are available for a given meaning if that meaning is to be unequivocally signified; thus it is always necessary to establish the historical parameters of a structurally required ideology.

Philosophical reflections operate on previous philosophical reflections and spontaneous observations. Moreover, they often penetrate spontaneous observation as its operative ideologies. There is thus a relation of interpenetration between philosophical and spontaneous forms of ideology. This is such a vast area for analysis that my remarks must be severely restricted. All I want to do is to argue that the beginning of our understanding here is the concept of the specificity of cultural practice. Philosophical work, of whatever kind, is carried out under a definite social structure and in definite socio-geographical contexts. This structure and context will produce certain ideologies peculiar to the work. These ideologies will form part of the ideological grid of the reflecting observer (the rest being formed by ideologies picked up from elsewhere). The observed appearances here are the apparent observations given by spontaneous observation. The products of philosophical work are thus incredibly complex, reflecting "professional" ideologies, the practical contexts of philosophical reflection, the nature of the observations analysed, the ideologies embodied in the analysed observations, and, above all, the social structure of the practice of philosophical reflection. What prevents the products of philosophy being composed of a myriad of contradictory elements is the fact that there is usually correspondence between many of their determinations. For example, the social relations underpinning the reflections of news editors today are often much the same as those underpinning the reflections of the junior reporters. This will tend to be the case in concentrated and centralized production systems with a narrow economic goal. Similarly, the ideologies of the editor and of the junior reporter are often much the appoint the junior reporter, so it is no accident. Apparatuses of cultural production rarely thrive on ideological pluralism today, as in the past. Perhaps, what gives academic life its current relative pluralism is the relatively independent nature of universities, the relative lack of bureaucracy in academic production and the relative independence of the occupation of university lecturer. This pluralism, is, of course, very relative. In fact, despite the myths of academic freedom, the produce of teaching and research contains ideologies which seem to fall into very standard patterns. The mythical, vast range of idiosyncratic thoughts is non-existent today, if it ever existed at all. In a developed social formation, even the most independent thinker is subject to social considerations affecting many others in a similar manner: the philosophical products being correspondingly similar. If we take the most independent thinker of all, which of course is always oneself, we only need to note the number of Ph.D.s begun in the 1970s on the nature of subjectivity, ideology and consciousness whose authors were all unaware of each other's existence. This is not the result of sheep consciousness, as many old professors (with ethnographies under their belts) have observed, but the result of commonly effective social conditions (e.g. the lack of grants and access enabling empirical work, and the politicization of science) and of the observed deficiencies in the existing work (e.g. the empiricism of sociology, its banal theoretical efforts of the 1950s). This section could well be concluded by observing that it is only the scientist's professional ideology which justifies the view that scientific theory is aloof from practical influence and spontaneous observation, and, conversely, it is only the ideology of the jealous layman which justifies the view that science is pure abstraction with no practical relevance.

Social Relations and Class Formations: the Complexity of Society's Ideological Map

Marx and Engels said that hitherto history has been a long sequence of class struggles. Marxists have often taken this too literally and ignored the relations which have divided classes within themselves and the shared events which have united classes in a common cause. Recently Marx's distinction between the technical and the social same: indeed, the people who appoint the editor also, effectively, features of the division of labour has been resurrected (Althusser and Balibar, 1970; Rancière, 1974; Hindess and Hirst, 1977). This distinction is vital for a more adequate mapping of the social distribution of ideologies. As Poulantzas has put it, classes are not football teams with ideological number-plates on their backs (Poulantzas, 1973, p. 202). Poulantzas criticizes Lukacs on this score, yet he himself does not get much further than mentioning the existence of class fractions. Indeed, Poulantzas himself could be accused of seeing ideologies as football players with class number-plates on their backs. Marxism must break from a monolithic conception of the class-ideology connection. The two concepts that will enable the development of theory of ideology are (1) the concept of the dual nature of social relations, and (2) the concept of the relative autonomy of the political and cultural practices (a concept already outlined).

Rancière has most sharply reminded us of the modern political significance of Marx's conception of the dual nature (or "double articulation") of social relations (Rancière, 1974). In a polemic against Althusser, Rancière points out that the social division of labour in a university takes both technical and class forms. Lecturers and students are divided by their technical functions in the process, but at the same time, these technical functions express class relations within the superstructure. Thus lecturers are not just teachers, but also historically the propagators of dominant class ideology and science, serving the terms of reference of the social system. Rancière himself uses the terms technical and social. I would prefer to draw the distinction in terms of technical and class relations since both are very much social forms. An easier example to grasp is the manager–general labourer distinction in a factory. This distinction involves different "detail functions" within the productive process and also contains different functions within the production of capital. In addition, these different aspects of the social relations between managers and labourers are conjointly articulated: the class relations constitute, and only operate through, the technical relations and the latter express and reinforce class relations. Finally, it must be added that such a set of social relations must also be seen in its societal and historical contexts; contexts which will affect the intrinsic divisiveness of these relations.

Now, let us look at the implications of this conception of social relations. The fundamental focus here must be upon the social relations of economic life and from there we can look at the role of political and cultural practices. Even if we supposed a completely homogeneous population (in terms of age, sex and race), a particular economic class structure must, on the basis of our conception, become complicated by technical divisions. For example, technical divisions will divide a class within itself (skilled worker, general labourer and casual labourer, or financial capitalist, industrialist and *entrepreneur*). Hence ideologies will arise which reflect these technical relations. These could include ideologies related to occupational status and consumption patterns based on different incomes. Now, because a productive process is a technical unity, some ideologies will arise which reflect this unity (e.g. ideologies of the need for mutual co-operation based on functional or technical interdependence). Since the totality of productive processes is united by its national nature within an international social division of labour, we can also see that there is an economic basis for ideologies of national unity, co-operation and interest. We might add that because of the increasing development of international society there is also the basis for international ideologies of unity, co-operation and shared interest, and for international ideologies dividing producers on a technical basis.

Now, still supposing a homogeneous population in terms of age, sex and race, we can consider political and cultural implications. Given technical divisions within the economy, groups are formed within classes with their own distinctive economic interests, ideologies, patterns of consumption and life-styles. Because these distinctive life-patterns and interests are also in opposition to each other, political organizations and cultural practices will develop which encapsulate (*inter alia*) these oppositions. Groups organize to establish their power as social units and to create situations of leisure and culture. The technical divisions of the economy thus fix themselves at the political and cultural levels. Once established, the political and cultural relations between technically founded groups themselves form the basis for the emergence of ideological differences and the picture is further complicated. Now, it must be remembered that the political and cultural extensions of technical divisions must also express, at the very same time, the political and cultural extensions of class divisions. Thus working-class political organizations also embody the political effects of the technical division of labour; it is the same for working-class cultural practices.

We must now introduce the fact that classes only exist in conflict and that, therefore, to protect its domination and to fix its hegemony, the ruling class will often deliberately play upon the technical divisions within the subordinate classes and the political and cultural extensions of these divisions. Probably more commonly, the interests pursued by the ruling class, whether economic, political or cultural, will bear no relation to any working-class need for unity and solidarity and will thus inadvertently accentuate divisions within that class. Regarding socialist politics, although political organizations, such as trade unions, are based upon the technical division of labour, they do express working-class interests and hence are to be supported. However, just as it is in the long-term, structural interest of the ruling class to maintain divisions amongst the subordinated classes, it is in the long-term structural interests of the subordinated classes to minimize technical divisions (and their effects) and to create economic, political and cultural solidarity. This also applies to the realm of cultural practices. The working classes need cultural practices which operate for unity not for division. It is vital to realize that the Marxian theoretical understanding of society posits that ideologies arise from political and cultural social practices as well as from the economic sphere. Thus, if the superstructural realms are ridden with class and technical relations, they will generate opposing ideologies which have features of both a class and technical kind. Not only will the main classes have different substantive philosophies about what should be done politically and what is enjoyable and valuable culturally, but these differences will also result in different forms of approved politics and culture.

How far this complicated map of social relations and their corresponding ideologies is opened up to its full extent and how far it is closed down to its most fundamental features is naturally dependent upon the nature of the mode of production and its stage of development. It is necessary to study the structural changes which encourage solidarity as well as those which divide. On the basis of Marx's analysis in *Capital*, one must suppose that capitalist economies open the map up and accelerate the plurality of ideologies as they develop. If capitalism means increased division of labour, increased administration, increased political control, increased development of cultural facilities and increased individualization, then this must be the case. Because of this, there is also a counter-tendency to produce a mass society, a tendency based on increased socialization of production, political power and means of communication, and on the need to prevent the advance of cultural pluralism with all its bad effects for mass production. Clearly, any model of socialism for an advanced capitalist society is naive and unworkable if it assumes class homogeneity in the realm of ideology and ignores the effects of "mass society". It would have to build devices into the blueprint to ensure a full political and cultural democracy as well as social ownership and cohesion. The development of capitalism seems to involve the maturation of political and cultural contradictions as well as those of the economy. If this is so, class unity under socialism will also mean advanced forms of political and cultural pluralism.

And, as if this is not complicated enough, we must now withdraw our artificial simplifying assumption of a homogeneous population. Differences in age, sex and race based on biology and developed in social forms in earlier modes of production cannot be ignored. In terms of the economy, there are great divides between ages, sexes and races according to their differential employment in the productive process. Class divisions and ideologies divide the ages, sexes and races in terms of their social function within the reproduction of capital. Thus young, black male immigrants in Britain are over-represented in the unemployment figures, whilst the passivity of middle-aged Asian women colludes with their employment in exploitative conditions. Women in general have been denied important roles within both ruling and other classes. So have blacks and Asians. Children are imprisoned daily in schools until at least the age of 16. Old people are consigned to an unproductive retirement. These differentiations also have a technical basis and form, some jobs being best done by certain kinds of people. On the whole, then, a developed capitalist economy creates social divisions according to non-property criteria. Age, sex and race are the most important criteria perhaps, but we must also recognize that social divisions also exist in terms of town versus countryside and intellectual versus manual labour. All these criteria of social differentiation are non-property features of social stratification founded upon the economic process, and subsequently articulated in the processes of politics and culture. They constitute real social relations, when put into practice, and generate contending ideologies founded upon them. These contending ideologies and the consequent association of their adherents result in political and cultural practices and organizations. These practices and organizations are articulated in forms reflecting their class character, but which are not solely founded on class relations. They often exist outside the major class forms of political organization and culture and sometimes they develop inside them. Whatever happens it should be clear that ideologies of sexism, feminism, racism, black consciousness, children's power, etc., have a solid structural basis in the economy and a basis which usually has developed political and cultural extensions. Discrimination of such a kind within the economic, political and cultural systems of a society is not peripheral to class politics because it is jointly articulated with the class structure. Socialists must, therefore, learn from others and recognize non-class forms of oppression for themselves, and, on the other hand, they should also attempt to show groups formed to fight such oppression that the latter has a class character within an exploitative mode of production. Class unity must express the interests of all its members for it to be politically substantial.

In conclusion, my conceptual advances offer us a theorized understanding of what we already knew empirically and intuitively: that the complexity of ideological differentiation in modern capitalist societies is structurally rooted in the social relations of production and their corresponding political and cultural structures. Ideologies of nationalism, occupational groups, women, immigrants, children and urbanism can now be seen as integral aspects of social development and not as features tangential to the main dynamo, the class struggle. A class and its ideology are complexly articulated today. Some ideologies unite a class with other classes and other ideologies divide it within itself. Moreover, situations of inter-class unity and intra-class division are found across the whole spectrum of society—in economics, politics and culture. Simple class maps of social ideology must obviously be abandoned for they have no longer any basis in reality and have no justification in Marxist theory.

The Transference and Maintenance of Ideologies

The question of transference cannot be examined in depth here. All that needs to be emphasized is that people bring their ideologies to situations which are new to them. They do not enter them *tabula rasa*, to become the innocent victims of deceptive appearances. The ideologies engendered in previous experience may collude with new situations and their necessary ideologies, or they may conflict and a practical resolution will be required. Worsley has elucidated this notion reasonably well in the following passage:

> Thus industrial studies have shown how people import social relations from the outside world into the factory, crossing the "permeable" membrane between work and non-work: such imports include racist beliefs, ideals of class-solidarity, of orientation towards privatised instrumentalism. But the language of "export" and "import" is insufficiently dialectical to catch the interpenetration that occurs. . . . (Worsley, 1974, p. 12)

The interpenetration of ideologies of different origins has been excellently illustrated in *Workers Divided* (Nichols and Armstrong, 1976). It is this interpenetration which makes the reading of discourse such a hazardous business in many cases. I would suggest that the difficulty can be overcome, however, by the analyst having a clear conception of the ideologies under study and by taking sufficiently large samples of the discourse to make clear differentiation possible. Bearing in mind the very possibility of interpenetration is itself a crucial step forward.

This simple insistence that the classical interpretation of Marx's theory of ideology in *Capital* overlooks the fact that people bring ideologies into practices, has important ramifications which enable us to present a processual picture of ideology in social formations. These ramifications and the concepts on which they are based offer us a complex, Marxian resolution for the sociologists' problem of how to conceive of the relation between structure and process. The following are of the greatest importance:

1. Some ideologies pave the way for mystifying appearances to perform their dirty work. The ideologies imbibed from early family life, school and public communications prepare the worker and the housewife for their subordination to the dominant economic structure. Research is required which shows how labour-power is ideologically trained for its economic functions, and which demonstrates that *certain ideologies are necessary pre-conditions for the successful operation of structural mystifica-*

tion. Experience of the appearances convinces many that bourgeois ideologies are valid; to understand this validation we not only need to know how and why social relations present deceptive appearances, but also how and why certain ideologies prepare people to be deceived.

2. New social practices and institutions (collection of practices) are only set up under the guidance of specific ideologies. These ideologies are not necessarily class ideologies—they could arise from occupational divisions or (structurally based) racial differentiation. Research needs to investigate the ideologies concretized in the setting up of important new social institutions (e.g. the National Enterprise Board) and to contrast these ideologies with the actual effects of the new practices. Clearly the important thing here is to ask questions, such as, what are the origins of the ideology in question? and, which group or class's version of it becomes institutionalized and whose versions are ignored? A particularly interesting topic in this area is the role of differing ideologies in the setting up of a socialist society. Which ideologies are carried by the class(es) which makes the revolution?

3. There are some practices which allow people time and space to exchange ideas. Ideology modification can thus occur. Marxists have ignored this realm and symbolic interactionist sociologists only partially dealt with it when they studied the ideological changes involved in fluid 'interaction contexts'. At least, however, the symbolic interactionists did appreciate the importance of human interaction in altering states of subjectivity. Many repressive governments also appreciate the point too, and consequently make great efforts to prevent such fruitful associations. My version of Marx's theory of ideology enables us to conceive of the importance of "social intercourse" (Marx's phrase) in generating (of itself) ideological change. Of course, it is necessary to study the social relations (and the corresponding political regimes) which tend to inhibit or encourage social intercourse. But, in the light of my formulations, it seems important to study the structurally founded interaction contexts which promote ideological changes of various kinds.

4. It would seem to be a logical conclusion that some social formations work in such a way as to limit the variation of experience available to people. Thus, conversely, capitalist forma-

tions tend to involve a relatively high degree of personal mobility, a quick rate of change and a high rate of conscious conflict. These conditions probably apply differentially within such social formations, of course, and so agricultural workers and housewives seem to experience them to a lesser degree than skilled technicians. It seems to me that, where such conditions are applicable, the role of structurally generated mystifying appearances is lessened and we must look more carefully at the spread of ideologies which can see beyond the appearances, at the role of conflicts and political 'contracts' in establishing new norms, at the increased importance of mass communications, and at the decreased importance of community-based social intercourse in generating ideologies.

Regarding the maintenance and development of existing ideologies, it is vital to bear in mind that ideologies are constantly reproduced by their generative social relations. However, where such relations also generate contradictory versions of an ideology, the institutions of ideology maintenance and development have a great importance in favouring one version. All I want to emphasize here is that the cultural practices of a society are the place to begin studying this process. We need to study their origins, current organization and social functions. Who mans the powerful positions in the structure of cultural practices? Who are the teachers, the editors and the artists, and what do they think? The maintenance of ideology by political force is normally only of secondary importance but is pushed to the forefront in times of crisis. I would assume that force is rarely a successful way of defeating a well-rooted ideology: that is, however, something which remains to be investigated thoroughly. Perhaps more important than force is co–optation and bribery (in a broad sense). The successful political integration of oppositional groups into important, established structures is probably the third most important condition for ideology-maintenance, after the reproduction of those very structures themselves and the control of the main cultural institutions. Force often only really comes into its own after these three conditions have proved unsuccessful. It may, however, be more fruitful not to see the operation of these four conditions in an evolutionary, chronological way and to assume they all operate (to differing extents) on a regular basis in all societies.

A Scientific Method of Reading Ideology

Having elucidated the concepts necessary for the precise application of a scientific, historical materialist method of reading ideology, I shall now outline that method in terms of chronologically ordered stages which are geared to producing increasingly precise approximations to the nature of the ideology being investigated. A complete application of the method would go through each level of approximation. Each level is concerned with establishing the social meaning of the discourse studied and the part played by the ideology under investigation. Both the elements of an ideology—the signifying unit and the signified meaning—and the relation between them are of social origin and form. Our proposed method is directed towards reading the presence and form of a specific ideology within its encoded state in a determinate discourse, a reading which proceeds via the establishment of the practical, social basis of that ideology and therefore the precise nature of its signification. Instead of implicitly assuming the social meaning of the discourse in order to discover its constituent ideological codes, our method endeavours to make that assumption explicit and to examine its validity. Since decoding a discourse requires assumptions about the meaning of its terms, a method claiming scientific status must check the validity of those assumptions. This checking must involve the analysis of the essential structure of the studied ideology necessitated by a specific social structure and an analysis of the historical forms of appearance of the ideology in similarly structured social contexts. In other words, through historical comparison and the analysis of social structures, we ascertain the meaning of the ideology, the significance it can bear, and the contexts in which it appears. This method, which could be described as an historical materialist semiology, provides an answer to our initial question: yes, we can produce a reading of ideology in discourse which is much more than a series of subjective impressions. The stages in the application of this method are as follows:

First approximation: solid impressions

Beginning with the researcher's initial spontaneous impression that the ideology is necessitated by a particular social structure and is active within a specific discourse, it is necessary to establish that this impression has some socio-historical basis for its existence. (Other reading methods do not even get this far since they refuse to investigate their assumptions about the social meaning of a discourse.) To do this, the researcher should eclectically and imaginatively refer to a series of relevant contemporary sources and thus carry out a 'pilot' study of the ideology in question. Thus, if one's impression was that, in times of structural collision between the interests of capital and the interests of labour, an ideology is generated within the ranks of capital to the effect that "the workers are causing trouble, disrupting production and threatening the national interest, on a misguided basis, mainly because of the subversive leadership of left-wing militants", and that this ideology was re-presented within the discourse of news reports in the press, the researcher should check this impression as a totality. This involves:

1. Checking that the powerful journalists (e.g. editors and main-feature writers) actually hold this view through the examination of editorials and features or through interviews if possible.
2. Checking the apparent reality of the workers' activities to see how far this ideology is valid, to see what grasp on reality it has actually got and to determine how the workers' activities could be seen differently.
3. Checking that the ideology is not just a one-off occurrence by reference to recent news reports (say of famous strikes within the last ten years), to other discursive sources (e.g. novels, magazines, television news, popular opinion), and to current news reports of other forms of political conflict (e.g. reports of student demonstrations and of conflicts abroad).
4. Investigating the requirements of the social relations involved (e.g. briefly examining capital/labour relations and the relation of the press to capital), and finally
5. Checking the extent of the ideology's appearance across the range of national newspapers and through time (say, a week's newspapers).

Where this pilot study entails the reading of discourse, no special esoteric techniques are needed. This reading is done on the basis of the commonsensical techniques used by the existing reading methods described in Part Two of the present work. Beginning with provisional assumptions and guesses about the social meaning of the discourse, the researcher examines them by reference to the repetition of signifiers (as in content analysis), to the internal structure of the discourse (as in structuralist semiology), to the repressed opposite discourse whose traces are reflected in the studied discourse (as in Derrida's approach), and to the prior discourse of the same type in whose absences the present studied one is articulated (as in symptomatic reading). In short, the initial reading of the presence and form of the ideology within a modern discourse is guided by a provisional theory of the social origins of the ideology and carried out by the techniques geared to describing its linguistic form. In this way, the investigated ideology is distinguished from its encoded form through reference to social structure, contemporary context, the structure and repetitions of the coded discourse, possible alternative encodings, and recent previous discursive expressions of the same ideology. Thus a first approximation to the specifity of the investigated ideology is crystallized out of an initial reading of some of its contemporary discursive appearances.

Second approximation: theory

If there is good evidence to suggest an historical and logical link between structure, context and ideology, the research must now deepen the theoretical understanding of that connection. Here the main job is to understand the necessity of the ideology to the social relations involved and thus to distinguish its essential substance from its contingent features which, perhaps, reflect other structures and other contexts. This analysis will no doubt raise various thorny questions and develop questions previously suggested in the pilot study. Thus, in our example, the researcher would question whether a focus on 'leaders' was a result of personalizing journalism or a genuine element of the ideology necessitated by the class structure and social relations of capitalism. Different aspects of the ideology may be linked with different structures in the capitalist social formation. Particularly important would be the examination of the influence of contemporary economic and political conditions on the form of the ideology. In our example, it would be important also to examine the reporting of the unrest of subordinate classes and political groupings in socialist societies and the documentation of peasants' revolts in feudal societies in order to establish which elements of our ideology reflected capitalist structures of domination and which elements reflected structures of domination in general.

Third approximation: history

Having determined the social relations which necessitate the ideology in its totality, the researcher selects a period from the past where those relations were operative and discovers whether the ideology is operative within the same type of discourse (if the same type is not available, then the nearest equivalent). In our example, news reports of nineteenth century strikes and unrest would be adequate historical resources. Again the researcher would check the relations between structure, context and ideology. Reading the first discursive instance will involve using the 'bridging assumption', the basic general theoretical premise of the logical connections between structure, context and ideology, as filled out with substance by the first two stages of the research. As in the first stage of the research, the ideology is 'read off' from the social structure and context and identified in the discourse through the commonsensical techniques of looking for the structure, repetition, absences and repressed alternatives within the discourse. Unlike other reading methods, ours proceeds from the social relations of life rather than the apparent forms of ideology (to paraphrase Marx). The readings of the third stage advance our understanding further since they are armed with the substantive content of the ideology as approximately understood from the first stage and with the theory of its specificity as developed in the second stage. Again, constant reference to the practices and events reported must be maintained to illustrate the uniqueness and partiality of the examined ideology. The number of historical instances taken will vary with the kind of discourse examined, but the essential point is to build up a knowledge of the operations of the ideology in its necessary historical milieu, a knowledge which convinces the researcher that he/she has exhausted the main questions and established the essence of the ideology. In our example, therefore, one may study the press reports of famous nineteenth century strikes and workers' movements (e.g Chartism) and of early twentieth century conflicts (the pre-war struggles and the General Strike). It may also be instructive to check news reports or documentation of political conflicts of early British capitalism which do not directly relate to class relations because it is important to establish that the ideology does not arise, in its essential form, from other social relations. It is vital that the ideology is proven to originate historically as well as logically with the emergence of its constituent social relations. It can be seen clearly that this whole method of reading essentially involves a constant dialectical to-ing and fro-ing between the socio-historical context and the ideology which hopefully deepens our understanding of the connection between them after each cycle.

From the historical investigation, the researcher could instructively build up a *socio-historical register* of the vocabularies available to the ideology in question, vocabularies which should tend towards a re-presentation of the generative structure but which could vary immensely with the context of both the ideology–structure connection and of the discursive expression of the ideology. There are often many different ways of saying the same thing. This socio-historical register of situated vocabularies will aid the researcher in understanding contemporary uses of old terms and will aid the researcher's audience in scrutinizing his conclusions from the final contemporary analysis.

An additional heuristic tool would be a *logical map* of the internal structure of the ideology, linking all its constituent ideas and images, and specifying its as yet unstated but logically necessary implications. This map is an abstracted account of the historical logic of the ideology and, again, will aid both the researcher and his/her audience in assessing the form of the ideology in its appearance in contemporary discourse. In an important way, this historico–logical map anchors the discovered, essential structure of the ideology and signposts its potential avenues of development.

Fourth approximation: the final analysis

Now the researcher can return to the present and analyse in depth another discursive expression of the contextualized, structurally generated ideology. Clearly, the research must await the reappearance of the reported events before beginning this final analysis, if it is the reporting of events that is being studied. Events rather than steady states will, of course, often be more helpful in providing regular, clear expressions of the ideology in discursive form. In the case I am using as an example, the researcher would study the press reports of a similar collision between capital and labour. This time the study will be in more depth and will probably use a month's reports from the whole of the national press. If possible, extensive interviews with powerful journalists would be carried out. Contemporary sources would again be checked out to examine other modes of expression of the ideology. Editorials and features will be systematically read. The nature of the activities reported will be carefully investigated where possible. Detailed theoretical and empirical analysis of the social role and internal imperatives of news reporting must also be carried out. Finally, the contemporary social context must be examined to determine its influence. These last three research practices are important as filtering practices, as researches which filter out extraneous ideologies which find their way into the discourse from the discursive practice itself and from the contemporary context; as researches which establish the appearances of the reported events and thus filter out what could be called 'situationally valid interpretations' or 'facts'. In the end, the researcher should be able to present a plausible case that he/she has identified the ideology in the discourse and linked its presence to its generative structure and context of appearance. Relating this back to the developed theory and the historical knowledge, an evidenced account of the nature and role of this ideology in social development can then be presented which gives us a sharper perspective on the workings of contemporary society.

Contemporary discourse can now be read in all its rich complexity as an embodiment of ideology, structure and context. Its language and style can be historically and structurally situated. We have a reading which is fully evidenced, which takes into account social structure, which is historically informed, which recognizes the role of inherited ideologies and contemporary significance, which takes into account the persuasive reality of appearances to be reported, which distinguishes occupational (or technical) ideologies from wider, class forms of ideology, and which grants language its fully social character. It is a reading which identifies the relations of signification (and their substantive vocabularies and meanings) constituting the social meaning of discursive artefacts, and which, therefore, enables us to go on to look at the interpretations of these discourses by public audiences. We now have a firm basis upon which audience interpretations can be judged as concordant or discordant.

Audience research at the moment is characterized by two things: a lack of sure knowledge about what is being interpreted, and consequently crude instruments of assessing the interpretations. The present work is not directed towards its re-assessment and reform, but my conclusions do offer some interesting developments. My research suggests the following techniques of determining audience interpretation:

1. The basic, substantive propositions of the ideology, embodied in abstract statements and word associations, could be offered to the audience for affirmation or denial and weighting.
2. These propositions could then be linked to a variety of contexts and personnel in order to discover the limits of the affirmation or denial.
3. The propositions could be placed within a variety of discursive contexts to see how the medium of communication varies the affirmation or denial.
4. The political implications of the ideology could be spelled out and proffered for affirmation or denial in order to establish the degree to which an ideology is consciously held.
5. The historical and structural background of the ideologies could be presented in order to establish the likelihood (and possibility) of a change of mind.

Audience concordance with the ideology would not, of course, prove any silly brainwashing thesis but it would provide a solid fact to be investigated in future research and recognized politically. Nor would audience denial prove the opposite. In either case, the nature of the questions asked on the basis of the historical materialist reading method would only provide valuable evidence of the extent, form and weighting of audience affirmation or denial of carefully delineated ideological formations.

In conclusion, the method advocated clearly entails much work. This will no doubt be completed piece by piece over time. The fact that existing readings do not get beyond first impressions leaves us with a task of some magnitude. Nevertheless, if the study of ideology is to join the ranks of the studies of economics and politics, to take its rightful place as the third member of the social science triumvirate, this task must be begun. Without a good knowledge of ideologies, as fully fledged forces of social development, the study of economics and politics is much diminished.

Notes

1. Compare this with the conceptions of Althusser and Balibar (1970) who limit political practice to revolutionary struggle, and Poulantzas (1973) who limits it to the struggle for victory in the "current situation" (the nodal point where social contradictions are condensed).
2. The combined energies of a society: a concept forged by Marx and Engels (1976a, p. 48).
3. It is these 'social relations of observation' which unify the appearances and ideologies into a given empirical form. This theory of the mechanism of formation of ideologies (both simple and complex) is perhaps the most important single development in this book. What distinguishes it from other approaches is (1) the distinction between appearance and ideology and (2) the notion of the social relations of observation as the decisive cause of any specific empirical mode of ideological appearance. These distinguishing marks are the keys which open the door to the analysis of complex ideological formations such as novels, images of deviance, laws and theories. The precise combination of signs in such a formation can only be understood through reference to the concept of the social relations of observation.

8   The Ideological Composition of Law

Economism in the Marxist Theory of Law

It is furthermore clear that here as always it is in the interest of the ruling section of society to sanction the existing order as law and to legally establish its limits given through usage and tradition. Apart from all else, this, by the way, comes about of itself as soon as the constant reproduction of the basis of the existing order and its fundamental relations assumes a regulated and orderly form in the course of time. And such regulation and order are themselves indispensable elements of any mode of production, if it is to assume social stability and independence from mere chance and arbitrariness. These are precisely the form of its social stability and therefore its relative freedom from mere arbitrariness and mere chance. Under backward conditions of the production process as well as the corresponding social relations, it achieves this form by mere repetition of their very reproduction. If this has continued on for some time, it entrenches itself as custom and tradition and is finally sanctioned as explicit law. (Marx, 1972, p. 793)

The above passage from *Capital* illustrates well the three most basic features of the Marxist theory of law. It indicates the centrality of the mode of production in any society and its consequent effects on inherited superstructural features such as law. It indicates the utility of the legal system for the ruling class, and their control over it. And, finally, it indicates that the main function of a legal system is to protect the reproduction of the economic system from external interference (e.g. from previously dominant economic classes, from political groups, from ideological conservatism or radicalism, from foreign intrusion). As Marx points out, sometimes the ruling class has to recognize the ideas, traditions and norms of other groups as law in order to ensure the reproduction of the economic system which that class benefits from.

None of these three primary features entails the conclusion that laws are epiphenomena of the economic system. Carefully formulated, they merely represent the theoretical platform, constructed out of the analysis of capital made by Marx, upon which the Marxist theory of law should have developed. Instead, what has happened is that the analysis of law in the Marxist tradition has been characterized by the most thoroughgoing economism one could imagine. Firstly, the legal system has been studied as a product of economic forces. Its other determinants have been neglected. Secondly, law has been converted into a mere function of ruling class economic interests. Other classes are rarely attributed with any historical role in the creation of laws. Thirdly, it has usually been said that the legal system is a machine which, of itself, reproduces the social relations and forces of production. The three primary features of the Marxian analysis of law, outlined earlier, have thus been reduced in validity and value. This reduction has been embodied in two main forms. On the one hand, the form and content of a legal system have been seen as reflexes of economic social relations and, on the other hand, they have been seen as instruments used by the ruling class in the class struggle with subordinate classes. The first form of reduction is a structuralist, passive one relying on Marxian economics. The second is a more active, political line focusing more on the politics of class struggle. Both are economistically conceived and both are natural tendencies of an analysis which begins with the economic and takes the nature of law for granted. Traditionally, Marxism has focused on the development of the capitalist economy and has thus only been concerned with law as it entered into the economic dialectic. Law as a form unto itself has therefore been neglected, as has the range of operation of that form. Increasingly however, Marxism is turning to the analysis of total social formations: a direction forced by Marx's neglect of the superstructural practices (and their relation to the economic) and the increasingly important role of politics, law and ideology in the maintenance of capitalist hegemony. Law will thus be explored in all its many facets as Marxism develops as a mode of social scientific enquiry.

Law as a reflex of the economic structure

Rooting themselves in Marx's observations on contract law as a juridic reflex of exchange relations (Marx, 1974, Chapter 2, for example), some Marxists carry out an economistic reduction by limiting the origin of law to economic relations. Thus, Karl Renner (the Austrian writer, and later President) saw legal norms and economic processes as mutually conditioning and subservient to each other (Renner, 1976, p. 58). Throughout his discussion, Renner assumed an economy–law dialectic which effectively excludes all else. "All economic institutions are at the same time institutions of law" (Renner, 1976, p. 57). In addition, Renner clearly implied (p. 55) that legal norms only arise out of "economic backgrounds". Renner probably never intended to compress the study of law into such a crude dialectic, but it was an inevitable effect within his own work after he had refused to analyse the origins of norms or ideologies embodied in the law. Typically, his work was firmly grounded in *Capital* and consciously avoided resolving the question of the meaning of the base-superstructure metaphor. In resort, he weakly points to uneven relations between law and economy and refuses to assert a one-to-one movement or correspondence. My reading of Renner is given more support by the fact that his overall thesis is that "legal institutions" may remain constant in form yet serve different economic functions at different points in time. This tends to negate a more sympathetic reading because Renner seemed to think that he had avoided economism by allowing for a time gap between economic origin and economic function.

Renner's approach is not unfamiliar to students of early twentieth century European Marxism (his book was written in 1904 and revised in 1929). It is as if he saw the superstructure as a set of ideologies (e.g. ethics, philosophy, law), each of which has a relation with the economy (as a whole). Renner selected law and studied the relations of interpenetration between the capitalist economy and the concepts of private law. Public law entered the arena as an after-thought, or as a twentieth century development stimulated by the growth of the bourgeois state and originating from that state. A picture of a discrete economy–law dialectic was thus presented where politics and culture were mere shadows in the background. Even more unfortunately, this picture is inaccurate for Renner conflated the social relations of capitalist production with their legal expression in the law of contract. Thus, he defined the economic process as "an external, technico-natural event" (the "substratum" of the legal norm) and the legal norm as "an inherent relation of wills" (Renner, 1976, p. 58). These two aspects of economic life are of course intertwined in practice. This notion of the economy–law connection fails to grasp Marx's distinction between class relations and technical relations and fails to see that ideology and legal practice mediate between social relations and legal norms. For Renner, legal relations actually *are* social relations. Moreover, they are social relations founded upon technical relations! But how do the physical movements involved in exchange result in the laws of contract? The gap between the two is too great and can only be bridged by using the concepts of social relation, ideology and legislative practice. In other words, to answer the question one had to understand the movements as social acts within a social practice, a practice whose repetition generates, internally, an ideology of contract which is eventually legalized by the holders of social power in specific historical circumstances.

Writing a little later than Renner, in 1924, Eugene Pashukanis[1] chided his comrades for thinking that the mere introduction of class struggle into the study of law was sufficient to justify the description of the study as materialist or Marxist. He thought that it was necessary to study the apparently universal forms of law (what Renner called the legal institutions) as well as the contents (or instrumental aspects). Law was more than a weapon used by the rulers in the course of struggles with lower classes, it took forms which appeared to straddle different epochs. Pashukanis argued, obviously bearing in mind Marx's discussion of categories in the introduction to the *Grundrisse* (Marx, 1973), that the category of law only obtained its fullest historical meaning in capitalist society, a society where the different facets of the legal form bloomed in full flower. This was because legal relations, as Pashukanis called them, were reflections of economic social relations, and in particular the relations of commodity exchange, and because exchange relations reach their height of development in bourgeois society. Consequently, law would not die out or wither away after a socialist state was set up because, as Marx pointed out in the "Critique of the Gotha Programme" (Marx and Engels, 1973), commodity exchange would still occur in such a state. This would necessitate the continued existence of basic legal concepts, albeit temporarily and in a form which reflected the dictatorship of the proletariat. Moreover, argued Pashukanis (foreshadowing modern Soviet penal policy), criminal behaviour was a question of medical pedagogy not a matter for social engineers and therefore, for a time, criminal law and procedure would also be needed (until it disappeared at the hands of the doctors and psychiatrists).[2] Hence, the new socialist state should not abandon bourgeois law overnight and, indeed, cannot. Rather, socialists should open up the history which constitutes the real significance of bourgeois legal categories, an act which hails and hastens the disappearance of the social relations upon which these categories exist: "the laying bare of the roots of ideology is the true index of its, approaching end . . ." (Pashukanis, in Hazard, 1951, p. 124).

In contradiction to Reisner's[3] view that law was just one form of ideology, Pashukanis thought that juridic concepts, as opposed to what he called "technical regulations", were only part ideological (by which he meant subjective or psychological-illusory); they were also in part objective and rooted as valid reflections of social relations. Basing himself (like so many others) on Marx's analysis of commodity fetishism in *Capital*, Pashukanis likened juridic concepts to theoretical categories such as commodities, value and exchange-value, arguing that they were "distorted forms of ideas wrapped in mystery" (i.e. ideological conceptions) and also (amazingly) "abstractions from which we can scientifically construct economic objective reality" (in Hazard, 1951, p. 131). Given that Pashukanis misunderstands Marx's categories, he must misunderstand law. Categories such as commodity and value are not illusory in Marx's view, rather they are categories which adequately represent the nature of the economic reality (both latent and manifest) of capitalist production. Does Pashukanis intend concepts such as right, contract, ownership, etc., to have scientific validity in this sense? Hardly. He has fogged the issue in trying to defeat Reisner (whose conception of the exclusively ideological nature of law led to an emphasis on the "revolutionary legal consciousness" of the workers' Soviets rather than a reliance on the pragmatic, social engineering of the Leninist party-state). From here, Pashukanis did indeed run into problems in his analysis of law. In deliberately excluding ideology from his subsequent analysis, Pashukanis was left with a view of law (like capital) as a social relationship wrapped up in mystery, a form of social relationship based on the social relations of commodity exchange:

> A juridic relationship between subjects is merely the other side of the relationship between the products of labour which have become goods [commodities—C.S.]. (Pashukanis, in Hazard, 1951, p. 140)

Thus Pashukanis rejected the view that law is rooted in class ideology and interest and located the essential source within exchange relations.

But what did Pashukanis mean when he said that legal regulations are social relations between subjects? Did he not mean that they are composed of relations of signification which specify the relative powers of legal personalities? He could surely not have meant otherwise, i.e. that legal relations are the *real* relations between people in practice? From his many other remarks in his essay, "Theory of Law and Marxism," it is clear that Pashukanis actually shares that part of my view which sees legal regulations as social relations of signification or ideological formations which specify the relative powers of structurally constituted units. But his desire to escape from the political significance of the ideological component of law and from the political component of law (as ideologies sanctioned by social authority or, in modern times, the state) led him to conceive of legal regulations economistically as social relations between subjects arising from the social structures of commodity exchange. At a time when the state in Russia was becoming more and more powerful, when exchange relations were far from disappearing and when the ideologies of many sectors of Soviet society were antithetical to those of the ruling group, Pashukanis' position was no more than a sound reflection of his social circumstances.

In my view, laws in modern societies are ideological formations given legal form and sanction by the state. Pashukanis, as I have said, could not recognize the ideological content, but also he did not recognize their political content as ideologies sanctioned by the state. Hiding behind a critique of jurisprudential Positivism, he was able to excuse the maintenance and, indeed, development of bourgeois law in revolutionary Russia carried out by a state which intended to expand rapidly the production and exchange of commodities. For

Pashukanis, the state was merely a secondary and misleading feature because it was essentially the expression of bourgeois relations of production. He could therefore dismiss its political and ideological role in the creation of laws and argue (for example) that the individual subject is constituted by commodity exchange and not by state legal decrees:

> State authority introduces into the legal structure precision and stability, but it does not create the premises of that superstructure; these are rooted in material—that is to say, in production-relationships. (Pashukanis, in Hazard, 1951, p. 147)

Thus, much of the planning law of the later period (following the proclaimed pursuit of a planned economy in 1926) could only be understood by Pashukanis as "technical regulation" because for him truly juridic regulation must die away as bourgeois exchange relations decline. As the conceptions of the NEP were replaced by the notion of a planned economy, Pashukanis lost favour to those who saw law as an instrument of class rule (in this case, an instrument to be used by the state "in the interests of the working class", i.e. for an expanded economy). As Carr puts it:

> When Pashukanis, at the moment of the adoption of the five-year plan in April 1929, wrote that "the role of the purely juridical superstructure, the role of law, is diminishing", and that "regulation becomes more effective as the role of law becomes weaker and less significant", he was still speaking the language of the first years of the revolution, now overtaken by the advent of planning. The grandiose five-year plan imposed on Soviet law, the imperative obligation to support and enforce it. (Carr, 1976, p. 397)

Pashukanis' partial recantation in 1930 involved him recognizing the role of the state in sanctioning law and in creating "technical regulations", but he still insisted that juridic concepts arose out of the market economy. It is not surprising that he disappeared in 1937, especially since in 1936 Stalin had announced the disappearance of the working class as a proletariat and the achievement of the first phase of communism: if the market economy had disappeared (and most of its consequent classes), the continued existence (and rapid expansion) of law 'disproved' Pashukainis' theory.

Pashukanis' insistence that "wherever we have the primary stratum of the juridic superstructure, we find that the juridic relationship is generated by the material production relationships" is a classic example of economism in Marxist theory of law. It is based on a plausible but narrow reading of Marx. Its political naivety was demonstrated by Pashukanis' ineffectiveness in the Russian Revolution. Renner and Pashukanis were not the last Marxists to fall foul of economism but they are the most important in terms of the theory of law.[4] It is not surprising when Western commentators state that Marx held that "the mode of production determines all non-economic phenomena. Marx consistently maintained that base and superstructure stand to each other as a cause to an effect . . ." (Lloyd, 1972, p. 632). Tumanov, a modern Soviet student of law, forgets this when he rebukes bourgeois jurists who make the accusation of economism (Tumanov, 1974, p. 108). However, he is right to say that:

> A marked imprint is left on law by various factors like the political conditions, the dominant ideology, and in some epochs, by religion, the national mentality, historical traditions, etc. (Tumanov, 1974, p. 109)

This is too vague however; even though it clearly recognizes the complexity of the ideological component of law. I would like to leave this discussion of economism by positing the more precise view that ideologies embodied in legal form can be generated in political and cultural practices (past and present). Law is not just a reflex of economic structures but also a reflex of political and cultural relations. Nor is it the case that private law reflects the economy whilst public law reflects politics and culture. Such an artificial schema is totally inadequate: each piece of legislation or legal concept must be examined independently for its economic, political and cultural roots. A fortiori, there is no way that public law can be seen as either a pure result of the expansion of the twentieth century state (Renner), or as a body of non-law (Pashukanis).

Law as a weapon of the ruling class forged in the class struggle

Some Marxists have limited their general conception of law to its functions (for the ruling classes in history) as an instrument of class domination in situations of class conflict. Like economism, this tendency contains many valid arguments and insights, but, again, it is too limited a perspective to form the basis of a general, Marxian concept of law.

A classic statement within this tendency comes from the Russian Commissariat of Justice in 1919:

> It is self-evident that all codes of bourgeois laws, all bourgeois law as a system of norms (legal rules), have had the same part to play, namely to maintain by organized force the balance of interests of the various classes of society to the advantage of the ruling classes (the bourgeoisie and landlords). . . . In the interests of conserving strength, of bringing isolated actions into conformity with one another, and of centralization, the proletariat must work out rules for curbing its class enemies, for establishing a method in struggling with its enemies and must teach itself to rule. (Quoted in Hazard, 1951, p. xxiii)

No doubt such statements are typical of a revolutionary period or of groups that think such a period is round the corner. But by no means do all laws function for the ruling class, nor did they all originate in the class struggle. This is so fantastically obvious that I refuse to waste time exemplifying it. I suppose that the vast majority of Marxists would agree with me, if pushed, but nevertheless empirical studies recurrently focus on the origins and functions of laws in terms of class relations. Again, perhaps this is because law often only becomes of interest to Marxists when it interferes in the classic economistic dialectic of capital versus labour. This would explain why laws relating to industrial relations, economic crimes, housing, riot control and safety at work are most commonly selected for Marxist analysis (e.g. Beirne, 1977; Hay et al., 1977; Thompson, 1977; Hadden, 1975; Spicer, 1976; Pearce, 1976; Linebaugh, 1976; Petras, 1977). Such studies are of great value to the understanding of law as are those studies, like Renner's, which examine the correspondence between legal form and economic structure. And, I must add, some of them are more economistic in their understanding of class struggle than others. But, nevertheless, is this all there is to the Marxian conception and analysis of law?

A good illustration of the problems raised by narrow class analysis can be found in Quinney's *Critique of Legal Order* (1974). Having said that "the legal system is an apparatus created to secure the interests of the dominant class", Quinney defines that benefit as accruing to the ruling class in the cause of dominating the subordinate classes (1974,

p. 52). Thus, criminal law establishes domestic order for the ruling class, in Quinney's view. Consequently, the "crime control program" of the US government in the late 1960s and early 1970s is seen by Quinney as the construction of "a new reality of crime":

> This reality is an obvious attempt to perpetuate the existing social and economic order, in further oppression of those who suffer from a class-dominated society. (Quinney, 1974, p. 105)

Not surprisingly, Quinney concludes that, with socialism (note: not communism), classes, bureaucracy and centralized authority disappear and so too does state law; although he does, shortly after, mention that some functions of the socialist community may best be "served on a general state level" (1974, pp. 190, 191). One can agree with the general tenor of Quinney's position and the (very) general truth of many of his propositions, but the analysis leaves out so much that it eventually becomes quite oppressive itself. Quinney's book should be compared with the more subtle analysis of Douglas Hay for a full understanding of my position (Hay et al., 1977).

More illustrations of this tendency could be found, especially from activist newspapers, but let me move on by pointing out that law is always under the control of the ruling class in a broad sense but it does not always originate in economic class conflict, function well for the ruling class, reflect the full range of ruling class opinion, remain immune from the lawyers and bureaucrats who administer it, or serve economic ends.

Perhaps, the socialist movement was too entranced with economism to break easily from the two tendencies discussed here. However, over the last few years there are signs that the break is being made (see some of the articles in Carlen, 1976). Faced with laws which reflect racist, sexist, nationalist and urban ideologies, and influenced by women's movements, black groups, immigrant groups, etc., the Marxian theory of law is moving out of its slumber. This movement has been stimulated not the least by the obviously political nature of much modern legislation all over the world. No longer can socialist theorists fall back onto the economic structure and the class struggle in the simple-minded way that characterizes some of the existing work. Certainly, new issues need to be related to economic relations and class conflict—but not reduced to them. Law must now be located in its full existence, which means looking at its political and cultural origins. New weight is therefore thrown onto the ideological component of law: this component must be understood in order to grasp the effectivity of politics and culture. Legal enactments must be seen as reflections of contemporary culture and as reflections of political manoeuvre, as well as reflections of economic structure. This will involve the recognition that the analysis of class relations and ideologies must be complemented by the study of class fractions, political parties, political cliques, bureaucrats, cultural movements, cultural groups, and all their corresponding ideologies.

Advances in Modern Marxism

It was necessary to go into some detail in the previous section in order to be able to place the more recent writers in a proper historical perspective. We should now be able to see where they have made advances over the essentially Bukharinist, mechanical materialism of Renner and Pashukanis. It will be noticed that no longer are we limited to the economic structure and the class struggle in our explanations of law. The relative autonomy of the state and the ideological nature of law have become much more important than ever before. The thrust of this advance can be understood better by brief reference to the work of Gramsci, an Italian Marxist writing in the 1920s and 1930s.

Gramsci, like all Marxists, believed that many laws reflected economic relations and that law itself was eternally and generally a weapon of class domination. But his distinctiveness is well summed up by his biographer, Fiori:

> Gramsci's originality as a Marxist lay partly in his conception of the nature of Bourgeois rule (and indeed of any previous established social order), in his argument that the system's real strength does not lie in the violence of the ruling class or the coercive power of its state apparatus, but in the acceptance by the ruled of a "conception of the world" which belongs to the rulers. The philosophy of the ruling class passes through a whole tissue of complex vulgarizations to emerge as "common sense": that is, the philosophy of the masses, who accept the morality, the customs, the institutionalized rules of behaviour of the society they live in. The problem for Gramsci then is to

understand *how* the ruling class has managed to win the consent of the subordinate classes in this way; and then to see how the latter will manage to overthrow the old order and bring about a new one of universal freedom. This is no abstract analysis of capitalism in general, or of the general meaning of exploitation, however. Gramsci is principally concerned with the much more concrete reality of Italy and Italian history: he is trying to see how the Italian bourgeois state was formed, and what part the intellectuals played in the process. (Fiori, 1970, p. 238)

The role played by law in the winning of consent was important. Gramsci distinguished between two major superstructural "levels": "civil society", which was an ensemble of private organisms, and "political society" or the state (1971, p. 12). Civil society performed the function of maintaining the hegemony of the ruling class (domination by consent), whilst the state exercised coercive power. The law figures in both these levels, according to Gramsci. Firstly, "juridical government" as state coercion:

. . . "legally" enforces discipline on those groups who do not "consent" either actively or passively. This apparatus is, how- ever, constituted for the whole of society in anticipation of moments of crisis of command and direction when spontaneous consent has failed. (Gramsci, 1971, p. 12)

The legal apparatus thus operates coercively to maintain hegemony, *and* directively in periods of ideological and political crisis. Secondly, the legal enactments educate and adapt the masses to the goals of civil society (as defined by the system through its ruling class), to the realms of "morality and custom".

The dynamic of a legal system was termed by Gramsci: "the juridical problem". This problem is that of "assimilating the entire grouping to its most advanced fraction" (Gramsci, 1971, p. 195). In modern capitalism, this means the problem of assimilating the intermediate classes, the proletariat, the industrial reserve army and even fractious sectors of the bourgeoisie to the hegemonic domina- tion of the multinational bourgeoisie and their national political and cultural representatives. In short, Gramsci argues that the general function of law, whether it relates to crime or custom, is to render the ruling group homogeneous and to create "a social conformism which is useful to the ruling group's line of development" (1971, p. 195). Clearly, Gramsci is moving well beyond Bukharinist economism in his analysis of law towards a position which can cope with the ideological heterogeneity of modern societies. Gramsci does not stress the economic structures themselves so much as the ideologies which they generate or which maintain them at the political and cultural level. The economy–law dialectic of Renner is rendered crude by this new reference to the intervening conditions of ideology, state power, the intellectuals, hegemonic fractions and class conflict. One of the most interesting points here is that Gramsci points to the ideological function of law in unifying fractions of the ruling class in practice, as well as to the classic Marxian argument that law conceals the reality of the social structure for the masses. Gramsci is going further than Marx, however, in that ideological mystification through the law is seen as not just an effect of structures whose appearances conceal. This mystique has to be *won* by the ruling class for its devices and, therefore, the propaganda campaigns, speeches, books, ceremonies, procedures and 'dirty tricks' of the organic intellectuals of the bourgeoisie are vitally important in the construction of conformism and the mystique of legal enactments. Legal mystification could be undermined, if the organic intellectuals of the lower classes were active in defeating hegemonic propaganda and demonstrating the thoroughly social and oppressive nature of bourgeois law.

> The conception of law will have to be freed from every residue of transcendentalism and from every absolute; in practice, from every moralistic fanaticism. . . . In reality, the State must be conceived of as an "educator", in as much as it tends precisely to create a new type or level of civilisation. Because one is acting essentially on economic forces, reorganising and developing the apparatus of economic production, creating a new structure, the conclusion must not be drawn that superstructural factors should be left to themselves, to develop spontaneously, to a haphazard and sporadic germination. The State in this field, too, is an instrument of "nationalisation", of acceleration and of Taylorisation. . . . The Law is the repressive and negative aspect of the entire, positive, civilising activity undertaken by the State. The "prize-giving" activities of individuals and groups, etc., must also be incorporated in the conception of the Law; . . .
> (Gramsci, 1971, p. 247)

Thus it is that the practice of the politicians and the intellectuals is crucial to the understanding of the legal form as one of the key apparatuses maintaining hegemony of the ruling classes.

From Gramsci, we must move to the French structuralists. But before that, it is necessary (if only briefly) to mention the chronologically intermediate work of Otto Kirchheimer, a member of the Frankfurt school of Marxism who emigrated to the USA in the face of fascism. Kirchheimer's book *Political Justice* (1961) is very important because it firmly establishes the political nature of law. Kirchheimer argued that political and ideological tensions between fascism and bourgeois democracy, and between bourgeois regimes of all kinds and communist/progressive opposition, have become internationally intense in the twentieth century. This increased intensity, he said, has "caused all regimes to reinforce police and informal institutional controls over their subjects' associations and political activities" (Kirchheimer, 1961, p. 16). This has meant an increased significance for law and legal procedure as a political force. Echoing Gramsci, Kirchheimer observes that "the ideological fight for domination over people's minds" entails the courts in important political activity. Even in bourgeois democracies where the executive has not got direct control of the courts, there are the biases of underlying assumptions and procedures and the indirect pressures of the propaganda of the mass media. Thus the political trial is an ideal way of "eliminating political foes" since it carries legitimacy as a branch of "due process". Linking the courts with other agencies such as military action, informal violence, bribery, the church preachings and mass media propaganda, Kirchheimer sees the political trial as a functional authentication of political repression. It is a new political weapon in the struggle for "spontaneous assent", operating through its selection of suitable targets for public degradation and criminalization. Linking clemency with asylum, Kirchheimer shows how even remote legal practices effectively serve the hegemonic chariot of political justice in societies ridden with economic, political and cultural divisions.

In an important discussion in *Reading Capital* (1970), Balibar re-introduces the economistic problematic and moves away from it to a minor degree. His discussion is rooted within the soil of an economy–law dialectic handed down from *Capital*. He does differ from Renner, however, in several ways, notably in distinguishing clearly the physical-technical aspects of practice from its class elements. And, unlike Pashukanis, he focuses on production rather than on the market. Balibar correctly sustains the view, contra Renner and Pashukanis, that the social relations of production are quite distinct from their ideological expression in legal concepts and decisions, noting however that it is difficult even to talk of class relations in the production sphere without referring to legal concepts which reflect those relations (such as ownership). He goes on to establish the Marxian nature of the view that a dislocation is possible between the realm of law and the realm of economy (and its concomitant ideologies). Balibar asserts a term subsequently adopted by Hirst (1976a, b): the "non-correspondence" between law and the social relations of production. This is not merely a shift in verbiage but an indication of a new direction in Marxism based on Althusser's conception of relative autonomy (which is really only a fancy way of stating how dialectical materialism sees any thing): a direction which, in the work of Hirst (1976a, b, 1977), Hirst and Hindess (1977), and Hindess (1977), threatens to lead to the conceptualization of the political as totally autonomous and dominant. Balibar did not go that far, and merely defines law as a second-order concept, relations of production being of the first order. Balibar fails to define law, however, and also fails to specify the precise location of law in a social formation. What does determine "the generation of the instance of law" is left unaddressed and his remarks drift into the old question of the kinds and forms of law demanded by the capitalist economic structure: a relevant and still unexhausted topic, but one which should have been dealt with before the flood. Balibar's discussion thus marks a definite regression in the theory of law.

Balibar's colleague, Louis Althusser, briefly mentions law in his essay on ideology (1971) (discussed earlier in Chapter 2). This discussion reflects the modern drift to open up Marxism but does not really advance us very far. Althusser merely points out à la Gramsci that the realm of law belongs to both repressive and ideological state apparatuses (ISAs). Like Gramsci, he sees the legal machine as both coercive and educative.[5] The state apparatuses of violence act as guarantees of the indoctrination function, and act in themselves as enforcers of ruling class power and interest. Going further than Gramsci, and reminding us of many of Pashukanis' remarks, Althusser sees the ISAs as indoctrinating the mass with the fundamental bourgeois ideology of the free subject. Althusser of course overdoes it and, unlike Gramsci, leaves no room for class conflict and counter-propaganda until his famous postscript. Most importantly, though, Althusser does stress the importance of class struggle within the ISAs: this presumably applies to the legal machine as well as to the schools and newspapers. Whether Althusser would extend the ideological composition and function of the law as an ISA to include the whole range of social ideologies is an interesting question. I am sure that he would, but his conception of the range of those ideologies is narrower than mine in that he focuses on those which originate in the capitalist economic structure. His *Essays in Self-Criticism* (Althusser, 1976) do, however, seem to extend his conception of relevant ideologies and, also, seem to share my view that some of those ideologies derive from political and cultural relations. Thus he points to the role of bourgeois political relations in generating the category of the free citizen (p. 204), and emphasizes the importance of the superstructure in aiding and protecting economic reproduction (p. 203). He now clearly sees that the reproduction of capital is a self-contained economic process and that it needs a superstructure dominated by ruling class ideologies and interests in order to sustain itself in the face of workers' challenges.

Like Pashukanis and Althusser, Nicos Poulantzas stresses "the institutionalized fixing of agents of production as juridical subjects" (1973, p. 128). Juridical relations, he says, set up individuals as such and deprive them (juridically) of their economic position and class membership (the key matters in deciding what *actual* powers they have in society). This legal individualization reflects the separation of the workers from the means of production and sustains it through the device of contracts of employment. Poulantzas then advances beyond this basic, Marxian position and argues that the "juridico-political instance" itself generates an ideology, an ideology which is central to the dominant ideology of the capitalist mode of production. He does not say much about this ideology which, from our point of view, is of great interest. But he does say:

> Here, the separation of the direct producer from his means of production is expressed, in ideological discourse, in extraordinarily complex forms of individualist personalism, in the setting-up of agents as "subjects". (Poulantzas, 1973, pp. 128, 129)

What promised to be the advance we were looking to thus eventually turned out to be a reiteration of Althusser's argument, but in a more explicitly economistic form. Poulantzas concludes his argument on this point by saying that the individualization in the law masks the class system and the unity of interest of workers. Competition thus produces isolation. This competition, surprisingly, is said to be "the effect of the juridical and the ideological and socio-economic relations" (1973, p. 131). Thus law is vital for Poulantzas in masking the class struggle and representing it at the superstructural level as clashes of individual interest. I doubt if this argument is correct as well as interesting for by its very nature the capitalist mode of production atomizes labour into separate detail-functions and generates competition in every nook and cranny. Juridical concepts of the individual would merely seem to *anchor* these developments and may well originate elsewhere (e.g. in Roman law and in the rise of the bourgeois class against the divine collectivism of the feudal aristocracy). I doubt if one can see competition as the effect of juridical ideology.

Poulantzas' view, that juridic relations constitute people as subjects and thus isolate individuals within their socio-economic practice, is important because it is upon this basis that he argues that the state constitutes in political practice the hegemony of the bourgeoisie (1973, pp. 133–141). On the foundation of a false but real isolation, articulated and constructed in juridical relations, the state is able to build a political ideology (and practice) of unity of interest and thus its hegemony over the subordinate classes. Thus combining a little Althusser with a little Gramsci, Poulantzas provides us with a further development of the theory of law. Law in capitalist social formations is the device which conditions individuals for their subjection to the ruling class. It separates them ideologically from their class, gives each of them powers, rights and interests, constitutes the key concepts of dominant ideology and organizes a system of penalties and rewards. Thus legally constituted the nation is ready for its state.

Like Althusser, Poulantzas locates law at the centre of bourgeois ideology and gives it a major role in the reproduction of the total social formation. Unfortunately, like much of Althusser's writings, Poulantzas' work seems to neglect the challenges of the working class in shattering the veils of ideology. If the legal system was tied in more closely with the apparatuses of mass communications, it would be a more plausible case: "the law provides the structure of the private subject's house and the mass media provide the furniture".

Maybe. I personally doubt if the law is quite as effective ideologically as Althusser and Poulantzas seem to think. "The law is an ass" is also an ideology that has its adherents, as does "one law for the rich and another for the poor". Law is so expensive and technical these days that its hegemonic functions must not be overstressed: it may be of more value in integrating the ruling class around its procedures, ideologies and slogans. "Law and order" campaigns seem to be an effective way of uniting a ruling class separated by its diverse egoistic interests, as well as of drawing some "spontaneous assent" from the masses for repressive action. What concerns me more is the ideological component of law and the French Marxists have made an important advance in suggesting that ideology may have political and cultural sources. Ultimately, they unfortunately tend to locate the origins of legal ideologies in the economic structure and give insufficient attention to other sources of legal ideology. Their contribution lies in a structuralist and functionalist extension of the Gramscian thesis, in the theorization of the effects of legal ideology. This theorization is, however, often very one-sided. It tends to ignore the role of class conflict, structural contradictions, social intercourse, and proletarian culture (and, for that matter, middle class culture) in generating and distributing subordinate class ideologies in opposition to the ruling ideologies.

Recently, echoes of Gramsci, Althusser and Poulantzas appeared in Hay's essay "Property, Authority and the Criminal Law" (Hay et al., 1977). He argues that the eighteenth century English ruling class was able to maintain order without a massive police-military machine and without any great increase in the use of judicial terror. This was done through the astute manipulation of the ideology of Law, says Hay. For him, Law was "an instrument of authority and a breeder of values" which replaced the weakened "divine right of kings" ideology (Hay et al., 1977, p. 58). Sounding much like a Gramscian hegemonic institution, the Law was a lynchpin of social order. Hay focuses not so much on the law itself but on the ideology of Law, the popular understanding of Law which meant its Majesty, Wisdom, Terror and Divine authority. Popular belief in the divine and magical justice of the law was sustained, says Hay, by ceremonial public hangings and the careful use of the pardon. As Hay puts it:

> An ideology endures not by being wholly enforced and rigidly defined. Its effectiveness lies first in its very elasticity, the fact

that men are not required to make it a credo, that it seems to them the product of their own minds and their own experience. And the law did not enforce uniform obedience, did not seek total control; indeed it sacrificed punishment when necessary to preserve the belief in justice. The courts dealt in terror, pain and death, but also in moral ideals, control of arbitrary power, mercy for the weak. In doing so they made it possible to disguise much of the class interest of the law. (Hay *et al.*, 1977, p. 55)

Of course, one may doubt whether the ideology of the Law and the ideologies embodied in the law were gullibly received by the masses of eighteenth century England, especially in the urban centres. However, Hay's essay is an important contribution in that it suggests the emergence of an ideology of Law outside the economy and documents the various devices used by the ruling classes to cultivate and sustain this ideology to their own benefit. The notion of the appearances of law as something that of itself could give rise to an ideology about the legal system as a whole is an interesting one. His descriptions of its cultivation resonate with my own insistence that people can present and develop appearances which are structurally created beforehand in practice. Mystification is rarely a pure effect of the economic structure. What is needed now is the demonstration of the origins of legal ideologies in the political and cultural conditions of the day, as well as their economic contexts and class functions.

The developments in the modern Marxist theory of law are encapsulated in Alan Hunt's essay of 1976. Insisting that law is an important mechanism of ideological domination as well as of sheer coercion, Hunt argues that the legal system of the bourgeois democratic state legitimizes and mystifies the class rule of the bourgeoisie. Quite rightly, he also points to the fact that the continued effectiveness of such a legal system depends on its ability to express the rights, powers and interests of subordinate classes. Here Hunt has made an important advance, one hitherto unanalysed by Marxists. He has greatly opened up the question of hegemony in relation to law. Extending his remarks a little, one could say that the effectiveness of law as an ideological force, as a means towards ruling class hegemony, depends upon its ideological encapsulation of a consensus constructed outside itself in other economic, political and cultural practices. This raises the question of the possibility of a legal system solely dependent upon coercion. I doubt if this is possible.

Even a highly coercive fascist state requires an ideological alliance between the ruling class and other classes (and class fractions). A legal system without an ideological base is as inconceivable as a repressive military dictatorship with "due process". Law without some hegemonic class bloc is merely naked power and thus no law at all. Law is not only ideology backed by instituted social power, it is also instituted social power articulated in and reinforced by ideology. Marxian analysis must not neglect either side of the equation.

On the ideological component of law, Hunt restates the fetishism thesis by arguing that laws do not reflect the truth of social relations but rather their phenomenal forms of appearance. Thus an employment arrangement appears in the law as a consensual contract between equals rather than what it really is, an expression of the conflicting interests of parties of unequal power. On this basis, Hunt says that legal rules have an "ideological dimension". The conclusion is correct, but in my view the basis is wider than that posited by Hunt. Like most Marxists, he does not distinguish between ideology and appearance. I would argue that not only does law embody the appearances of reality produced by social relations, but also it embodies those appearances *as they have been seen and interpreted* by the classes and groups who make the law. Thus, not only does the contract of employment individualize what is essentially a class relation, but it also individualizes it in a way which expresses the dominance of the employers and their ideological grasp of the apparent relation between individuals. The ideological grasp of the employees of this apparent relation is usually subordinated in the negotiating situation, and, therefore, the final legal document expresses their views to a lesser extent. My general point is true even where there are militant employees. In that case, their view would more likely represent the relation in its true light, as a class relation, and, therefore, clauses which may victimize individuals or divide the workforce would often be severely restricted. In short, yes, social relations in capitalism often deceive in appearance, but their observers are not always deceived because "they have minds of their own", minds which sometimes accurately reflect contradictory class interests.

On the sources of ideology in the law, Hunt tends to stress the appearances of economic practice, but, most importantly, he recognizes that some laws are generated out of political relations. Thus, like Kirchheimer, he points to laws which protect the state itself. I want to see this line of enquiry developed to cover the institutions, agents and structures of cultural practice. Those laws which arose to protect and legitimate ruling class ideology itself, the institutions of ruling class culture, and relations between the educators and the educated should be studied, along with those laws which arise out of conflict in culture. The role of law in relation to cultural practices is greatly neglected. Such laws are often explained away as outcomes of economic or political conflict, when on some occasions they are mainly generated by differences over cultural matters.

There we leave the advances of modern Marxism in the theory of law. In the light of these developments away from economism, I shall now briefly make some observations of my own on the ideological component of law.

The Ideological Nature of Law

> The law in its majestic impartiality forbids rich and poor alike to sleep under bridges, to beg in the streets and steal bread.
> (Anatole France, quoted in Hunt, 1976, p. 184)

Law has rarely been explicitly defined as a concept in Marxist theory and one is often left with the impression that empiricism has prevailed. That is, law has usually been dealt with as "the law in the books". This is understandable but seems unsatisfactory since it is a definition which takes the state's word for what counts as law. However, perhaps the implicit definition is the correct one—after all, is not the point about law that it is what the state says it is? Subjectively, the law may be what you think it is, but surely objectively it is a collection of ideologies, sanctioned in the correct manner by the institutionalized executors of social power, which define the socially permissible modes of social intercourse? It is distinguished from ordinary ideology by its political backing. It is distinguished from politicians' speeches and policies by the fact that it has received political backing in the manner laid down by custom or constitution. It is distinguished from administrative decisions not by due process or rights of appeal but by the fact that it expresses approved rules of conduct in a general form and by the fact that these rules have been agreed upon in the proper manner by the proper persons in power. What counts as the 'proper' mode of law-creation is, of course, itself a matter in the control of the powerful.

This definition will cover stateless societies which are often excluded by Marxist definitions which usually suppose a state. It will allow for minority legal systems which operate within a nation-state: these systems only ever operate by permission of the social power-holders. Judge-made law is included, since the judiciary are institutionalized as executive agents of social power. Inoperative or unenforced rules are also included: as properly sanctioned ideologies they are laws, even though their existence may discredit the legal system.

Definitions of law which point to the necessity of collective consensus, which see it as an expression of some transcendental force, which depoliticize it, which reduce it to mere decisions of the powerful, or which limit it to those ideas which serve ruling class interests—all such definitions miss the precise sense of law as a conjoint expression of power and ideology. The crucial questions about the origins of law always relate to the power bloc behind the legislation, the nature of the problem this bloc wants to solve, the ideologies in which this problem is perceived and understood, and the political opposition to the proposed legislation. Law is a hybrid phenomenon of politics and ideology: a politico-ideological artefact.

It may be argued that some ideologies are sanctioned by the power-holders in a different manner to that laid down as necessary for legal enactment and that these ideologies are often more effective than a statute or judge's decision. An example of this is a government incomes policy which is sanctioned by a political pact between the party in power, the trade unions, the employer's representatives and media-influenced 'public opinion'. My definition may thus seem to collude with the state in playing down the fact that modes of social practice are often controlled without legal enactment or procedure. I do not think it does. That is the whole point about law, as it is now and as it always has been. Law is a public, ideological front which can often conceal the true workings of a social formation. It is very much an ideological means of controlling social practice: sometimes more practical means of social control are necessary. Law depends on some kind of ideological consensus amongst a number of classes and class fractions: that consensus cannot always be produced on important issues or problems. In such situations, social control has to go on behind the law's ideological curtain. In short, the use of law is not always culturally possible and therefore not politically expedient and, in political practice, politics is always in command. Law lies in the cradle of political practice and is, therefore, subject to the pressures and imperatives of politics. This is the answer to Balibar's question: as an instance in a social formation, law is a politico-ideological phenomenon produced in a form of political practice, that practice geared to the creation, definition and maintenance of power relations. As such it is only one weapon within a whole armoury.

It is important not to overstate the political sources of law. Thus, I use the phrase "sanctioned by the instituted social powers" rather than "created by". Legislation and judicial decisions are always political since their immediate causes are the legislators and the judges, agents of political practice, and their immediate purpose is the resolution of conflict but, less immediately, the balance of class forces, economic necessity, ideological pressures and political pressure groups are always other important causal considerations. Moroever, something Gramsci said should not be forgotten:

> . . . once the conditions are created in which a certain way of life is "possible", then "criminal action or omission" must have a punitive sanction, with moral implications, and not merely be judged generically as "dangerous". (Gramsci, 1971, p. 247)

It does not concern us here which problems are treated punitively and which are dealt with by restitutive law, but what is important is to realize, with Gramsci, that once a mode of production is established, along with corresponding modes of political and cultural intercourse, the law of the land must develop in order to regulate that social formation. In other words, legal enactments mostly respond to social problems and are not simply unilateral political declarations of ideology. To a certain extent, therefore, the social system dictates to judges and legislators. Only to an extent though; what is vital is the recognition that problems only appear in a certain manner depending on the social structural context in which they exist and are only perceived through the ideological grids of the people observing them. Thus the system may require legislative action, but it does not dictate to legislators how they are to see the problem or how to deal with it. This fact often reduces parliament to a "talking shop" (Lenin's phrase) and judicial decisions to wonders of cultural ignorance: the system often goes on without them.

It is a false argument which mitigates the political and ideological nature of law on the grounds that much law is "technical". In its most sophisticated form, the argument would be that most legal enactments today reflect technical problems within social practice and thus are little to do with class relations. However, this is not only a politician's viewpoint (whether bourgeois or Marxist); it is also a false one. Technical relations of practice are always bound up with the class relations of practice. Thus, in economic life, the reorganization of production is not simply a technical adjustment but one which affects the classes and class relations articulated conjointly with the technical relations (see Bettelheim, 1974, for a good analysis of this issue). The distinction between law which reflects political ideology and law which is a mere technical instrument is made in both modern Western and Russian legal systems. It is a spurious distinction which often works to conceal the political and ideological nature of so-called technical instruments.

If it is possible to sum up these brief remarks on the nature of law in one argument, I would say that law is only an instrument of class rule through the mediating arenas of politics and ideology and that, therefore, it is not just an instrument of class rule. It is also, at the very same time, an instrument of party politics, a protector of revered ideas and an agency for the prevention of social chaos. Moreover, it can only successfully operate on the basis of a politico-ideological consensus (whether spontaneous or constructed). Law is all of these things at the same time and that is one reason why class rule has continued for as long as it has.

All the remarks I made earlier (in Chapters 2 and 7) about the origination of ideologies outside the economic structure (as well as inside it) apply to the origins of ideologies embodied in legal form. Ideologies arise out of economic, political and cultural practices and thus not only reflect class relations but also the technical divisions encapsulated within class relations. Law does not, therefore, just contain bourgeois economic ideology. It also reflects the ideologies of fractions of the bourgeoisie and the ideologies of other classes— through the political activities of these classes and class fractions. Moreover, it reflects the ideologies of occupational groups, minority groups and pressure groups. And, in terms of the range of ideologies, law expresses ideologies relating to the family, morality, the environment, political representation, immigration, communication, public association and so on—as well as ideologies relating to the economy. Law is truly an ideological form of the fullest complexity. Having said all this, it must be reiterated that law does not reflect these ideologies equally. Some classes, some occupational groups, some pressure groups and some individuals have more power than others in the legislative process. It is not as pluralistic as other ideological forms because it is subject to the political process and, hence, the relative ability of different classes and groups to establish their ideas as law. Political success requires money and power as well as potent ideas, even more so than other fields of superstructural practice. Thus law as an ideological form is less pluralistic, than, say, the novel or music. It is a much closer reflection of class inequality than other forms. It tends to express the ideologies of the dominant class and their political and cultural representatives. I want to render a Marxian analysis capable of dealing with all forms of law, law as it exists in a complex society, but I most certainly do not want to deny that law is still a major weapon of class domination. When the chips are down, the essential function of the legal system is revealed as itself: the reproduction of class power.

Now it is necessary to turn to the inner determinations of law, for like all things, it is not just an effect of externals. It is also necessary to say something about the peculiarity of law as an ideological form. These two matters are of course connected.

Legal enactments are partly ideological and partly political forms. In their ideological being, they exist as discourses. In their most developed form these discourses are written down and carefully circumscribed. They take on a magical form as sacred texts: the canons of social order. In quantity, the magic of their expression is compounded by their bureaucratic organization in a whole range of statutes and law reports and by its professional production in a language peculiar unto itself. Legal discourse in modern societies is thus bureaucratized magic expressed in legalese. It is therefore not only a discrete phenomenon but downright impenetrable: unless one has been initiated in the ancient skills of finding and reading the law, skills only available, of course, to the legal profession and its initiates. Legal discourse is worthy of study in itself by students of contemporary culture: if they can wrest themselves away from the 'high' culture of novels and the 'approved' culture of the proletariat. As an impenetrable discourse it ranks second to none: at least sociology does not use Latin.

The privacy of legal discourse (embodied in its impenetrability) stands in stark contrast to its essential peculiarity, which is to delineate power relations within a society in terms of the most general social ideologies available to that social formation. (Perhaps this is the secret of the lawyer's self-imposed "omnicompetence" noted by Riesman (1957): he is in possession of the code which enables him to tell us in general what we can and cannot do.) In its discourse, law does not designate power relations in terms of the actual class (or group) version of the ideologies at work in the legislative process. Rather, it designates them in the terms of a general discourse abstracted from that sectional version. In this way, the actual definitions and ideas which produced the legal proposal are usually concealed in the final discourse and the proposal, being stated in abstracted terms, takes on a universal, moral character separated from its current economic, political and ideological thrust. Thus, in modern times, the latest attempts to suppress the unionized power of the working class, in order to prise more surplus value out that class, can be seen to take the form of legislative proposals to protect the freedom of the individual from the collective pressure of 'the closed shop'. What is essentially a matter of class power and interest becomes transformed into a legislative proposal which raises the universal moral question of the individual versus the collective. And, of course, as individuals we can all sympathize with the freedom of the individual, especially if the other issues at stake are minimized and distorted by the mass media.

It is insufficient to object that this legal abstraction from specific, historical ideologies is merely a characteristic of bourgeois ideology in general. Certainly, bourgeois ideology focuses superficially upon the appearances of capitalist social relations and thus talks in terms of 'the individual', 'liberty', 'property' and 'equality': that is, the liberty of the individual to be exploited equally by those who own the productive property. But all ruling classes express their own interests as abstract, universal interests, as Marx and Engels point out in *The German Ideology* (1976a). Moreover, and this is the finer point, one does not need to present one's own interests as universal interests in an abstract way. These interests can be presented as universal in a quite concrete and practical way. Economic policy is often presented in this manner: thus the interests of capital are openly presented to the populace by bourgeois politicians as the interests of the whole people. No: it is the demands of the legal form itself which require the universalization and moralization of private and seedy self-interest to be presented in an abstract manner. Law must command some kind of consensus. It must thus express itself in a general manner. Therefore, legal discourse signifies within the terms of the general ideologies reflected by the dominant social relations rather than within the terms of the specific versions of those ideologies held by the dominant classes and their representatives. Consequently, law signifies in terms of the freedom of the individual rather than the freedom of the bourgeoisie to expand their capital at the expense of the working class, or the freedom of the workers to work for capital or starve. Similarly, it signifies in terms of the sanctitude of property in general rather than the sanctitude of the productive property of the bourgeoisie or the sanctitude of the labourer's only productive property, his health. Freedom, property and equality are key general ideologies arising from the general nature of capitalist social relations and are expressed as such in various branches of bourgeois law (freedom of the individual, freedom of association, etc.). *The generic social function of law is to express, regulate and maintain the general nature of the dominant social relations of a social formation.* It is therefore only natural that it does this through the discourse of the general ideologies necessitated by these general forms of social relation. It is the peculiarity of legal discourse as a social form that it should signify in this way. Law must always delineate the power relations of social practice (or the permissible modes of social intercourse) through the general ideologies necessitated by the dominant social relations of a society.

This argument clearly cuts across any simplistic reduction of legal discourse to an expression of bourgeois ideology. If the argument is taken a step further, this becomes even more obvious. What I want to suggest is that some of the key items in the legal lexicon are overdetermined in modern society in that they not only reflect the general ideologies of its social structure but also the imperatives of any moral code. It seems to me that it is an inevitability that a moral code (and law is one such thing, sanctioned by social power) must talk in terms of right and wrong, duty and neglect, obligation and fulfilment, and guilt and innocence. How could a moral discourse talk otherwise, given that it is a discourse which prescribes the acceptability of modes of social intercourse? Thus property rights is not simply a concept which reflects a social structure with private property. It also reflects the notion of right. If I am correct, then, our modern legal dictionary is becoming less of a mysterious puzzle. Some of its concepts relate, through ideology and power, to the social structure, others relate to the imperatives of moral discourse. Of course, what is actually said to be reasonable conduct, or neglect, or criminal behaviour (and so on) is an historically situated matter determined by the social forces at work rather than by any discursive imperatives.

A substantial part of legal discourse is not even particularly legal, of course, but is merely descriptive of the facts to be dealt with. This part of the discourse is difficult to evaluate when it exists in a judicial decision, for what count as "the facts of the case" are the product of the filtering mechanisms of the trial and pre-trial investigations. Facts can be constructed either by accident, by the court procedure or by lies, just as much in the legal system as in any other form of social practice. In any case, whether true, false or somewhere in between, "the facts" are a substantial part, or reference point, of legal discourse.

One further aspect of the form of legal discourse is that it usually contains doctrines and concepts which express the general ideologies of social relations of a prior epoch. That is, some of its key elements may have originated in earlier historical contexts. This does not mean that they are fossilized residues or forms isolated from modern social life, although they could be. Very often such concepts or doctrines correspond with modern needs in a way which their proponents could not have imagined. Thus the concept of trespass (*vi et armis*) derives originally from the feudal ideologies of landowners, reflecting feudal relations of production where territoriality and battles for land were crucial features. A writ of trespass in the twelfth century enabled plaintiffs to recover damages for forcible entry into land, or (at a later time) into goods held in the person's possession. It gave birth to the modern law of torts (civil wrongs such as negligence) and to the modern law of theft which began as a trespass into goods held on bailment). It still remains of course, but in a much more restricted sense of unlawful entry. Thus the legal conception of trespass has had an interesting history where its functions have been largely hived off as property relations expanded and developed but where it retains the essence of its original meaning. Clearly, to understand the modern functions of this type of concept it is necessary to study the development of the meaning of the concept right from its historical roots.

Legal discourse is thus an ideological formation of some complexity and richness containing contemporary general concepts, the language of moral discourse, descriptive accounts and references, and doctrines and terms from the distant past. There is no doubt that it contains sufficient internal complexity for us to imagine that its internal dialectic is purely ideological, purely a matter of continually reconciling concepts and doctrines. It most certainly provides an interesting game for lawyers to play with, and part of its magic must surely lie with the fact that it provides a mass of principles, concepts, statutes and case decisions all relating to specific issues and needing to be sifted and applied to a present situation. However, one must not forget that as a system of discourse which is linked to the social structures of the day, law only works through its successful regulation of that social system in terms of the interests and ideologies of the dominant social classes. Thus the inner dialectic of law rests here. Law designates power relations in terms of general ideologies reflecting a social structure which divides people economically, politically and ideologically. Its internal dialectic is fired by the eternal contradiction between its generalities and the specificities of contemporary social problems. Lawyers, of course, will see it differently and posit legal history as the history of a set of concepts developed solely by lawyers. In my view, law moves within, and is moved by, its relation to the problems posed for it by the social structure. This relation is mediated practically, in the form of the institutions of law creation and enforcement. The central tensions within law enforcement and law creation are thus set by the relation between legal discourse and social practice. The history of law is the history of this relation as it is mediated by the legal profession, the legislature and the law enforcement agencies.

Finally, as an instrument of social change or development, the law's internal character is important. One cannot just talk of the intractability of certain social contradictions or of the manner of enforcement. As a discourse, law takes a general form and, therefore, it is in principle, and sometimes in practice, useful for all-comers.

Law can thus be pulled in directions other than those intended by the legislators. It can become an instrument for the mitigation of the harsher effects of the class structure and other inequalities.

We have looked at the social determinations of ideologies embodied in the law and commented upon the nature of legal discourse. It is also necessary to say something briefly about the ideology of Law. The legal form hitherto has always been seen as something supernatural, magical, God-given and sacred. Perhaps today, it is also seen as an expression of objective rationality or True reason. Many people today, and presumably in the past, have seen through this mystical veil and perceived the secular nature of law. The ideology of Law as something above the mundane run of things is still popular however. What is the basis of this ideology? It seems to me that the inner structure of legal practice and its key social function in attempting to maintain order combine to give legal discourse and institutions an external appearance as something special and mysterious. Professional secrecy, esoteric language, grand ceremony, special clothing, carefully structured courtrooms, the rituals of legislation and the occupational status of the judge are all internal factors which work to present the appearance of magic. But I think that the reasons run deeper than these factors which are only superficial conditions. What we have to consider is that, in essence, law is little different from political policy, administrative decision and military strategy. In itself therefore it would be seen for what it is, a form of political control, without much difficulty. Now clearly such transparency is contrary to the interests of ruling classes who always want to give their directions some universal legitimacy. It is also contrary to the interests of lawyers who need special status and esoteric services in order to continue—who would pay so much for mere political administrators? Lawyers' interests are, however, secondary and depend on the main condition which is the structural necessity of all ruling classes to obtain some kind of consent for their direction and supremacy. Consent can be obtained much more easily if the rulers' main policies and principles of administration can be seen as the expression of something transcendental, whether this be a God or Absolute Reason or the Necessity of Order. The production of this mystification of law began a long time ago and we inherit some of the older illusions. However, the mystification of the nature of law (as a form) is still necessary today and will be as long as there is class domination. In short, the ideology of Law is an ideology *necessitated* by political relations of domination: it enables them to continue on a regular basis. Lawyers develop this ideology to a fine point because it is in their interests to do so. But they cannot conceal the fact that law is little different from other means of political control. Despite their insistence that law is distinguished by its 'proper' constitution, it is clear that what counts as proper is a political question and not one for God or True Reason. It is also clear that the ideology and rituals of propriety within legal practice serve an important function in concealing the sectional nature of law-making.

The law is a rich combination. Not only does it conceal politics through its magic, its rituals of propriety, its moral universals, its esoteric language and its historical longevity, but it has the added benefit of sharing in all the legitimacy that the state as the executor of social power has managed to acquire for itself. Since the remote state has a magic of its own and since the rulers of a society have the available tools to create the impression that they are worthy, the law basks in the sunshine of the rulers' patronage and charisma. In this way, we have the nice paradox that law avoids the dirty images of politics and shares in its good side. Law's structural position enables it to be presented as an expression of universal truth under the aegis of beneficent and meritorious authority.

Perhaps because law holds out so many fake promises, people feel all the more disillusioned when they are broken. To begin with, the ideology of Law offers us truth, magic, impartiality and merit whilst denying the filthy side of politics. Secondly, the specific ideologies within legal enactments tell us what the world ought to be like on the basis of illusions about what it is like. Both these ideologies, those of the inside and those of the outside, are of course closely interlinked. When they collapse as effective grips on one's mind, then the whole ideological edifice collapses like a pack of cards. It becomes crystal clear that the whole business—the discourse, the procedure, the ceremony, the ritual, the prestige, the magic—is part of a colossal façade. Of course, the legal system coerces, punishes and executes 'criminals' and of course it may leave many ordinary people without access to civil remedy and therefore in financial difficulty. The legal system has its instrumental side. But it has this other aspect—as Law—its ideological side. This aspect is a complete and utter façade. If we take modern capitalist society, for example, it is no exaggeration to say that the legal system is first and foremost a means of exercising political control available to the propertied, the powerful and the highly educated. It is the weapon and toy of the hegemonic bloc of classes and class fractions whose rough consensus it sustains. As such, it lies hidden beneath a heavy shroud of discourse, ritual and magic which proclaim the Wisdom and Justice of The Law. This shroud is of central importance to our social formation. Once it is torn into tatters, that hegemonic bloc of classes and class fractions which sustains the rule of capital is in trouble, because inequality and domination can only be justified mystically and that is precisely the ideological function of the law.

To sum up, legal discourse represents an historically constituted unity of politics and ideology and therefore stands for something much wider than itself. As a representation of social structure in the language of general and moral ideology sanctioned by the institutionalized executors of social power, it is a significant feature of all social formations mapping social history at the same time as it redirects it. It is a form which is central to ruling class hegemony because of its cultivated sacredness. It is an emblem of the universal pretensions of a ruling class and an abstracted expression of the concrete interests of that class and its allies.

Reading the Ideology of Legal Discourse

Lawyers' methods

Lawyers recognize the problem of reading legal discourse. Their concern is, of course, a practical one. They need to know the meaning of the legal instrument in order to advise clients, make judicial decisions, make new statutes and teach law students. They are not concerned with its social meaning so much as its technical and practical meaning, its implications for what one can or cannot do. Our concern in reading the ideological nature of legal discourse envelops this technical interest; it does not ignore or supplant it. One could not understand the social significance of a legal instrument unless one understood its technical significance (its meaning in itself), precisely because the social significance of the discourse is embodied in its technical meaning. This is true of all discourses: thus, the social ideologies (or significance) in a news report are embodied within its descriptive account. What lawyers in fact do is to turn a blind eye to the social significance of the legal instrument. Concentrating on the purely technical aspect, they consign the rest to "politics". This is not to ignore the fact that many lawyers are concerned about the social nature of law, it is merely to say that the classic legal methods of interpreting legal discourse are not concerned with its social significance. I should add, however, that this would appear to be changing very slowly, as we shall see.

Taking a recognized student's textbook on the basic principles and organization of English law (Hood Phillips and Hudson, 1977), let us just glance at the lawyers' methods for reading statutes. To begin with, these methods or principles are themselves of legal status, being enshrined in the common law and to a certain extent in statute (Hood Phillips and Hudson, 1977, Chapter 11). They are said to be necessary because of "the imperfections of language and draftsmen": it is nothing to do with clashes of ideology. Moreover, they are only what judges say they do—there seems to be some doubt that judges actually do use these principles of statute interpretation. In my experience of studying law, judges seem to interpret statutes in a way which suits their ideological definition of the correct result and then rationalize their interpretation after the event. However, lawyers will tell you that the following are the principles of interpreting statutes:

1. Commencement: an Act comes into operation on the receipt of Royal Assent.
2. Some statutes define their own terms and some general terms are defined in the 1889 Interpretation Act. These statutory definitions do not apply if a "contrary intention appears in the context".
3. Judicial precedents interpreting an Act must be followed, subject to the rules about following precedents.
4. If, by this time, the meaning is still unclear, one makes a "literal interpretation", reading the words according to their literal meaning at the time of the enactment. "Clear and unambiguous and logically complete" statements are to be taken as conclusive evidence of the legislature's intention.
5. If ambiguity prevails, one must try reading the words in the

context of the whole statute.

6. Failing that, we use the "Golden Rule", which is that, if literal interpretation is impossible, the judge must read the statute in the light of the legislature's intention as it is expressed therein. This rule covers "logical inconsistency" within a statute or between statutes.

7. Failing that, the "Mischief Rule" says that the judge must look to the "mischief" (the social problem) to be removed in order to establish Parliament's intention.

8. Under rule 7, the courts can use the history of the previous law in order to understand the purpose of the new statute, but they cannot resort to "social, political or literary history, such as parliamentary debates, reports of commissions, etc." It is not clear why this rule exists but it certainly illustrates the kind of reading lawyers do. This rule may change soon in the UK as there have been various recent judicial suggestions that "preparatory materials" should be permitted and that statutes should contain a summary of their purpose.

9. Ther are various "intrinsic aids" within statutes which can be used, e.g. the long title, the pre-amble, schedules, etc.

10. If the statute fails to mention certain situations, facts or items to be dealt with, the judges cannot "fill the gap".

11. The repeal of a statute does not revive any former laws or affect other legal rights.

12. There are various "presumptions" which apply unless the statute says otherwise, such as that the Act applies to the UK, that the Crown is not bound by it, that the "common law" is not altered, that there is no intended restriction of individual liberty, that no deprivation of property (without compensation, at least) is intended, and so on.

Hood Phillips and Hudson comment that the "important practical question"—which rule will the judges use?—is unanswered. Two things are clear to me: (1) that these rules are sufficiently flexible to allow a judge to justify more or less any interpretative reading of an operable statute (and thus the frequent judicial frustrations of parliamentary intention), and (2) that the guiding thread of these rules is a sham. The guiding thread is to apply Parliament's intention. Firstly, this is a philosophical naivety, to believe that a discourse only means what its proponents intended it to mean. More importantly, the judges actually deny themselves any realistic access to parliamentary intention and allow themselves a series of assumptions which give them a great latitude in defying parliamentary intention. Therefore, it seems to me that these rules are largely a façade behind which judges can point the law in the directions which suit them. These directions will not necessarily run against those pursued by Parliament, but when they do there is room for manoeuvre in interpretation.

So, the judges' reading principle, look for Parliament's intention, is one that gives them flexibility. In our terms, it is clearly not even in the running as a mode of reading legal ideology. Of itself, it *is* a piece of legal ideology centring on the individualistic notion of the authoring subject. It is a technical ideology which has political functions within legal practice and which is not concerned *at all* with the social nature of legal discourse. This practice is merely concerned with the legal nature of legal discourse.

Lawyers and law teachers usually recognize these rules of interpretation, but also usually recognize that a judge can invent an interpretation if he so wishes. Lawyers, especially law teachers, are "judge-conscious". They tend to fetishize judges, basking sycophantically in their majesty and glorifying in the gossip about them. In reading judges' decisions, law teachers often seem to base their readings on their assumptions about the judge's political prejudices. What the judgement is taken to signify is that meaning which is consistent with the judge's known prejudices and attitudes. There is a whole school of jurisprudence, the American "Realist" school, which sees law as that which the judges declare it to be. In this sense, a legal decision is always pending and never extant. If the Realists could logically have a reading principle, which they cannot, it would be to read the law in terms of the judge's ideas and the courtroom interaction at the trial. Despite the jurisprudential cynicism of the American Realists and many law teachers, their readings are still only geared to deciphering the legal meaning of legal discourse. What else could one expect? The role of lawyers and law teachers is to determine what the law is and to expound it, not to read its social significance as an ideological form. However, as social scientists we cannot do without a reading of the technical (or legal) meaning of legal discourse. It would appear that even lawyers cannot give us a sure answer about such a reading (and then they gibe about the tendentiousness of social science!). I shall show shortly that an historical materialist reading of law is probably better than the lawyers' reading for establishing even the technical meaning of a legal instrument. But, now, I must also reflect on the inadequacies of existing social science reading methods for the reading of ideology in legal discourse.

The methods of social science

To avoid reiterating the discussion in Part Two of this book, let me summarize the matter very tersely. The most important thing to realize here is that even the most advanced methods of reading ideology, such as semiology, would not stand a chance of reading legal discourse, unless they deserted their own methodological premises. Content analysis would get nowhere by establishing that the word reasonable was repeated seven times in a statute. Information theory could not even get a foothold since it would be allowed no preparatory knowledge of legal codes in order to establish the amount of information transmitted. Speculative criticism could, of course, speculate on the social significance of legal discourse, but all it could produce is speculative polemic. Structuralist semiology, with the exclusion of matters extrinsic to the discourse, could not possibly decode the message within a statute or series of statutes. It could merely identify scattered presuppositions embodied in the Act or Acts. It could have no clues as to the meanings of words such as reasonable or negligence without recourse to extrinsic judicial decisions. It could have no inkling of the judicial presumptions involved in statutory interpretation. All it would have is a raw statute (or case report) which, on its own, is as impenetrable as the Sphinx's smile. Althusserian symptomatic reading would not be strictly applicable to legal discourse since such a discourse is not a theoretical system. Even if it was applied, it would have no means of reading the problematic of the statute since statutes do not have theoretical problematics. Neo-structuralism in general makes some sense, however, in directing us to prior legal discourses in whose absences a present discourse would be inscribed, and to prior legal traces inextricably linked to present traces.

Existing social scientific modes of reading ideology reveal their staggering inadequacies when placed against a discourse such as that of the law. Yet, I would suggest that, like many lawyers, most social scientists 'know' what the law means. But how? I believe that their 'knowledge' is acquired according to principles which they dare not admit, principles which take into account all sorts of inadmissible evidence such as the social functions of law, the political ideology of the judiciary, the nature of the current political parties, and so on; principles which are included explicitly within the method of historical materialist or scientific reading of ideology.

The scientific reading of ideologies in legal discourse

Legal discourse appears in the form of statutes, case law, tribunal decisions and legal instruments. Its highly condensed mode of super-abstraction combined with legally filtered 'facts', especially in a developed form in an old legal system like ours where every concept has its own history, would seem to defy existing reading methods. However, the following account of the application of the historical materialist method of reading ideologies to legal discourse should indicate that it can be rendered accessible to sophisticated social science enquiry.[6] I shall relate myself only to case-law and statute in order to simplify matters.

First Approximation

Gaining solid impressions in this area again involves a process of checking an initial spontaneous impression that a particular ideology is operative within a specific social context and structure, and active within a particular legal discourse. The general reasons for the procedures adopted in the case of legal discourse apply to all studies of ideology: we are concerned to check the initial impression as a totality. In this instance, the following tasks are necessary:

1. Determining the provisional meaning of the legal discourse for oneself through a careful reading of the case report(s) or statute(s) in question, and its legal antecedents.
2. Substantiating this reading by reference to parliamentary debates and committee reports, or to transcripts of the court proceedings (where possible).
3. Ascertaining the nature and purpose of the statute or judicial

decision by reference to commentaries in legal journals and textbooks, newspapers, television programmes and magazines.

4. Checking the ideologies of the judges or legislators through published interviews, stated policies, reports of other recent decisions, social science research and personal interviews where possible (and if needed).

5. Investigating the facts of the problem to be resolved. It will be difficult with judicial decisions to get beyond the case report and media commentaries because at this stage of the research a full investigation in the field will probably be a luxury (in terms of time and money).

6. Contrasting the legal discourse with the other discourses on the problem in order to establish how extensively the studied ideology is appearing and in which circles it receives support.

7. Determining briefly the social role of the legislators in similar situations throughout the history of the society in question.

Second Approximation

As with the study of ideology in any other form of discourse, it is necessary here to theorize precisely the logical necessity of an ideology within a specific social practice, and thus to separate out the merely contingent aspects of the ideology which may arise from the discursive practice itself or the contemporary context. This level of analysis, therefore, involves theoretical reflection, comparative sociology and some reference to national history.

Third Approximation

The historical stage of the research is concerned to trace the social development of the connection between structure and ideology right back to its roots, and thus to specify different historical forms taken by the ideology in differing contexts. In the case of legal discourse, there will often be excellent documentation of earlier expressions of the ideology in a statute or case. It is important here not to convert this stage of the research into a lawyers' history of the law by simply looking at a series of legal enactments within a particular field of law and discerning the doctrinal developments. Certainly, the stages of a law's development appear to be relevant but, in fact, they are not always, for what we are studying is the historical development of an ideology in correspondence with its generative structure, as it manifests itself in specific social contexts. We are studying ideology, not law, to put it crudely. This means that our ideology may appear across a range of legal areas (e.g. contract, tort, land law, family law, etc.) and enter into a range of legal doctrines. What we must firmly establish is the nature of the ideology and a selection of its important manifestations in legal discourse. We are out to show that the ideology is necessitated by specific social relations and that its different legal contexts of appearance give it a range of phenomenal forms.

Again, a socio-historical register of the ideology's available legal vocabularies can be usefully constructed, along with an historico-logical map of its internal structure and potential development. The only difference that arises with legal discourse is that certain forms of the ideology's expression will have been repealed by statute or negated judicially. This should always be pointed out in building the register and the map. However, since we are concerned with sociological possibility rather than legal possibility, we must be careful to retain features of the ideology which can be resurrected later in new forms.

Fourth Approximation

The final analysis, the return to the present, in this instance involves a more intensive and more wide-ranging study of the expression of the ideology in contemporary legal discourses. In the first stage of the research, only a limited sample of legal manifestations had been taken. The procedures now will be much the same as in the first stage, only with more depth and a larger sample of legal discourse. At this final stage, more depth will be needed especially in the areas of discovering the legislators' and judges' ideologies and of determining the nature of the practical problem facing the law-makers. Now we are at the final stage it is important to filter out ideological influences arising from contemporary context and legal practice in themselves. It is vital to be able to specify the precise operation and limits of our studied ideology. The study of the problem to be resolved will already have served to separate out the appearances of reality from the ideology at work and to demonstrate the line and effect of the legislative ideology in the practical context concerned. Of course, these analytic stages can never separate out in reality all the different ideologies inextricably condensed in a legal discourse.

However, they can prove as far as is possible that the discourse is indeed a condensed unity of diverse ideological determinations.

Thus armed with a knowledge of the specificity of an ideology, its previous legal manifestations, its social contexts of use, its generative social relations, its referential context, its practical location in a discursive legal practice and its position in a contemporary historical conjuncture, we are able to read its appearance in legal discourse. Law can thus be rendered in its neglected aspect as a complex cultural form embodying a significance for structure, context and history.

Notes

1. A Russian scholar who, in the 1920s, became a Director of the Institute of Soviet Construction and, in 1936, a Vice-Commissar of Justice before being discredited and removed in 1937. This discussion is based entirely upon Hazard (1951, introduction and pp. 111–226). Unfortunately, the translation in Hazard is appalling, being completely ignorant of Marxist concepts. The above discussion involves a reading of this translation which is familiar with the Marxian texts and debates and, therefore, hopefully correctly represents Pashukanis.
2. Compare this with Taylor et al. (1973, 1975), Hirst (1975a, b) and Arthur (1977).
3. Mikhail Reisner, a Russian professor of law, was a follower and acquaintance of the idealist philosopher, Petrazycki, who has so much influenced the modern Polish socialist sociologist of law, Adam Podgorecki (see his Law and Society, 1974).
4. For modern economistic commentaries on economistic Marxism, see Arthur (1977) on Pashukanis, and Taylor et al. (1975) on Renner.
5. Althusser explicitly recognizes Gramsci's work on this topic.
6. This account follows the general outline of the method in Chapter 7, and will therefore be more condensed.

9 Summary and Final Reflections

> Even today most Marxist theoreticians conceive of the efficacy of so-called intellectual phenomena in a purely negative, abstract and undialectical sense, when they should analyse this domain of social reality within the materialist and scientific method moulded by Marx and Engels. Intellectual life should be conceived in union with social and political life, and social being and becoming (in the widest sense, as economics, politics or law) should be studied in union with social consciousness in its many different manifestations, as a real yet also ideal (or "ideological") component of the historical process in general. Instead, all consciousness is approached with totally abstract and basically metaphysical dualism, and declared to be a reflection of the one really concrete and material development process, on which it is completely dependent (even if relatively independent, still dependent in the last instance). (Korsch, 1970, p. 71)

In this passage, Karl Korsch captures one of the main themes of the present work and one of the central problems of classical Marxist theory. Times are changing, however; more and more modern Marxism is giving the lie to the classical criticism that it reduces ideology to a mere effect of class interests and structures. This book is part of that change and attempts to capture in theoretical terms the undoubted fact that ideology is not only crucial to social existence but exists in definite social patterns which are remarkably stable.

What I have tried to understand and formulate is the fact that ideologies structure our understanding of the world out there and also exist as constituent and embodied features of that world, determining the way it presents itself to us. More specifically, I have been struck by the fact that, although some people hold their views constant whilst shifting their social position, many people, of varying persuasions, adopt the ideologies that seem to adhere to their location in the social structure. This phenomenon can in no way be attributed to bio-psychic deficiencies, nor can it be said that the socially produced psychological states of pragmatism, gullibility and uncritical apathy are responsible. These two approaches represent the Right and Left of the elitist approach to ideology. Moreover, the rootedness of ideology cannot be explained by the political ideologies of the people concerned: all political ideologies are susceptible to interference from other ideologies arising from their adherents' social situation.

What is probably the hardest thing to grasp theoretically is the fact that all understandings, ideas and perceptions are obviously perfectly sensible and necessary in specific social situations. I am alluding to what one might call the circle of social reality: things (people, events, matter, discourse) are seen in a particular way when perceived through the grid of a particular ideology, yet that ideology is at the same time active in the practice of another being and eventually embodied in the thing observed, so that the appearance of that thing matches its perception perfectly. If you like, this is the hermeneutic of a consensual culture. But, also, we can see that each ideology has its own natural milieu—that of its origin. 'Reality' is instantly recognizable within this milieu. There is an identity between appearance and percepting ideology which guarantees the social psychological phenomenon of 'recognition'. It is analogous to the spontaneous practice of driving a car. You look at the map and it tells you that after 15 miles you will reach Manchester. After 15 miles you see a signpost which says "City of Manchester" and you conclude that you are now in Manchester. You do not question the validity of the map, you do not raise cynical doubts about the sincerity of the signpost and you do not start asking passing pedestrians whether this really is Manchester. It is and that's a fact. The signpost was definitive: it concluded the matter beyond all doubt. It defined and concluded because you accepted the validity of the map: thus you can now go ahead and make empirical statements about what it's 'really' like in Manchester, because you are now there, or so you think. Without going into the process whereby maps obtain validation, it should be clear that ideological maps and significant social appearances can be dealt with in the same way. In the course of a specific social practice, we perpetrate and adopt specific ideologies and confront specific objective phenomena. These objective phenomena always present themselves in a manner determined by their own social context and function. Ideology and appearance thus come face to face. In a static, consensual cultural context, appearance fits ideology and ideology maps appearance. Recognition ensues and the subject is at one with the world in an orderly, peaceful, undisturbing way. Thus, when questioned, the individual defies all doubt, being certain of the sensibility, truthfulness and obviousness of the belief and being able to provide empirical evidence for it. There is, therefore, a very real sense in which understanding produces its own social reality at the same time as social reality produces its own understanding: this is the circle of social reality.

Cultural contexts, however, are today (at least) rarely static. The dominant circle is frequently broken and new sub-circles are formed. Recognition continues but different classes, races, sexes and associations are now using different maps and these maps do not all contain the same geography. What breaks the dominant circle has not yet been answered in social science. It is a question which has not yet even been posed properly, a question concealed by the insistence that those who leave the dominant circle are 'deviants' with a pathological state of mind. What is clear is that even modern, pluralistic capitalist cultures have only a limited number of tenable circles of reality. The reasons for this are two-fold. Firstly, the manifest form of things is dependent on their structural position and context: an appearance does not change in itself just because you look at it differently. That appearance will still continue to convince others. Secondly, ways of seeing are subject to powerful social pressures. Persuasion by the mass communication machine, the failures of unorthodox politics and the bribes of the economic system are all powerful forces which limit the number of different ways of seeing. Moreover, even when a new way of seeing is established, it needs its own socio-geographical vantage point in order to see the world from its point of view—and there are many social forces preventing those vantage points being created. All in all, the nature of the dominant circle of social reality, the nature and number of sub-circles, and the forms of social expression are founded within and limited by the mode of production and its corresponding political and cultural structures. The nature of a mode of production and the finitude and quality of its culture are totally bound up together.

Modern Britain is a natural environment for philosophical elucidations of the concept of ideology. This is due to the fact that we have a dominant class whose ideology is stagnant and rotten, yet still pervasive. As the oldest capitalist society, Britain has begun the slow death agony which inheres in the dialectic of capital. British capital grew in the Industrial Revolution, reached its profit-making peak at the height of British imperialism, declined in the face of competition, was (and is) baled out by the generous compensation of nationalization, and now, as a state property, staggers and twitches from one agonizing wound after another. What is true for the economic is also true for the political and the ideological. British culture has seen the rise of bourgeois ideology and is now witnessing its fall. From the brazen commercialism of its origins, through the self-confident moral hypocrisy of Arnoldism and the imperial period, through the gangrenous and decadent rectitude of the Edwardian period, through the shattering socialist challenges of the 1920s and 1930s, through the resuscitation of the Second World War and through its consequent, complacent political consensus, the ideology of the masters has now arrived at the stage where it is riddled with disease. Shattered profit rates, foreign competition and uncertain future now coalesce with socialist challenge and cultural fragmentation on an increasing scale. In such a situation, the political authoritarianism inherent in the state must increase, and so must the intensity of ruling class propaganda. Coercion and ideology increase in significance when bribery fails.

When, in 1972, I began my research into the press reporting of political demonstrations, it seemed to me that the challenges to the system by middle-class youth and organized labour between 1966 and 1972 had been met by an intensive, ideological campaign throughout the ideological apparatuses of the state and big business. This ideological counter-reaction was undoubtedly not the result of a class conspiracy but of the structural co-ordination of the whole range of ruling class interests and ideologies. My subsequent researches were intended to investigate the existence and influence of bourgeois ideology in the allegedly impartial, balanced discourses of news reports and judicial decisions. Once begun, the empirical research revealed that the existing Marxian conception of ideology was quite inadequate for an analysis of the integral role of ideology within the whole range of social practices. Moreover, the existing methods of reading ideology in its discursive forms were vague and seemed to be merely mystifying versions of commonsense techniques. It seemed that all one had was a basically subjective method based on pure impression. Empirical research may have been politically necessary at the time and may have brought political results. However, there was enough mindless empiricism already in the social sciences and I could not see how one could complete an empirical analysis of ideology without a concept of ideology and a method of reading it. If older sociologists object that this is just another theoretical text, I would reply that their attitude left us with the empiricist debris of attitude surveys, 'pop' philosophy and tribe studies, and that the political problems of the 1970s *demanded* theoretical re-examination and constructive advances.

The present work begins by re-looking at Marx's concept of ideology. I conclude that the old notion of ideology as a gaseous effect of the economic structure is inadequate and must be replaced by a conception of ideology as an integral and substantive element of all social practice. In this way, ideology is an active force within all aspects of social development and not just an animal that roams around the ephemeral reserves of the superstructure. By dividing social practice into three main types—economic, political and cultural—on the basis of their produce, it is easy to see that ideology is particularly important in the realms of political and cultural practice but not exclusive to them. From here, I collapse that old favourite of a distinction—language versus ideology—on the grounds that it is misleading and argue that ideology is a signification, constituted by a signifying unit and signified meaning in relation; a signification which could be simple or complex, recent or long-established, nationally shared or sectional and denotative or connotative. Language is now seen as one mode of signification by which ideologies are expressed, and, as their embodiment, a determinant of present and future forms of thought. It is no longer to be seen as a resource of pure, shared significance upon which the politically motivated consciousness draws in constructing ideologies. Any distinction between language and ideology on the basis of degrees of certainty about meaning is also baseless since even shared significations are rooted in social practice. I also collapsed the ideology–science distinction constructed in the classic Marxist–Leninist texts, which often gave science (like language) a privileged place outside of social relations. However, I did maintain that some ideologies were more accurate representations of reality than others and warranted the social label of science. Thus, although what counts as science is subject to all the economic, political and cultural determinations that affect the use of any term, relations of accuracy between discourse and reality are real phenomena.

Employing this wide definition of ideology, and frequently referring to complex ideologies as ideological formations, I argued that ideology must be distinguished from appearance. Classical Marxism reduces ideology to the appearances of social structure, just as it reduces ideology to falsehood. It seems to me that not all ideologies are false and that significations are quite different things from modes of presentation (or appearances). Significations or ideologies are phenomena which specify the meaning of things: appearances are the outer manifestations of situated phenomena. Commodity fetishism theory interprets Marx to say, in effect, that appearances are the same as the meanings given to them; I have therefore moved away from another of the orthodox tenets of Marxism.

On all these issues where I differ from orthodox Marxism, I would claim to be following the spirit of Marx's own analyses, if not to the letter. My own interpretation clearly develops out of a critique of Althusser which has led me to centre my analysis on the concept of social practice. I have thus resurrected some of the elements of the classical theory of praxis and combined them with some of the features of Althusser's interpretation, in a way which avoids the worst of humanism and the worst of anti-humanism and hopefully synthesizes the best elements of each into a new form.

On the basis of this understanding, as an element within social practice, ideology only appears in a form which reflects the structure of that practice. This form is not necessarily the original form of that ideology, which could have arisen elsewhere or in the past. Forms of appearance, as distinguished from essential forms, will be expressed in a way which reflects other ideologies brought into the practice and the social context and structure of the practice. Essential forms of an ideology are its basic structures of signification and are necessitated by specific social relations. Because of their general origin in practice, some ideologies are necessitated by political and cultural relations: ideologies do not just arise out of the economic system. As an element in practice, ideologies are always one of the determinants of its product. In this sense, all objects produced by human beings contain embodied ideologies. Ideology is an integral part of social practice, it determines its forms and is formed within it. Ideology reflects social structure and determines its emergence: not at the same time necessarily—the mutual interpenetration of ideology and structure is conditioned by the social contexts of its particular instances. Therefore, concepts of man as either creator or agent must be rejected: people can be creative or passive, or both, depending on the contexts, structures and conjunctures in which they live. Ahistorical Man must give way to historical men operating on the basis of specific ideologies in determinate, structured contexts.

The existing social science methods of reading ideology, known as content analysis, information theory (what I termed) speculative criticism, general structuralism, structuralist semiology and symptomatic reading, were critically examined and found wanting. Their central defects were an inadequate theorization of the concept of ideology, a reliance on a consensual concept of denotation, a neglect of social structure and history, an inability to specify the limits of particular ideologies investigated, and a mystifying system of concepts to justify essentially commonsensical techniques. Out of this critique and the preceding theory of ideology, I constructed the basic principles of an historical materialist, and more scientific, reading of ideology. This new method centres on the need, as Marx put it, "to develop from the actual relations of life the corresponding celestialised forms of those relations". Essentially, the method involves working back from firmly established initial impressions of the connections between an ideology, its generative social relations and the context of that ideology's form of appearance into the history of these connections in order to ascertain the structurally necessitated specificity of the ideology and the range of its historical forms of appearance. Armed with this theorized historical knowledge, the reading of the contemporary discourse can evidence its conclusion that the ideology is present within it. It has a solid basis for separating that ideology from all the other aspects of its form of appearance. It is a reading which is not based on mere appearances and which can reach beyond the surface because it has a good foothold in history. No magical techniques of reading are required: the commonsensical ones suffice. Doing explicitly and in detail what previous methods often did implicitly and superficially, the historical materialist reading thus fixes the ideology in its practical surround, determines its form of appearance and paves the way for a soundly based study of the interpretation of the ideology's appearance by a wider audience. Hence the search for an adequate reading method is over, at least to my satisfaction. No doubt readings will arise in the future which involve yet more esoteric and incomprehensible 'techniques', but in my view all our possible techniques are simple. It is our method that is crucial, and the only scientific method can be one which identifies ideologies on the basis of a theoretically and historically grounded understanding of their specificity as elements of consciousness originating and existing within determinate social practices in specific historical conjunctures.

To begin to understand the nature of ideology and to read its appearance with certainty allows us to begin a more sound study of the social forms which depend heavily upon it. Thus, as a form heavy with ideology, law can now be studied in some depth as more than a coercive instrument, as an expression of ideology. Without a developed theory of ideology the Marxist theory of law must be doomed to stagnate in the platitudes of economic determinism and class reductionism. Laws may be reflections of economic structures and instruments of class conflict, but they cannot be fully understood as such. A legal enactment is a hybrid form combining power and ideology: an ideological formation sanctioned, according to fixed and hallowed procedures for the creation of Law, by the instituted executors of social power. It originates within legalizing practices which are political in that they are geared to producing specific power relations. Once constituted, legal systems do not just produce laws, but exist as The Law. An ideology of legality develops which celebrates and elevates The Law to an exalted status as the expression of unity in the nation. It is most important to begin the study of the functions of the ideology of legality in concealing political acts and domination. The ideology of Law has a real basis, for laws are indeed expressions of a unity in politics and culture. This unity is the hegemonic bloc of classes and class fractions which carries sufficient support to establish a consensus of interests and ideas around its imperatives. All laws require some kind of consensus in order to operate successfully: if they fail, however, less formal and more pliable means of social control are available from the armoury of political control to which the legal system belongs.

As an instrument and expression of the politics and ideology of class hegemony, law is a key force in social development and must be studied carefully in both its political and ideological dimensions. Its ideological component is constituted by ideologies arising from economic, political and cultural practices, ideologies which not only represent classes in general but also class fractions, racial groups, political parties and cultural movements. Ideologies from a variety of sources, therefore, can find their way into the law, although, in practice, these ideologies tend to be those of the hegemonic class bloc and those which protect the reproduction of the dominant economic relations. As a discursive form, law is a highly developed and condensed expression of sectional ideologies in the language of moral universals. It is therefore extremely difficult to read the ideologies within it. Existing methods could not even begin. I have shown how the historical materialist method could. It is important now that law be analysed as an ideological force. Existing studies have focused on economic structure and the state. We cannot continue to ignore the third dimension: that of ideology.

The social and historical context demands that we re-examine the question of ideology and extend the boundaries of its study. In the advanced capitalist societies, we face a period of accelerating social crises where constant capital expansion and consequent automation will increase the amount of unemployment and the amount of unproductive labour (in the Marxian sense). This means that ideas and consequently politics must change. It also means that culture and politics will come to the forefront of the social theatre. The ruling classes will have to change their ideologies and political strategies or else capitalism will swing out of their control and into the hands of *petit-bourgeois* fascism. Moreover, they will try to change the ideas of the mass of the people, to keep control. The workers' organizations and socialist parties will have to change their ideas and strategies or else the transformation of capitalism will also fall into the same hands. They too will have to struggle for hegemony, the hegemony of the opposition. The unorganized, apathetic and hedonistic mass, also, will have to change its ideas in the face of increased available time or else it will screw itself into the ground (one way or another), driven by its own frustrations, pointlessness and emptiness (or it will form the basis of the developing fascist front). Whichever way one turns, ideas and consciousness are coming of age to take their place right at the very centre of social development. Never before in human history have the social ideologies of the *whole* society been so relevant to what happens next. Once it was only the ideologies of the elite that mattered and history went on with or without the consent of the people. That has changed: hegemony is central. The range of social ideologies now matters to the key phases of social development. There is only one thing that can stop it mattering and can thus arrest the course of social development: bourgeois authoritarianism. This must be fought at all points by the most effective means available.

These changes must be reflected in the theory and political practices of socialism. We cannot rest content with simplistic analyses of ideology which reduce it to an epiphenomenon of the economic structure, an instrument of class war or a mere moment in the evolution to a classless society. Nor can we reduce it to the analysis of the ideology of the subject, important as it is. The whole range of ideologies is now important to the movement of capital because of the ideological fragmentation produced by the economic, political and cultural changes of the last one hundred years. That range, its historic development, current social functions and likely future directions must be studied. We cannot keep focusing on the monolithic imperial ideology of *The Classic Slum* (Roberts, 1974) when the real world is the fragmented individualism of *Workers Divided* (Nichols and Armstrong, 1976).

So theory must develop, but not only to aid our understanding of the development of international capitalism. It must also develop so that we can begin to understand the place of ideology in socialist societies (present and future). The creation of a socialist mode of production may eliminate class divisions within the economy; however, on my theoretical understanding, this elimination of class relations does not of itself eliminate technical relations of production. Now, if stratification is firmly established politically and ideologically within the revolutionary movement, it is quite possible that political and ideological divisions will come to be articulated economically in terms of the technical relations of production. A new class system can thus arise on the foundation of a conjoint articulation of politico-ideological hierarchies and technical productive relations: a possibility entirely comprehensible in Marxist terms. This has happened in Russia and is developing elsewhere. In this way, the role of ideology is as vital to the future of socialism as is the role of the party.

In socialist societies, technically anchored inequalities, political hierarchy and ideological differences can congeal to produce a system which is as much in need of a ruling class hegemony and developed legal system as is a capitalist economy. As Mao might have put it, not all contradictions are explained by capitalism. There are always going to be technical economic divisions, political hierarchies and ideological differences at the onset of any socialist society. As Marx suggested in *Capital*, co-operation itself will also raise problems. Taking all these things together, it is clear that even a mode of production founded on social ownership, co-operation and rational planning does not remove all forms of inequality, nor does it remove the need for a state, or dissolve ideological differences overnight. How any form of socialism survives must therefore, logically, depend a great deal on how it deals with its power relations and ideological differences. This flows from my interpretation of Marx and is so startlingly obvious, one wonders why it has not been made clear before. Instead, political dissent and cultural conflicts seem to have taken many Marxists by surprise.

The practical relations that emerge in a society with a technical division of labour, political hierarchy and cultural (or ideological) conflicts, all combined and fixed into a new class system, will be the basis for further ideological differentiation and practical conflict. These differences of ideology and conflicts of interest must give rise to an organized state and an extensive legal system. Therefore, such a society, although not capitalist, would much resemble capitalism. It is interesting to note that, in Eastern Europe, the political and ideological basis of crime is nullified by economic charges and criminalization in much the same way as it is in Western Europe. Whether socialist societies must inevitably begin with a new class system is open to doubt, I think. The key question is: what makes politically and ideologically based stratifications cohere and conjoin with the technical division of production? In a rapidly changing situation of permanent revolution, fixity need not obtain perhaps. Cultural and political democracy could be established and the technical relations of production could be prevented from forming new class relations. Perhaps. Maybe a socialist revolution in a fully automated capitalist society with developed democratic politics and cultural pluralism also avoids the problem. But since that option is not on the horizon, and since socialist modes of production are, unsurprisingly, being created in the most undeveloped and oppressed societies, we must conclude that, in socialism, the generation of ideological oppositions on the basis of (economic) technical divisions, political hierarchy and cultural conflict is inevitable (especially where these divisions are combined). Consequently, order in such socialist societies will be dependent on dominant class hegemony, and the state and ideology will continue to be vehicles of domination for a long time yet. Therefore the nature of law in socialism is an issue of the most central significance.

Contrary to orthodox Marxism, I do not think that ideological differences, the state and law disappear with the arrival of socialism. They merely take on new forms until a more advanced stage of development is reached when the state can be dismantled, the ideology of Law abandoned and the practices of regulation democratized and demystified. Ideological differences will never disappear—hopefully—because socialism, and then communism, is precisely about the development of cultural capacities and forms. No: rather than discussing blueprints we should see that the state and law will continue for a long while yet and begin studying important topics such as the economic effects of political hierarchy and ideological divisions within a successful revolutionary movement. We must continue to study law, even in socialist societies, as a political expression of the ideologies prevalent amongst the class fractions combined in the hegemonic bloc; a political expression geared to the resolution of a whole range of social problems. And lastly, but not by any means least, we must look at socialist versions of the ideology of Law—the mysterious doctrines of "proletarian law" and "socialist legality". Even socialist societies need the mystique, ritual and legitimacy of legal control. And where demystification has occurred, for example in the people's local tribunals in Cuba and China, let us ask why it does not apply across the whole field of law to include political justice, and under what conditions is demystification politically and culturally possible.

References

Althusser, L. (1969). *For Marx*. Allen Lane, Harmondsworth.

Althusser, L. (1971). *Lenin and Philosophy and Other Essays*. New Left Books, London.

Althusser, L. (1972). *Politics and History*. New Left Books, London.

Althusser, L. (1976). *Essays in Self-Criticism*. New Left Books, London.

Althusser, L. and Balibar, E. (1970). *Reading Capital*. New Left Books, London.

Arthur, C. J. (1977). Towards a Materialist Theory of Law. *Critique* **7**, 31–46.

Barthes, R. (1967). *Elements of Semiology*. Cape, London.

Barthes, R. (1973). *Mythologies*. Paladin, St. Albans.

Barthes, R. (1977). *Image—Music—Text*. Fontana, Glasgow.

Bauman, Z. (1973a). *Culture as Praxis*. Routledge and Kegan Paul, London.

Bauman, Z. (1973b). The Structuralist Promise. *British Journal of Sociology* **24**, 67–83.

Beirne, P. (1977). *Fair Rent and Legal Fiction*. MacMillan, London.

Berelson, B. (1966). Content Analysis in Communication Research. In *Reader in Public Opinion and Communication* (B. Berelson and M. Janowitz, eds). Free Press, New York.

Burgelin, O. (1968). Structuralist Analysis and Mass Communications. In *Studies of Broadcasting* (The Radio and TV Culture Research Institute). Nippon Hoso Kyokai, Tokyo.

Callinicos, A. (1976). *Althusser's Marxism*. Pluto Press, London.

Carlen, P., ed. (1976). *The Sociology of Law* (Sociologial Review Monograph 23). University of Keele.

Carr, E. H. (1976) *Foundations of a Planned Economy 1926–1929*, Vol. 2. Penguin, Harmondsworth.

Cicourel, A. V. (1964). *Method and Measurement in Sociology*. Free Press, New York.

Cohen, S. and Young, J., eds (1973). *The Manufacture of News*. Constable, London.

Cornforth, M. (1974). *Dialectical Materialism,* Vol. 3. Lawrence and Wishart, London.

Coward, R. and Ellis, J. (1977). *Language and Materialism.* Routledge and Kegan Paul, London.

Culler, J. (1973). The Linguistic Basis of Structuralism. In *Structuralism* (D. Robey, ed.). Clarendon Press, Oxford.

Culler, J. (1975). *Structuralist Poetics.* Routledge and Kegan Paul, London.

Derrida, J. (1971). Semiologie et Grammatologie. In *Essays in Semiotics* (J. Kristeva *et al.,* eds). Mouton, Hague-Paris.

Derrida, J. (1972). Structure, Sign and Play in the Discourse of the Human Sciences. In *The Structuralist Controversy* (R. Macksey and E. Donato, eds). John Hopkins Press, Baltimore.

De Sola Pool, I., ed. (1959). *Trends in Content Analysis.* University of Illinois Press, Urbana.

Durkheim, E. (1964). *The Division of Labour in Society.* Free Press, New York.

Durkheim, E. (1970). *Suicide.* Routledge and Kegan Paul, London.

Eco, U. (1967). Rhetoric and Ideology in Sue's Les Mysteres de Paris. *International Social Science Journal* **XIX,** No. 4, 551–569.

Eco, U. (1971). A Semiotic Approach to Semantics. *Versus* **1,** 21–60.

Elliott, P. (1977). Media Organisations and Occupations: an overview. In *Mass Communication and Society* (J. Curran *et al.,* eds). Edward Arnold, London.

Evans, M. (1975). *Karl Marx.* Allen and Unwin, London.

Fiori, G. (1970). *Antonio Gramsci.* New Left Books, London.

Foucault, M. (1974). *The Archaeology of Knowledge.* Tavistock, London.

Genette, G. (1969). The Reverse Side of the Sign. *Social Sciences Information,* Vol. VIII, 169–182.

Geras, N. (1971). Essence and Appearance: Aspects of Fetishism in Marx's Capital. *New Left Review* **65,** 69–85.

Geras, N. (1972). Althusser's Marxism. *New Left Review* **71,** 57–86.

Glucksmann, A. (1972). A Ventriloquist Structuralism. *New Left Review* **72,** 68–92.

Glucksmann, M. (1974). *Structuralist Analysis in Contemporary Social Thought.* Routledge and Kegan Paul, London.

Gouldner, A. (1971). *The Coming Crisis in Western Sociology.* Heinemann, London.

Gramsci, A. (1971). *Prison Notebooks.* Lawrence and Wishart, London.

Hadden, T. (1975). *Company Law and Capitalism.* Weidenfeld and Nicholson, London.

Hall, S. (1973). The Determinations of News Photographs. In *The Manufacture of News* (S. Cohen and J. Young, eds). Constable, London.

Halloran, J. D., Elliott, P. and Murdock, G. (1970). *Demonstrations and Communications.* Penguin, Harmondsworth.

Hay, D., Linebaugh, P., Rule, J. G., Thompson, E. P. and Winslow, C. (1977). *Albion's Fatal Tree.* Penguin, Harmondsworth.

Hazard, J. ed. (1951). *Soviet Legal Philosophy*. Harvard University Press, Harvard.

Hegel, G. W. F. (1975). *Logic*. Clarendon Press, Oxford.

Hindess, B. (1977). Classes and Politics in Marxist Theory (Paper given at British Sociological Association Conference, Sheffield University). Now reprinted (1978) In *Power and the State* (G. Littlejohn et al., eds). Croom Helm, London.

Hindess, B. and Hirst, P. Q. (1975). *Pre-Capitalist Modes of Production*. Routledge and Kegan Paul, London.

Hindess, B., and Hirst. P. Q. (1977). *Mode of Production and Social Formation*. MacMillan, London.

Hirst, P. Q. (1975a). Marx and Engels on law, crime and morality. In *Critical Criminology* (I. Taylor, P. Walton and J. Young, eds). Routledge and Kegan Paul, London.

Hirst, P. Q. (1975b). Radical Deviancy Theory and Marxism. In *Critical Criminology* (I. Taylor, P. Walton and J. Young, eds). Routledge and Kegan Paul, London.

Hirst, P. Q. (1976a). Althusser and the Theory of Ideology. *Economy and Society* **V**, No. 4, 385–412.

Hirst, P. Q. (1976b). Economic Classes and Politics. (Paper given at Communist Party Conference, London). Now reprinted (1978) in *Class and Class Structure* (A. Hunt, ed.). Lawrence and Wishart, London.

Hollis, M. (1970a). The Limits of Irrationality. In *Rationality* (B. R. Wilson, ed.) Basil Blackwell, Oxford.

Hollis, M. (1970b). Reason and Ritual. In *Rationality* (B. R. Wilson, ed.) Basil Blackwell, Oxford.

Hollis, M. (1977). *Models of Man*. Cambridge University Press, Cambridge.

Hood Phillips, O. and Hudson, A. H. (1977). *A First Book of English Law*. Sweet and Maxwell, London.

Hunt, A. (1976). Law, State and Class Struggle. *Marxism Today* **20**, No. 6, 178–187.

James, C. L. R. (1963). *Beyond a Boundary*. Hutchinson, London.

Jameson, F. (1971). *Marxism and Form*. Princeton University Press, Princeton.

Keat, R. and Urry, J. (1975). *Social Theory as Science*. Routledge and Kegan Paul, London.

Kirchheimer, O. (1961). *Political Justice*. Princeton University Press, Princeton.

Korsch, K. (1970). *Marxism and Philosophy*. New Left Books, London.

Kristeva, J. (1969). La Semiologie comme Science des Ideologies. *Semiotica* **1**, 196–204.

Kristeva, J. (1971). L'Expansion de la Semiotique. In *Essays in Semiotics* (J. Kristeva et al., eds). Marton, Hague-Paris.

Kristeva, J. (1973). The Semiotic Activity. *Screen,* **14**, No. 1/2, 25–39.

Lane, M. (1970). *Structuralism*. Cape, London.

Lasswell, H. D. (1966). Why be Quantitative? In *Reader in Public Opinion and Communication* (B. Berelson and M. Janowitz, eds). Free Press, New York.

Leach, E. (1972). Anthropological Aspects of Language. In *Mythology* (P. Maranda, ed.). Harmondsworth, Penguin.

Leites, N. and Lasswell, H. D. (1940). *The Language of Politics.* Stewart, New York.

Levi-Strauss, C. (1968). The Story of Asdiwal. In *The Structural Study of Myth and Toterism* (E. Leach, ed.) Tourstock, London.

Levi-Strauss, C. (1972). *Structural Anthropology.* Penguin, Harmondsworth.

Lewis, J. (1972). The Althusser Case. *Marxism Today,* **16** No. 1, 23–28 and 43–48.

Linebaugh, P. (1976). Karl Marx, The Theft of Wood, and Working Class Composition. *Crime and Social Justice.* **6,** 5–16.

Lloyd, Lord. (1972). *Introduction to Jurisprudence.* Stevens, London.

Lovell, T. (1973). Anti-Earthquake Pill. In *Times Higher Education Supplement,* 14th September.

Lyons, J. (1973). Structuralism and Linguistics. In *Structuralism* (D. Robey, ed.). Clarendon Press, Oxford.

Mao Tse Tung. (1962). On Contradiction. In *Mao Tse Tung* (A. Freemantle, ed.). Mentor Books, New York.

Marx, K. (1955). *The Poverty of Philosophy.* Progress, Moscow.

Marx, K. (1972). *Capital,* Vol. III. Lawrence and Wishart, London.

Marx, K. (1973). *Grundrisse.* Penguin, Harmondsworth.

Marx, K. (1974). *Capital,* Vol. I. Lawrence and Wishart, London.

Marx, K. (1975). Notes on Adolph Wagner. In *Karl Marx: Tests on Method* (T. Carver, ed.). Blackwell, Oxford.

Marx, K. and Engels, F. (1973). *Selected Works.* Lawrence and Wishart, London.

Marx, K. and Engels, F. (1975). *Collected Works,* Vol. 3. Lawrence and Wishart, London.

Marx, K. and Engels, F. (1976a). *Collected Works,* Vol. 5. Lawrence and Wishart, London.

Marx, K. and Engels, F. (1976b). *Collected Works,* Vol. 6. Lawrence and Wishart, London.

McLennan, G., Molina, V. and Peters, R. (1977). Althusser's Theory of Ideology. *Working Papers in Cultural Studies* **10,** 77–105.

Mepham, J. (1974). Theory of Ideology in *Capital. Working Papers in Cultural Studies* **6,** 98–123.

Murdock, G. and Golding, P. (1973). For a Political Economy of Mass Communications. In *The Socialist Register* (R. Miliband and J. Saville, eds). Merlin Press, London.

Murdock, G. and Golding, P. (1977). Capitalism, Communication and Class Relations. In *Mass Communication and Society.* (J. Curran *et al.*, eds). Edward Arnold, London.

Nichols, T. and Armstrong, P. (1976). *Workers Divided.* Fontana, Glasgow.

Pearce, F. (1976). *Crimes of the Powerful.* Pluto Press, London.

Petras, J. F. (1977). Chile: Crime, Class Consciousness and the Bourgeoisie. *Crime and Social Justice* **7,** 14–22.

Podgorecki, A. (1974). *Law and Society*. Routledge and Kegan Paul, London.
Poulantzas, N. (1973). *Political Power and Social Classes*. New Left Books, London.
Quinney, R. (1974). *Critique of Legal Order*. Little, Brown and Co., Boston.
Ranciere, J. (1974). On the Theory of Ideology (the Politics of Althusser). *Radical Philosophy* **7**, 2–15.
Renner, K. (1976). *The Institutions of Private Law*. Routledge and Kegan Paul, London.
Roberts, R. (1974). *The Classic Slum*. Penguin, Harmondsworth.
Rusher, R. (1974). What is it he's done? Ideology of Althusser. *Working Papers in Cultural Studies* **6**, 70–97.
Saussure, F. de (1974). *Course in General Linguistics*. Fontana, Glasgow.
Slater, M. (1970). Levi-Strauss in Fleet Street. M.A. dissertation, University of Essex.
Smith, A. G., ed. (1966). *Communication and Culture*. Holt, Rinehart and Winston, New York.
Spicer, R. (1976). Conspiracy Law, Class and Society. In *Sociology of Law*. (P. Carlen, ed.) University of Keele.
Taylor, I., Walton, P. and Young, J. (1973). *The New Criminology*. Routledge and Kegan Paul, London.
Taylor, I., Walton, P. and Young, J. eds (1975). *Critical Criminology*. Routledge and Kegan Paul, London.
Taylor, J. (1972). Marxism and Anthropology. *Economy and Society* **1**, No. 3, 339–350.
Thompson, E. P. (1977). *Whigs and Hunters*. Penguin, Harmondsworth.
Tumanov, V. A. (1974). *Contemporary Bourgeois Legal Thought*. Progress, Moscow.
Veron, E. (1971). Ideology and Social Sciences. *Semiotica* No. **3**(1), 59–73.
Volosinov, V. N. (1973). *Marxism and the Philosophy of Language*. Seminar Press, New York.
Walton, P. and Gamble, A. (1972). *From Alienation to Surplus Value*. Sheed and Ward, London.
Willer, D. and Willer, J. (1973). *Systematic Empiricism*. Prentice-Hall, Englewood Cliffs.
Williams, G. (1975). *Proletarian Order*. Pluto Press, London.
Williams, K. (1974). Unproblematic Archaeology. *Economy and Society* **3**, No. 1, 41–68.
Williams, R. (1976). *Keywords*. Fontana, Glasgow.
Winch, P. (1973). *The Idea of a Social Science*. Routledge and Kegan Paul, London.
Winston, B. (1973). *Image of the Media*. Davis-Poynter, London.
Worsley, P. (1974). The State of Theory and the Status of Theory. *Sociology* **8**, No. 1, 1–17.
Young, J. (1973). The Myth of the Drug Taker in the Mass Media. In *The Manufacture of News* (S. Cohen and J. Young, eds). Constable, London.

Index